Make Showstopping Paintings Using Gorgeous Pressed Flowers

WATERCOLOR *flowerscapes*

KARLY MURPHY
Creator of kmpressed

PAGE STREET PUBLISHING CO.

PAGE STREET
PUBLISHING CO.

First published in 2025 by
Page Street Publishing Co.
27 Congress Street, Suite 1511
Salem, MA 01970
www.pagestreetpublishing.com

Distributed by Macmillan, sales in Canada by The Canadian Manda Group.

29 28 27 26 25 1 2 3 4 5

ISBN-13: 979-8-89003-166-2

Library of Congress Control Number: 2024933693

Edited by Alexandra Murphy
Cover and book design by Emma Hardy for Page Street Publishing Co.
Photography by Karly Murphy

Printed and bound in the United States of America

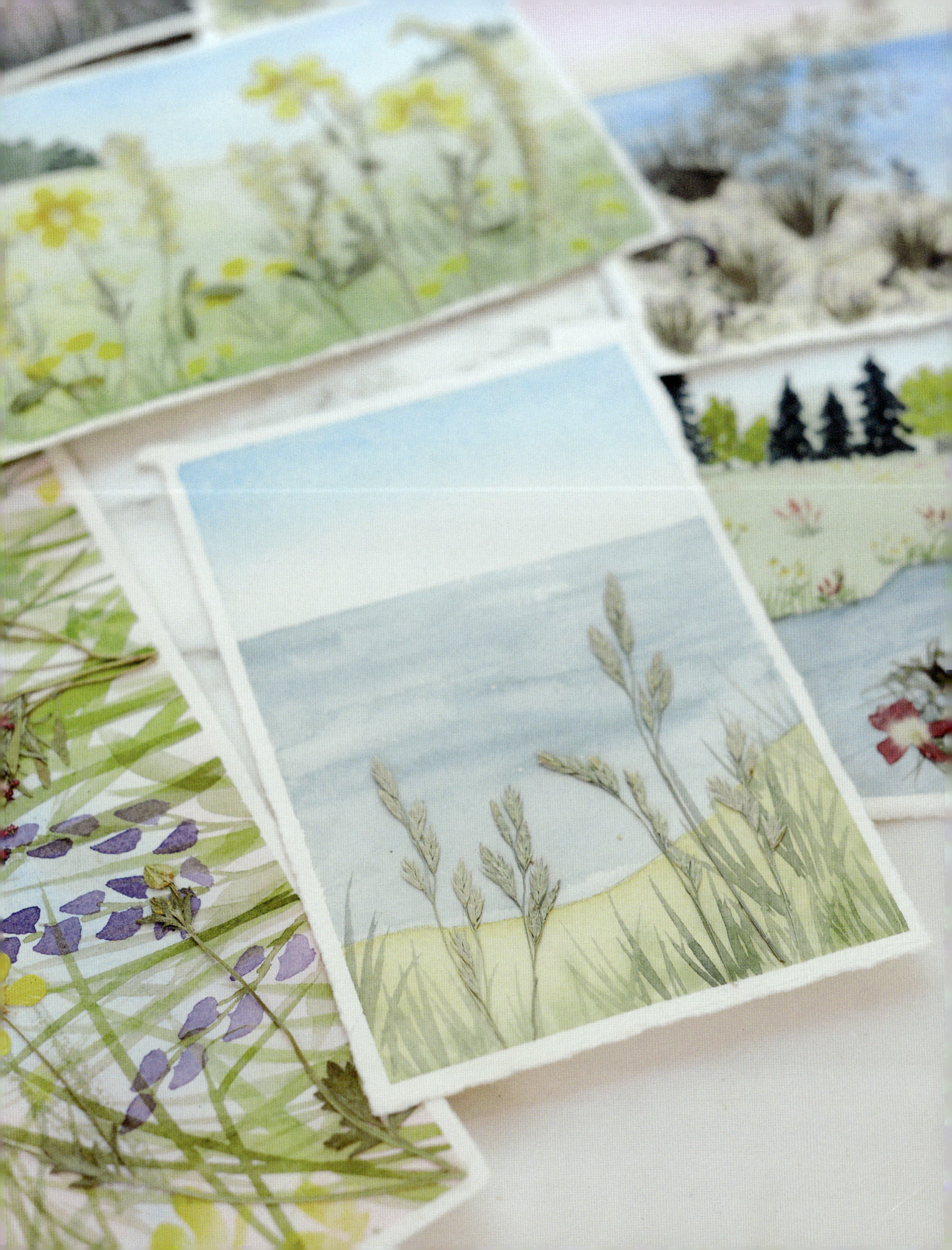

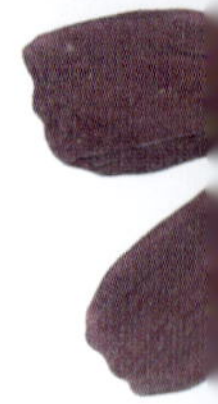

contents

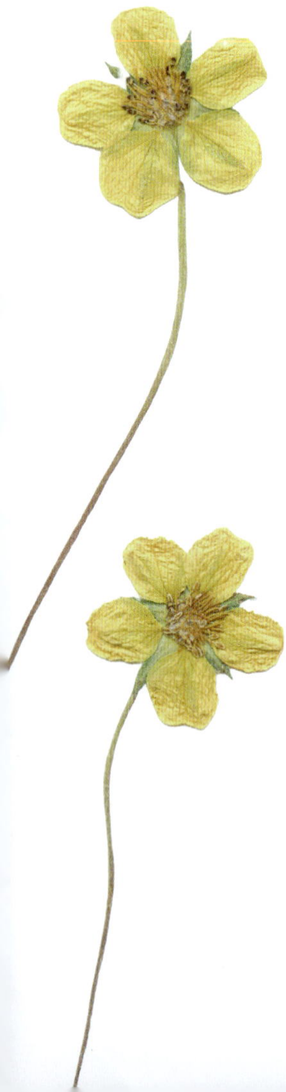

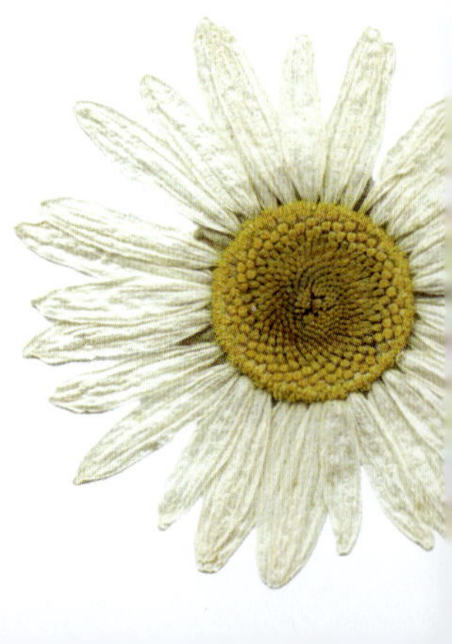

wildflower vistas · 75

mountain meadows · 109

shoreline scenes · 139

green thumb garden · 169

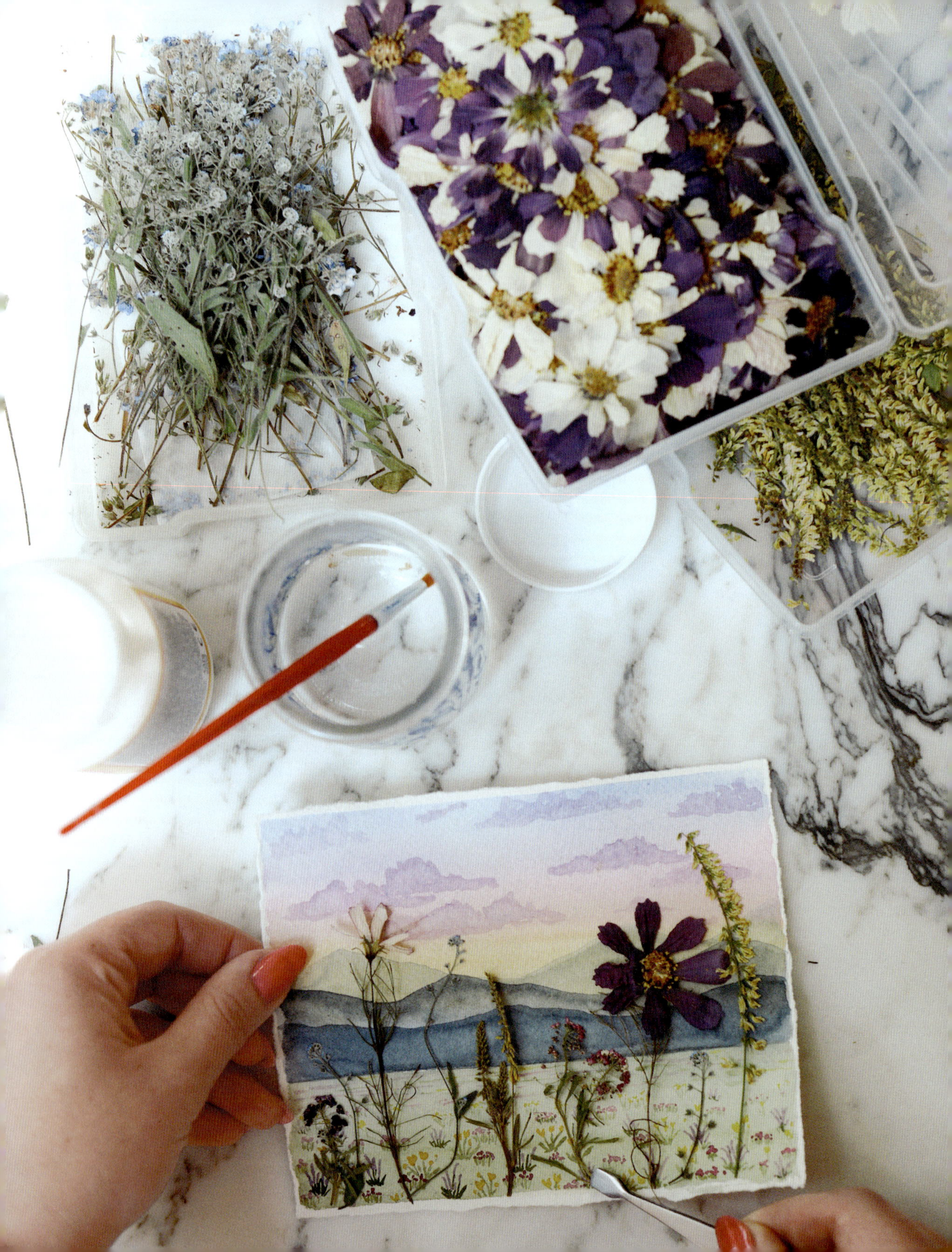

INTRODUCTION

I began pressing flowers about 10 years ago, deciding one late summer day that I would like to save the beautiful blooms I had grown from seeds in my garden. Back then, I tucked them into the pages of an old book and stacked a few more heavy volumes on top, rediscovering them on a cold gray day in winter. The shape, color and texture of these dried treasures, while different from the vibrant fresh flowers I had held in my hands all those months before, was captivating and beautiful. It transported me right back to those warm, lush garden days, even as the bleak winter dragged on outside my window.

Since then, I have honed my technique, advancing from a few old books to a small arsenal of handmade, purpose-built flower presses, and I've pressed thousands upon thousands of flowers. I have created artwork with those flowers in many shapes and sizes, but it wasn't until many years into my creative journey with pressed flowers that my watercolor flowerscapes were born.

"Watercolor flowerscape" is the name I chose for a mixed-media artwork combining pressed flowers with a watercolor painting, often of a scenic landscape. Combining the medium of watercolor with real pressed flowers creates a unique piece, bringing together a painting of a special landscape with pressed plants that enhance it. Imagine painting a landscape of a significant location and adorning it with a few flowers you pressed from the same area!

In this book, you will learn the essentials of flower pressing, including how to build your own flower press, as well as some watercolor techniques that combine well with pressed flowers. Then, you'll be able to put it all together in 20 unique step-by-step projects, ranging from simple to a bit more complex. Step-by-step instructions to paint springtime meadows, wild mountain landscapes, scenes by the sea and more domestic garden scenes await. Get ready to create beautiful mixed-media pieces inspired by the natural world!

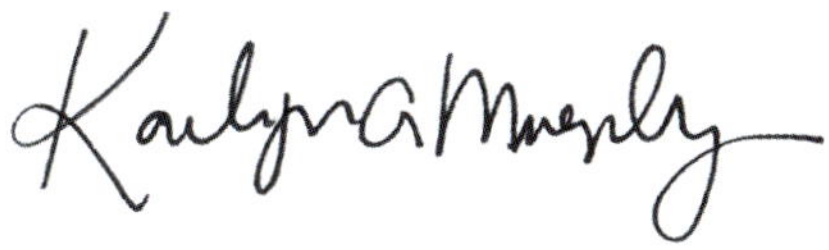

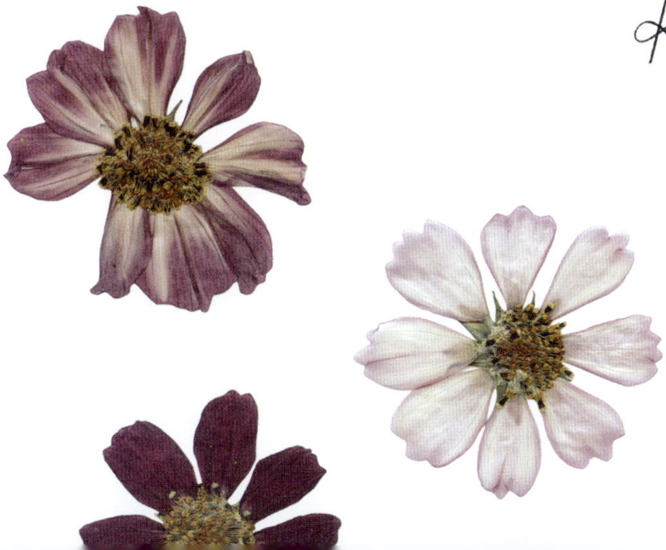

PART I

laying the foundation

Before creating a successful watercolor flowerscape, it is important to understand and practice the fundamentals of both watercolor painting and flower pressing. The landscapes in this book incorporate different watercolor techniques, brushstrokes, and elements to form the foundation of each artwork. Then, each project is finished with beautiful pressed plants! Learning to source, press, and mount pressed flowers is key before diving into your watercolor flowerscapes.

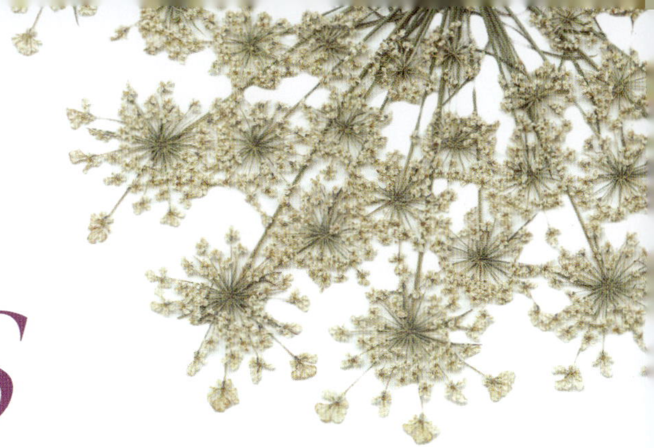

florals

Flower pressing is a centuries-old practice with both artistic and scientific significance. From a scientific standpoint, plants can be pressed as a method of preservation for future study; these pressed specimens are mounted to paper and kept in an herbarium, which is a collection of botanical material often associated with universities or museums. From an artistic perspective, pressed flowers are used to make pleasing pictures from botanical elements. *Oshibana*, which is the Japanese art of flower pressing, dates back to the sixteenth century, while flower pressing gained popularity in England during the Victorian era.

Pressing flowers has become a trend again in the modern era, with the increased ease of sharing inspiration and technique through modern search engines and social media. It is a relatively simple process, requiring few materials and a bit of patience, but it can provide years of enjoyment and experimentation.

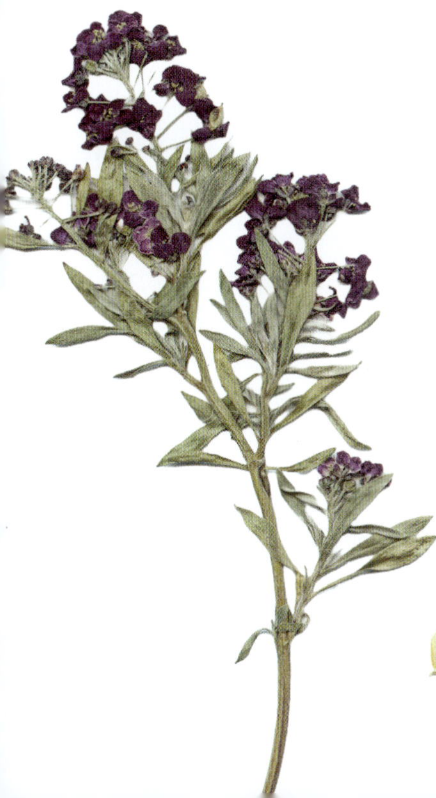

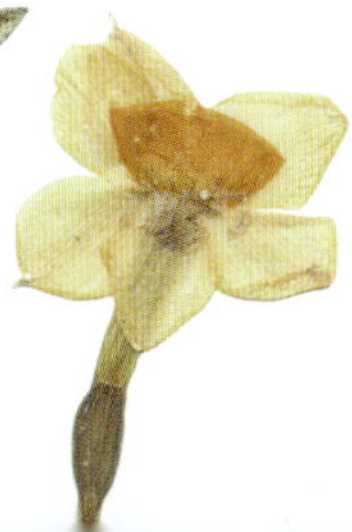

Pressed flowers are dried, flattened specimens, which can be quite fragile and require care. While a pressed flower will last much longer than a fresh one, its appearance and color will change over time both through the initial drying process and after. With care, pressed flowers will keep their form and details indefinitely, even if the color fades, so I like to keep this in mind when I'm selecting florals to use in my work. For instance, I find that an architectural flower with unique petals or leaves can be more interesting over time than a roundish flower whose distinguishing features are colors or markings.

Direct sunlight or even bright ambient light will quicken the process of color fading, so it is best not to display your pressed flowers in strongly lit areas. You can also use UV-resistant glass for framing your work to help mitigate these effects, and some artists choose to colorize their pressed flowers with dyes or paints to mask this change, but this book will focus on working with natural, untreated blooms. High humidity can also impact pressed flowers, causing mold and deterioration, so that is another important factor to keep in mind when pressing and displaying your flowers.

HELPFUL TOOLS AND MATERIALS FOR PRESSING AND MOUNTING FLOWERS

Flower pressing does not require complex tools or gadgets. However, there are a few useful household items to gather.

* A wooden flower press (instructions on building one appear on page 14)
* A pair of scissors or clippers
* A basket or bowl for harvesting flowers
* A craft knife
* Tweezers (I like blunt-ended ones rather than sharp or pointy types.)
* A craft paintbrush or two to use with glue (NOT one of your high-quality watercolor brushes)
* Mod Podge® (matte) or another pH-neutral adhesive
* Heavy paper (I like to use cheaper watercolor paper for mounting florals; if you aren't painting on it first, it doesn't need to be the high-quality cotton type.)
* Scrap paper or cardboard
* Wax paper or Glassine sheets

SOURCING FLOWERS

The first step to pressing flowers is to decide what flowers to use! In general, the thinner, flatter and drier the flower is to start, the easier it will be to press. Smaller flowers or those with fewer petals will contain less moisture than larger, denser ones, and the quick extraction of moisture under consistent pressure is the hallmark to a successful press.

Less moisture = quicker drying = better results.

I have found that garden flowers and wildflowers are some of the best options for pressing, and that is where I got started. Here is a list of some of the flowers and greenery I would recommend to those starting out; the most ideal options for watercolor flowerscapes are marked with an asterisk.

- Buttercup*
- Clover
- Cosmo*
- Fern*
- Forget-me-not*
- Grass*
- Hellebore
- Hydrangea (individual blossoms picked off from flower head)
- Larkspur*
- Pansy/viola
- Queen Anne's lace (also called wild carrot)*
- Sweet alyssum*
- Verbena*

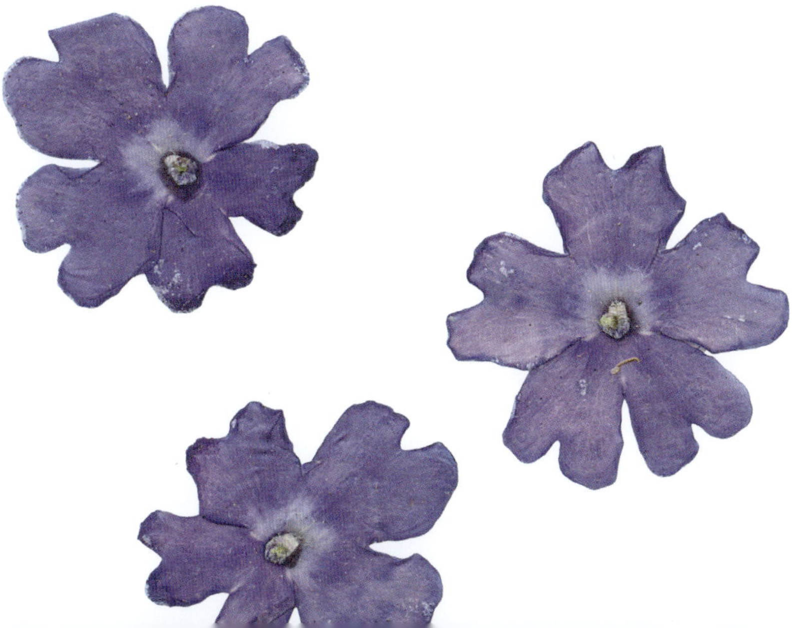

notes about harvesting

* Pick flowers on a dry day, after any dew has evaporated (late morning and afternoon usually work well). Surface moisture from dew or rain will be detrimental to your pressed flowers, causing browning or mold.
* Choose the best specimens you can find. Any blemishes or imperfections on the fresh flowers will carry through to their pressed result, so you want to start with the best possible blooms.
* Clip stems or remove blooms, using a basket or a similar container to collect your pickings, and be ready to press your specimens quickly so they do not wilt or shrivel.
* If you need to harvest flowers but can't press right away (for instance, if a rainstorm is coming so you need to pick your blooms before they get wet), you can place the stems in a jar or vase with a little water until you're ready. Just make sure you towel off the wet stems (or cut them away) when you are ready to press the flowers, so you don't introduce that moisture to your press.
* You should only pick flowers you have grown or have permission to pick. There are areas where picking wildflowers is against the law, such as within national parks, so it is best to check the laws in your area before you go. There are also endangered plants that are protected and illegal to harvest, so make sure to familiarize yourself with those as well.
* Queen Anne's lace, or wild carrot, is a great flower for pressing and grows abundantly in many places. Just be mindful of harmful look-alikes, such as hemlocks. If you aren't completely sure, you can source safe Queen Anne's lace from a florist or use baby's breath.

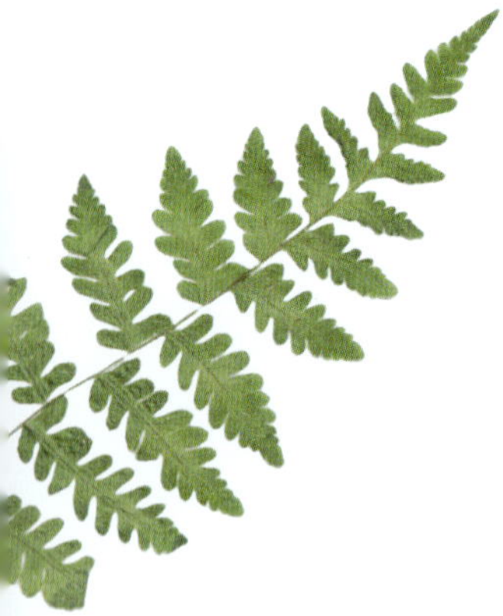

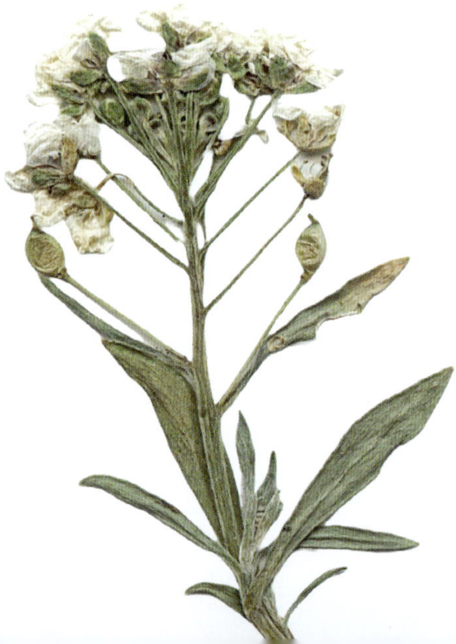

alternatives to harvesting

If you do not have a garden or the ability to harvest your own flowers, try seeking out a local flower farm or vendors at a farmer's market. You may be able to find some of the aforementioned flowers there. If you can't find a flower farm near you, there are some options available in the floral trade that are suitable for pressing: Astrantia, baby's breath, caspia, delphinium, hydrangea (individual blossoms picked off from flower head), larkspur, sea lavender. A good resource for those flowers might be your local florist or even a grocery store.

There are lots of other flowers out there that can also be pressed, but some pose more of a challenge. *Tropical materials* contain a lot of moisture and are very tricky to dry effectively without browning or mold. *Flowers grown from bulbs or tubers,* like daffodils, tulips, hyacinths, irises, lilies and dahlias also tend to contain a lot of moisture, which can make it difficult to achieve a good press. *Densely petaled flowers,* such as roses, ranunculus and peonies, can be extremely challenging to press whole; however, you can take them apart, press the petals individually and reconstruct them once they are dry.

If you are unable to source the flowers you want for your artwork, or if you don't want to wait, you can also find loose pressed flowers for purchase online. Marketplaces like Etsy are a good place to check for these materials.

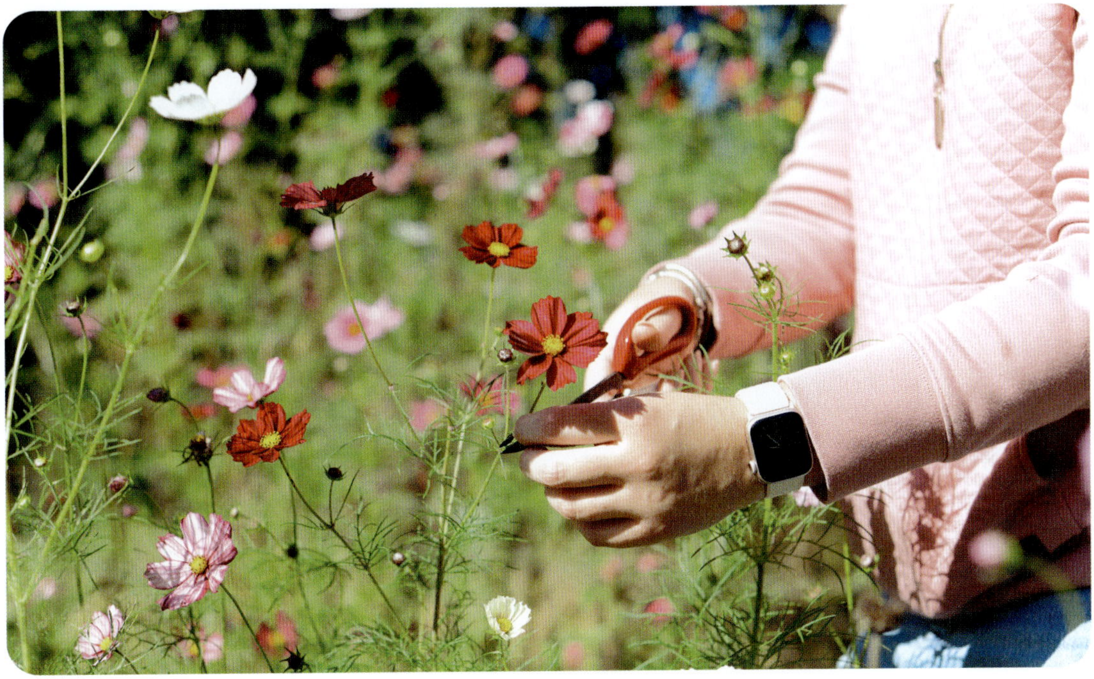

PRESSING FLOWERS

BUILD A FLOWER PRESS

A traditional flower press is my favorite tool for transforming fresh flowers into pressed flowers for artwork, and it is relatively straightforward to build one using just a few simple components and tools. If you aren't the DIY type, there are plenty of options to purchase a ready-made version online.

materials

2 (12 x 14" [31 x 26–cm], $^{3}/_{4}$" [2-cm] thick) pieces of wood (see Notes on page 16)

Scrap wood

4 ($^{1}/_{4}$ x 5" [0.6 x 13–cm]) carriage bolts (see Notes on page 16)

8 (9$^{1}/_{2}$ x 12" [24 x 30–cm]) pieces of cardboard

14 (9$^{1}/_{2}$ x 12" [24 x 30–cm]) couch sheets or other types of blotting paper (see Notes on page 16)

4 ($^{1}/_{4}$" [0.6-cm]) washers

4 ($^{1}/_{4}$" [0.6-cm]) wing nuts

tools

Pencil

Ruler or tape measure

Clamps

Drill and $^{3}/_{8}$" drill bit

Sandpaper (optional)

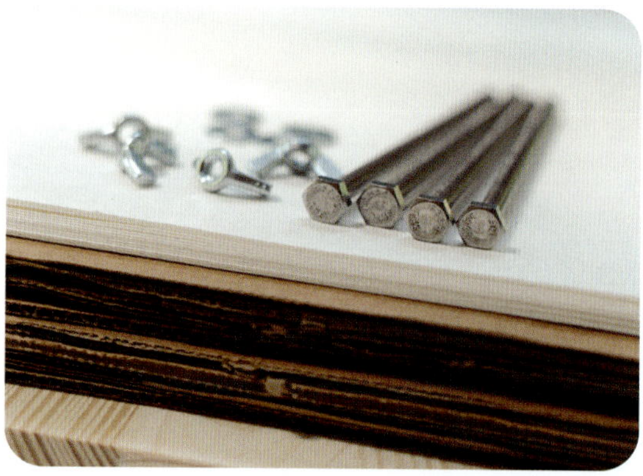

step 1

Using your pencil and ruler, make a 1 x 1-inch (2.5 x 2.5-cm) square mark from each corner of one of the pieces of wood. Place that piece of wood on top of the other, with the marked side up, and clamp them together. Place them on top of the scrap wood.

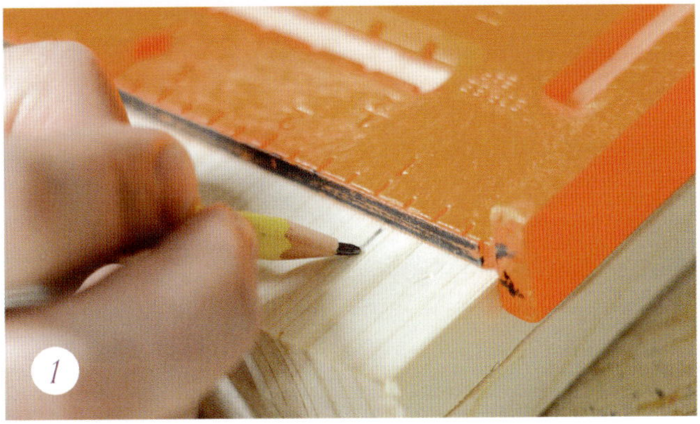

step 2

Using a ⅜-inch drill bit, carefully drill a hole through each of the four marks you made in step 1. Be sure to drill the hole straight down and through both pieces of wood. Remove the clamps.

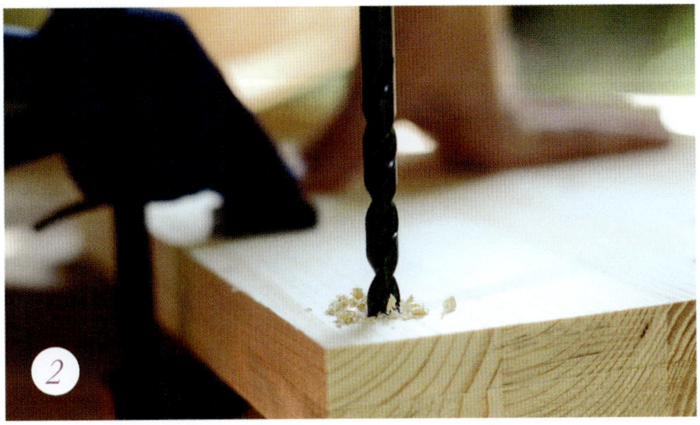

step 3

If desired, sand down any rough edges to your press and brush or wipe away the dust once this step is complete.

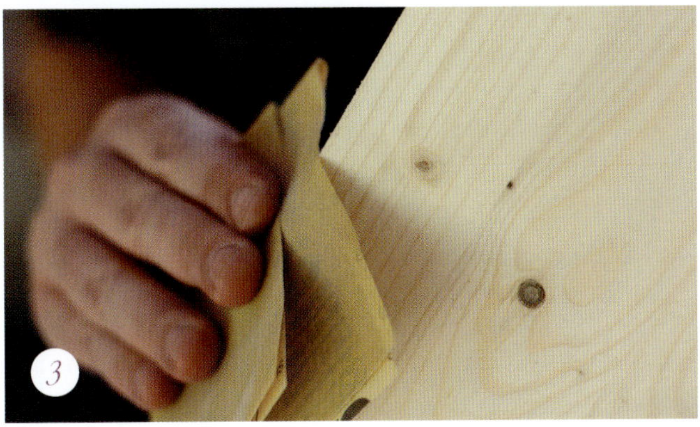

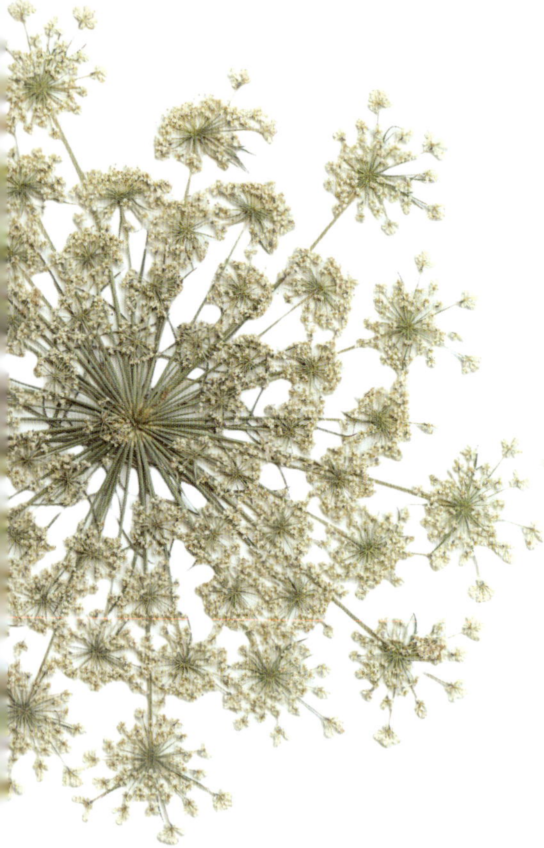

step 4

Insert the 4 carriage bolts up through the bottom of one of your boards so it sticks up vertically. Place your first layer of cardboard on the wood with the bolts. Place 2 couch sheets on the cardboard, then another layer of cardboard. Place 2 more couch sheets on top of the cardboard, then top with another layer of cardboard. Repeat this process until you have placed your final cardboard layer. Then, take your second piece of wood and carefully fit it over the 4 bolts. Place a washer on each of the bolts to lay on top of the wood. Then thread 1 wing nut onto each bolt. Tighten each wing nut down until it rests securely on top of the washer and holds all the layers together.

step 5

Your press is now complete and ready for action! We will open it back up and learn to press flowers in the next section.

NOTES

It is important that your 2 pieces of wood are the same exact size; you can ask to have them cut to size at the hardware store or, if you own the tools to do it at home, cut your wood carefully to size. You could build a smaller or larger press to fit your needs, with shorter or longer bolts, depending on the wood thickness and number of cardboard layers you use. These measurements are pretty standard for most of the presses I use in my work, but I do use tiny presses and one huge press, depending on which plants I am working with or if I am traveling.

Couch sheets (pronounced "kooch") are highly absorbent sheets designed to absorb water by crafters who are engaging in the papermaking process. They also work great for pulling moisture away from flowers in a flower press, so they are my preferred material for pressing. You can order them from papermaking or art supply stores online. With that in mind, other absorbent papers can also work, including newsprint (blank preferably), unprinted paper towels (no dyes or embossing, which can transfer to your flowers while pressing) or even plain printer paper. Just don't use anything with a waxy or shiny finish, like magazines or wax paper, as that will repel water and interfere with the drying process of your flowers.

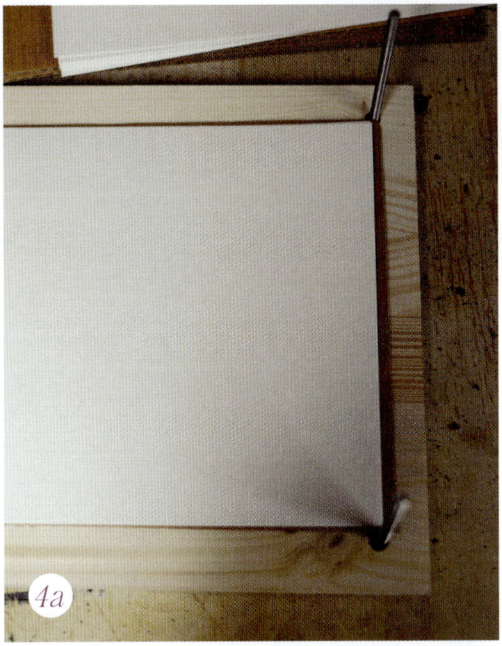
4a

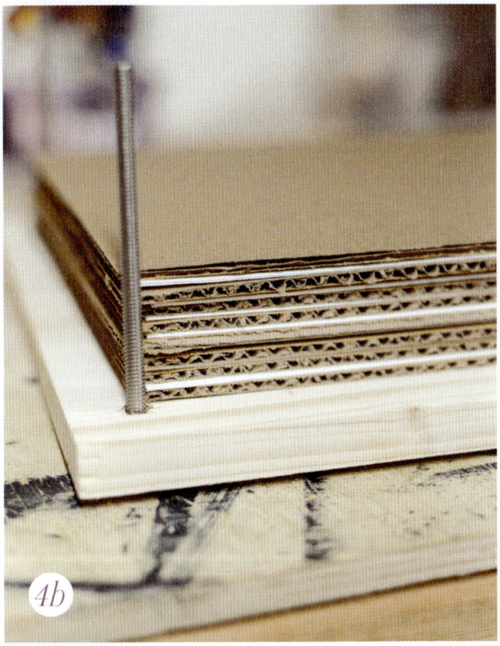
4b

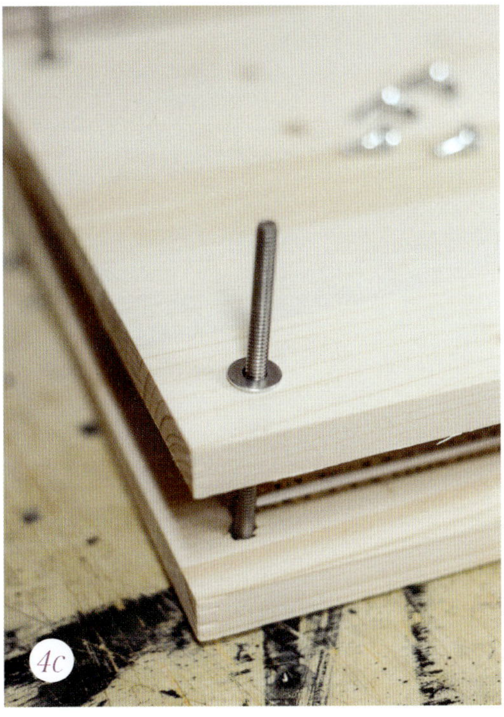
4c

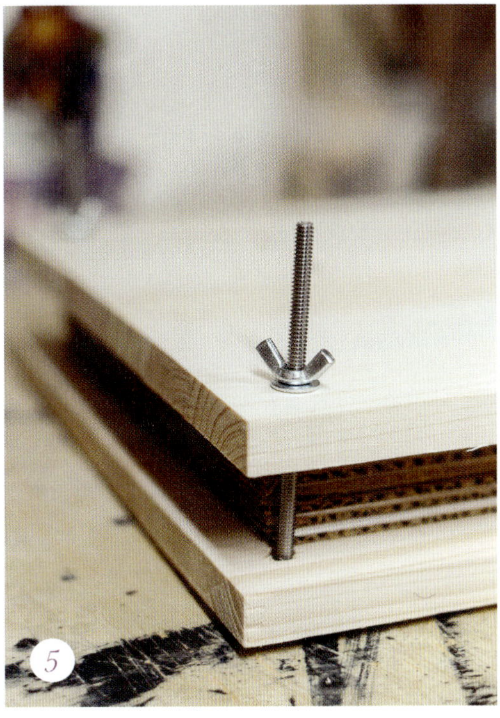
5

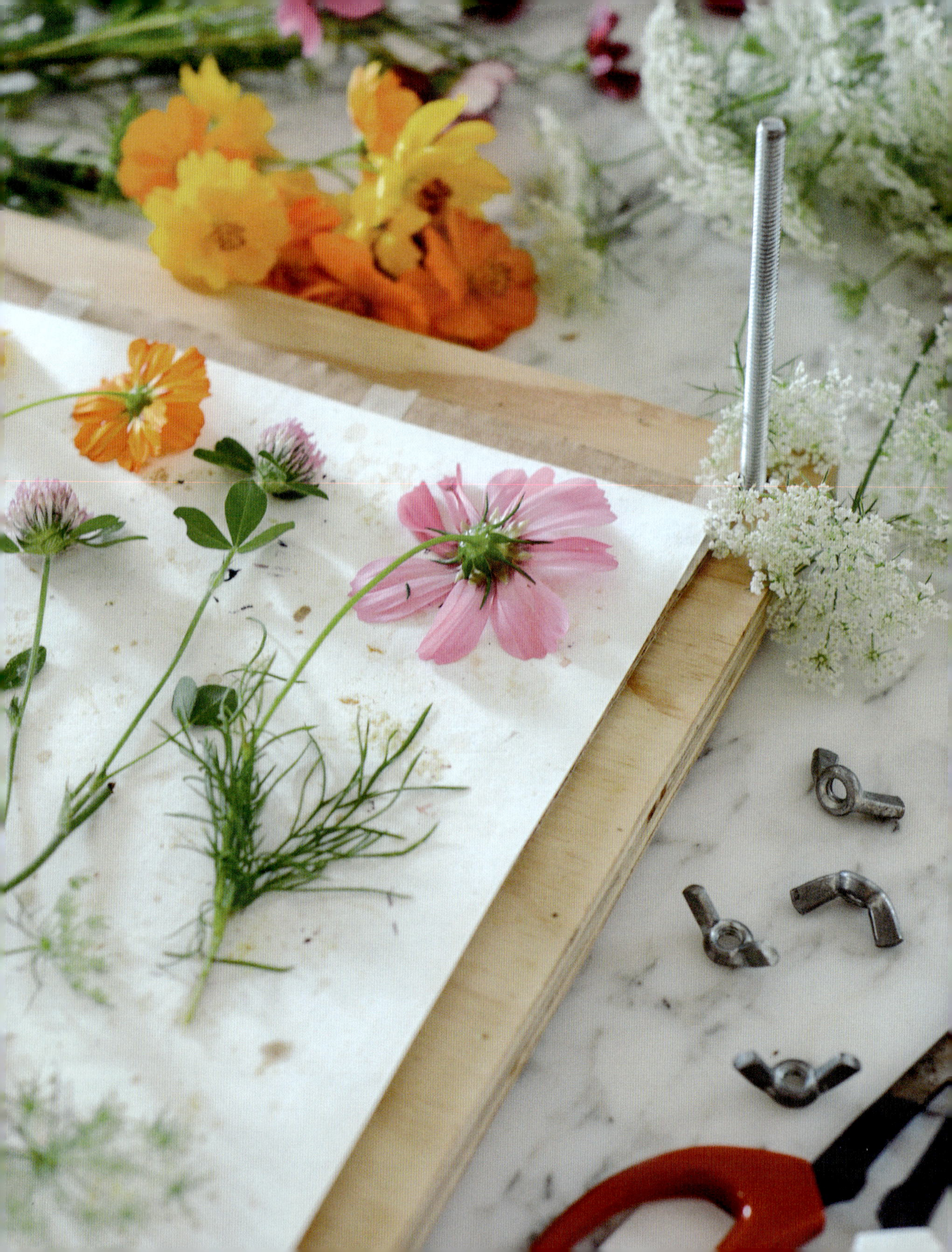

HOW TO PRESS FLOWERS

Once you have your flower press built and your floral materials sourced, it's time to get pressing!

step 1

Open up your flower press and remove everything but the bottom layer (1 piece of cardboard and 1 piece of couch paper on top of the bottom board).

step 2

Choose the first flowers you want to press. In general, it is best to keep each page/layer of your press at a consistent thickness, which means pressing flowers of the same type or, at least, similar thickness together. For example, if you try to press something very thin, like a pansy, with something that has a bit more thickness, like a daisy, there is a good chance your pansy will shrivel up because it won't have consistent pressure and paper contact.

step 3

Decide whether to press just the bloom (removed from the stem with your fingers or scissors) or the entire stem. Then lay your flowers across the paper (see image on page 21). Most of the time, I like to place my flowers face down on the paper, which I feel allows the petals and other parts to flatten a little more cleanly when the top piece of paper is added. Give each flower its own space; do not allow petals, stems or leaves to overlap, and don't crowd the paper too much. (More flowers in the same space means more moisture to be absorbed by the paper.)

step 4

Once your flowers are laid across the paper, place the second couch paper on top, followed by a cardboard layer. Then place another paper on top of the cardboard and repeat, filling each page and sandwiching the flowers between 2 sheets of paper. Continue adding flowers to your press until they are all tucked away or until you run out of space.

step 5

Fit the top board down over the bolts, and allow it to rest on your stack of cardboard, paper and flower sandwiches. Replace the washers and wing nuts on each bolt, tightening until everything is under secure pressure. There is a bit of a learning curve here; not enough pressure can make your flowers shrivel, but too much pressure can cause mold and browning, so don't tighten them aggressively once everything has been secured (no shifting or rattling).

step 6

The hardest step may be waiting! Flower pressing requires a lot of patience. The amount of time your flowers will take to dry and press completely will vary because it is dependent on many factors, including climate/humidity, flower type and paper type. Very thin, small flowers can dry out in a matter of days where there is low humidity, while larger or thicker flowers can take

4 to 6 weeks or more. The amount of time can even vary throughout the year. In general, I try to give my flowers about 2 weeks, but it's not always consistent. Furthermore, if you live in an area with constant high humidity, you may need to switch out your press papers throughout the drying time. By carefully removing your florals from dampened paper and placing them on new, dry sheets, you will help pull more moisture away and prevent mold/browning. I do not typically use this method since I don't like to disturb my flowers while they are still damp, but it is a good thing to try if you find yourself struggling often with browning or mold.

step 7

You can tell that your flowers are completely dry and ready when they feel more like paper than flowers and do not have any coolness or dampness to the touch. A pressed flower is often stiff, or at least less flexible than it was prior to pressing. If moisture is still present, the florals will feel cool and may be a little floppy or clammy. When in doubt, leave them in the press and check back in a week. There is no real harm in leaving them in the press "too long."

step 8

It is important to move slowly and carefully when unloading a flower press. You should also work in an area free from drafts, because pressed flowers are prone to blowing around in the slightest breeze (even if you just sigh too strongly near them). Another potential challenge is that as you prepare to remove the florals from the press, you may find that some have become stuck to the paper. If your flower is stuck, carefully try to peel the paper away, bending the paper at the sticking point, if possible, to allow the flower to pop loose. You can also use tweezers or a small craft knife to get underneath the flower and loosen it. You will find that pressed flowers can be quite fragile and require gentle handling.

step 9

Once your flowers are all out of the press, you will want to keep them safe until you are ready to mount them to paper. This means keeping them somewhere they can lie flat and not be jostled and broken. It's also important to protect them from sunlight, moisture and humidity. The solution can be as simple as placing them in a single layer between two sheets of paper or in an envelope or folder. You can also use small shallow boxes. I like to use small plastic boxes with lids to organize my small florals.

NOTES

The flower press can be reassembled without the flowers inside. The couch sheets can be reused many times, unless they become moldy or torn. I rarely replace mine but do keep extras on hand at all times just in case.

Many people over the years have used heavy old books to press their botanical treasures. While this is an option, it is not my favorite one for the majority of flowers because of inconsistent or inadequate pressure, unabsorbent paper and the risk of damage to your book. However, I do press very simple, small and flat materials in books at times, including my collection of four-leaf clovers, some autumn leaves and small ferns.

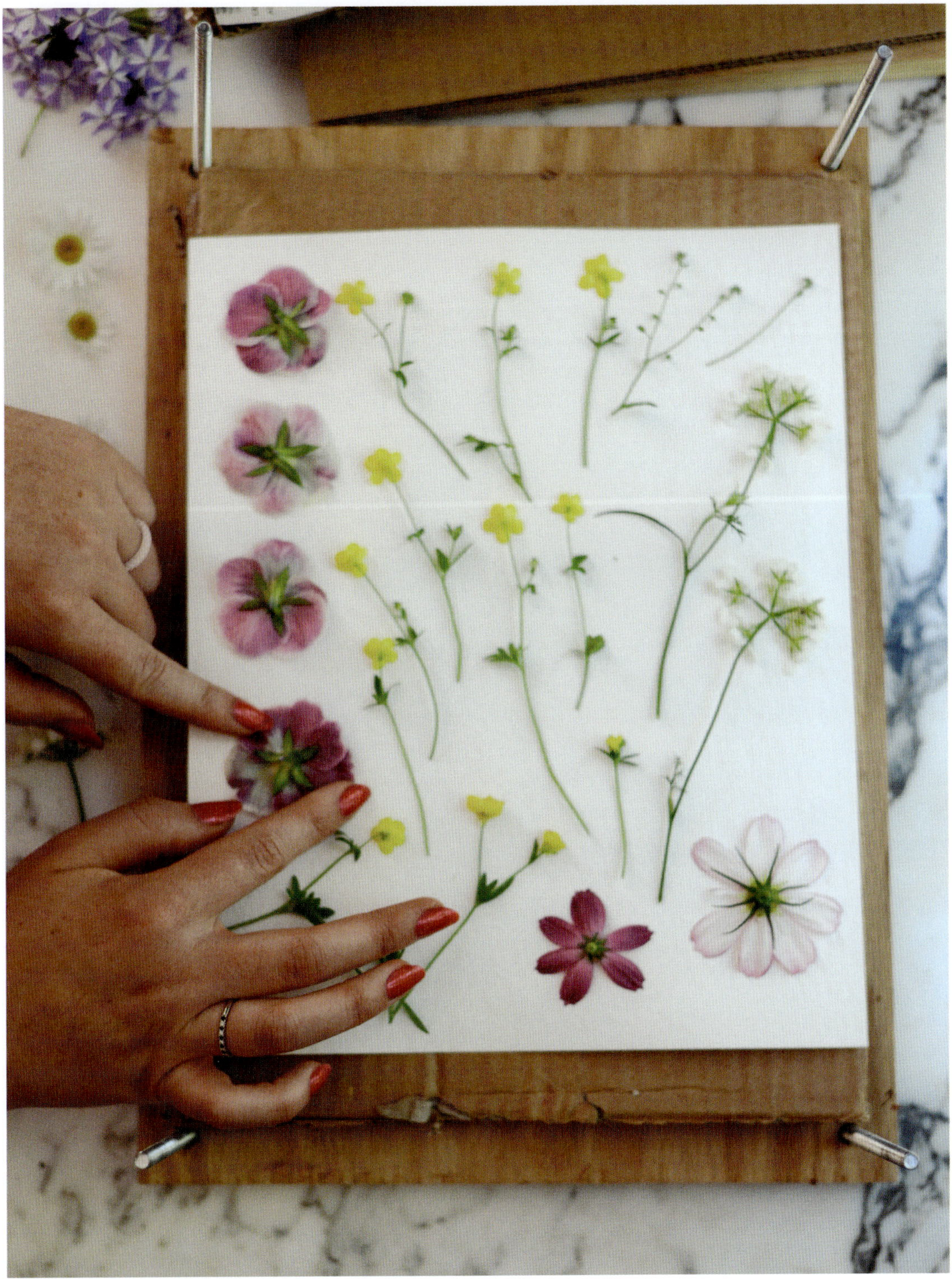

MOUNTING FLOWERS

Mounting flowers refers to the process of adhering them to your artwork. In this case, you will be mounting the flowers to paper—either to a blank page or to a painting you'd like to embellish. This section outlines the general approach you will use to create the projects in this book.

materials

Pressed flowers

Paper (I like stiff watercolor paper; cheap 140 lb [300 gsm] is fine if you aren't painting on it first)

Scissors

Tweezers

Scrap paper or cardboard

Cheap paintbrush for glue

Glue (I recommend Mod Podge)

Glassine or waxed paper

Heavy books

step 1

Choose one or more of your pressed specimens and decide what size you want your finished piece to be. Then cut a piece of stiff paper to size as needed. Gently use tweezers or your hands to lay the pressed material on the paper to find a layout you like. Even if you are only mounting one flower on its stem, you still want to do this step to confirm how you want it to look. Ask yourself questions like these: Is it centered on the page? Is the stem at an angle? Do I need to add any leaves or cut the stem shorter so it fits better?

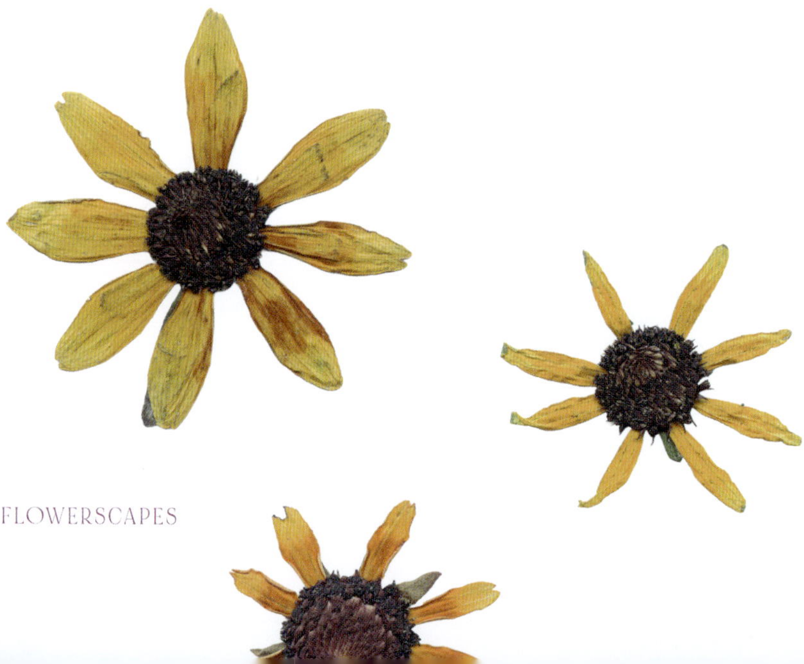

step 2

Once you have a layout you are happy with, pick up the specimen with your tweezers. I generally like to grab and hold my flower or plant at a less delicate area, which could be the stem, the center of the flower and so forth. Then, flip it face down on top of a piece of scrap paper or cardboard, still holding on to it with the tweezers.

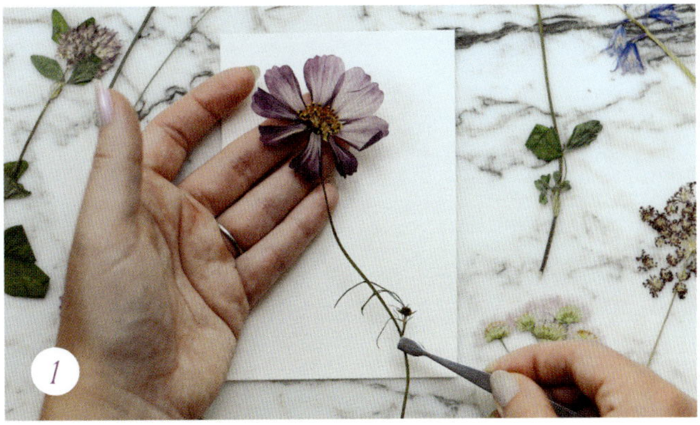

step 3

Dip your glue paintbrush (NOT one of your nice watercolor brushes!) in a little bit of Mod Podge. Gently and lightly paint the back of the flower with this glue. Work carefully but quickly; the glue can dry quickly, especially in a thin layer.

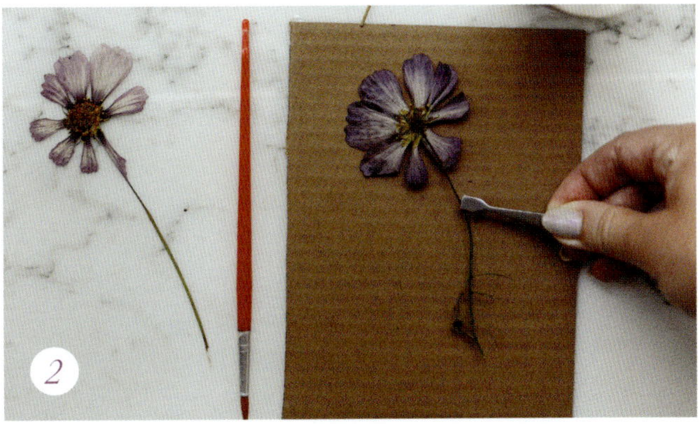

Depending on the size of the flower or plant you are mounting, you may want to move it around from time to time as you add the glue so it doesn't become stuck to the scrap paper or cardboard during this process. I find that when I am working with delicate items like ferns, this commonly happens.

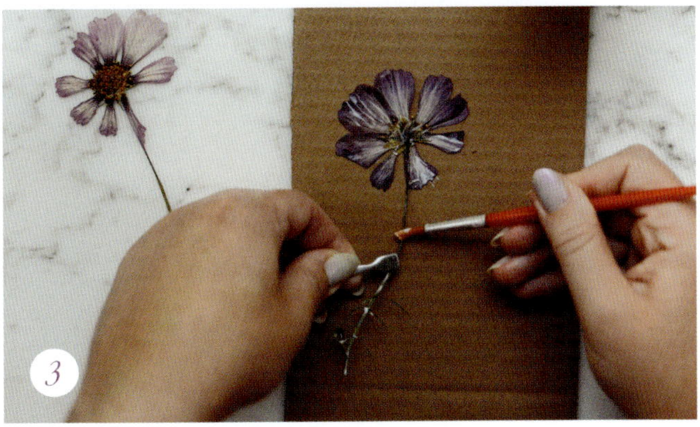

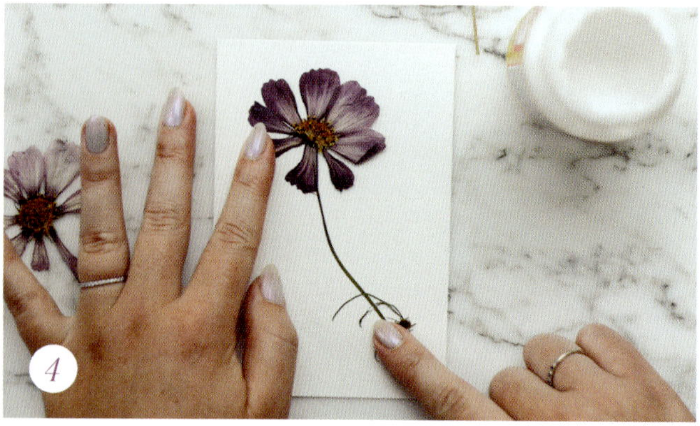

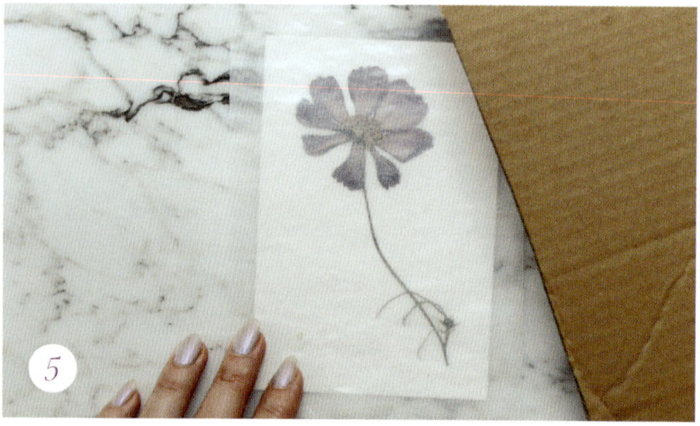

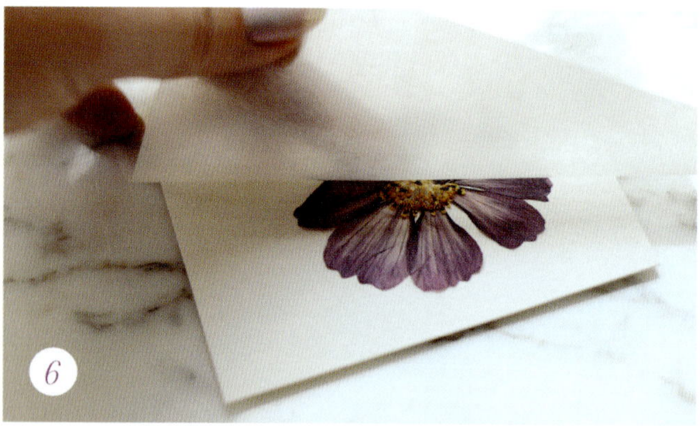

step 4

Once the back of the flower has a light coating of glue, pick it up and flip it right side up again before carefully placing it on the watercolor paper. You may need to use your free hand to guide it into place. Once the glue has touched the paper, try not to dislodge or reposition it. If you pick up your plant and try to realign it, not only will you have less glue, but also you will have glue marks on the paper. This part takes practice, so don't be discouraged if your first few attempts aren't perfect.

step 5

With the flower glued to the paper, use your fingers and tweezers to press down on it and make sure it is well stuck. Often when you are mounting flowers with their stems attached, they want to pop up or come unstuck. To help them adhere, take a sheet of Glassine or waxed paper and lay it on top of the mounted specimen. Then, add a sheet of cardboard and a heavy book or two on top to weigh it down. This helps ensure good contact and allows time for the glue to dry in place.

step 6

After 15 minutes or so, remove the books and cardboard from the Glassine or wax paper. Then carefully try to pull the Glassine or wax paper away. If it is stuck, move slowly to try to peel it without dislodging your mounted specimen. It shouldn't stick badly, but if you move too quickly, you could pull your pressed flower up.

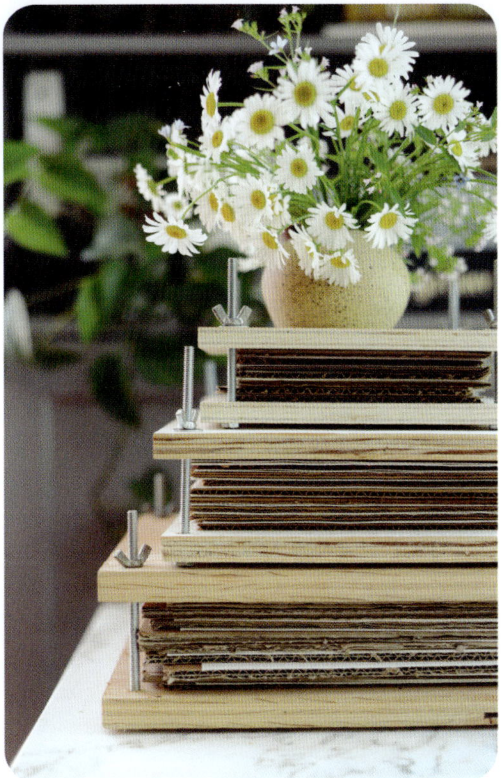

NOTE

For more complex arrangements involving multiple specimens, I like to complete the layout design, then remove and mount one specimen at a time so I don't lose or forget my design. It can also be helpful to snap a photo using your phone or camera before you begin mounting florals to reference as you work.

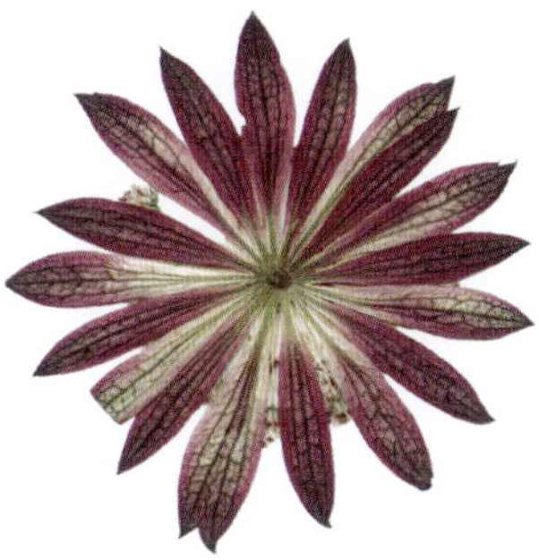

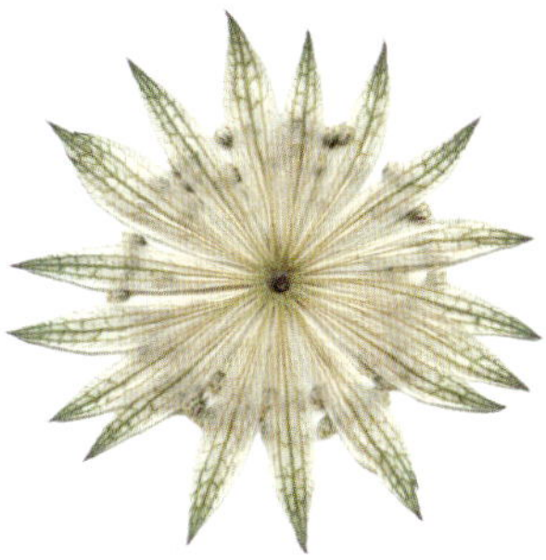

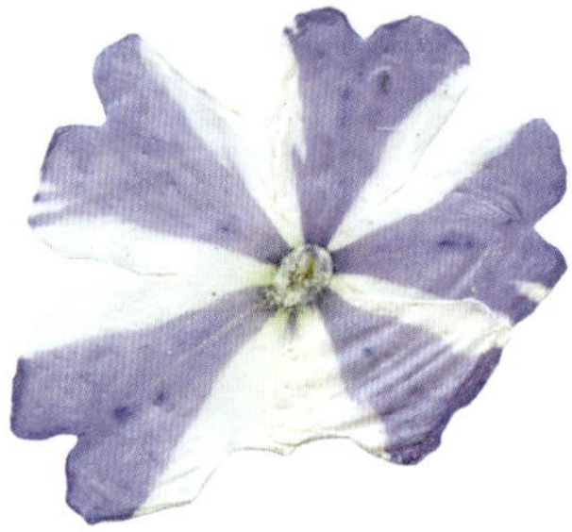

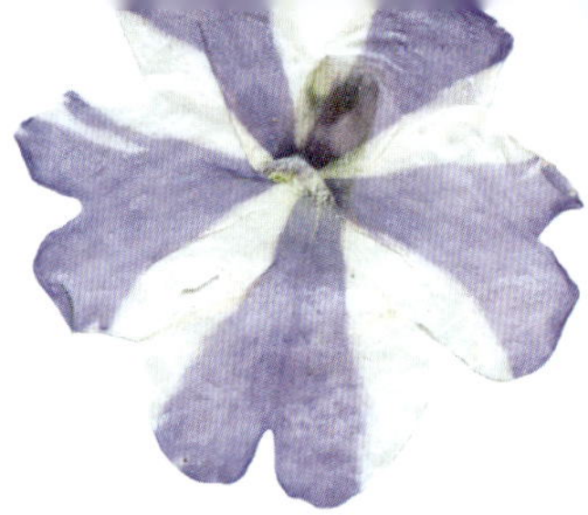

watercolor

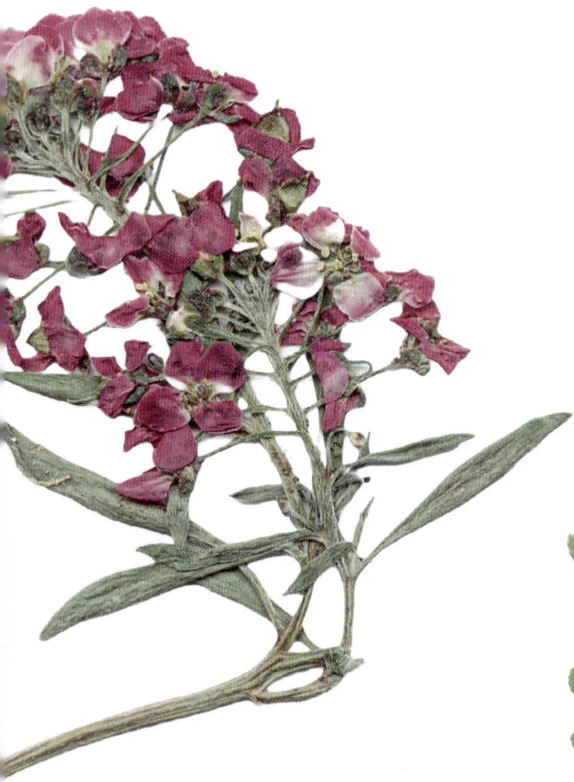

To create the watercolor flowerscapes outlined in this book, you will need a simple assortment of watercolor materials. With a few paints, a few brushes and some quality paper, you will be ready to go! In this section, I'll review some of my favorite supplies, along with some techniques and practice exercises, which I will reference throughout the painting projects in this book.

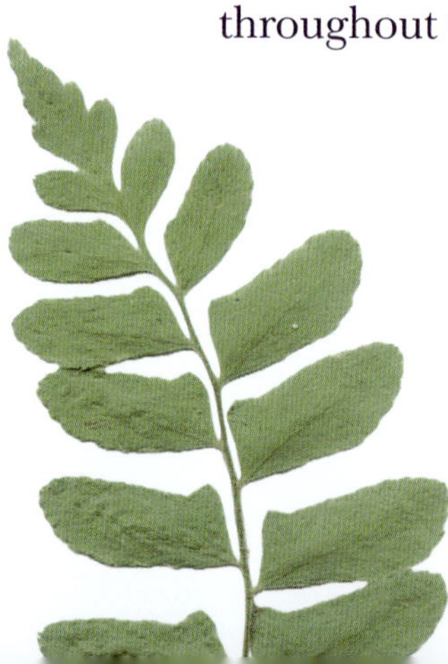

MATERIALS

watercolor paint

Watercolor paint comes in two main forms: tubes and pans. There are also varying levels of quality, from student-grade paints at a lower price point to professional-grade artist paints, which are more expensive. Professional-grade paints have more pigment and less filler than student-grade paints, but you can achieve great results in these projects with either grade level. In fact, I started painting my first watercolor flowerscapes with Winsor & Newton™ Cotman tube paints, which are their student-grade line, and I really enjoyed working with them. Many of the colors I reference here should be available in either grade across different brands, in both tubes and pans. I prefer to work with tube paints, so that is the method I will focus our attention on, but if you come to this book with a set of pan paints you already love, that's great too.

My palette consists of the following Winsor & Newton Professional Watercolours:

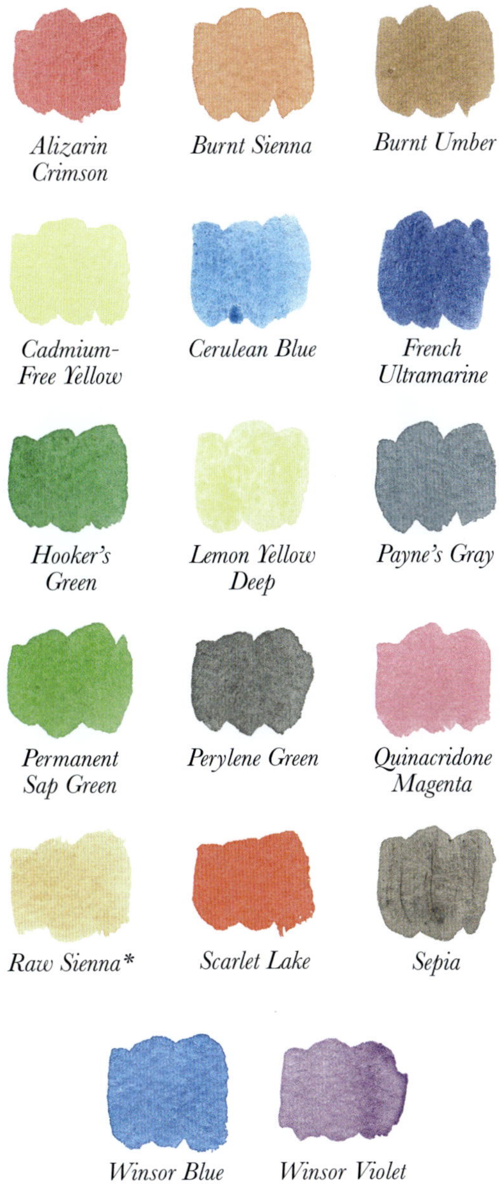

NOTE

The same pigments go by different names, depending on the manufacturer. Raw Sienna is a color I use frequently in this book, but not all companies' versions of Raw Sienna look the same. The Winsor & Newton Cotman version I use has a beautiful yellowy tone and works great as a sunny glow on the horizon, but other manufacturers' products may not give this same effect.

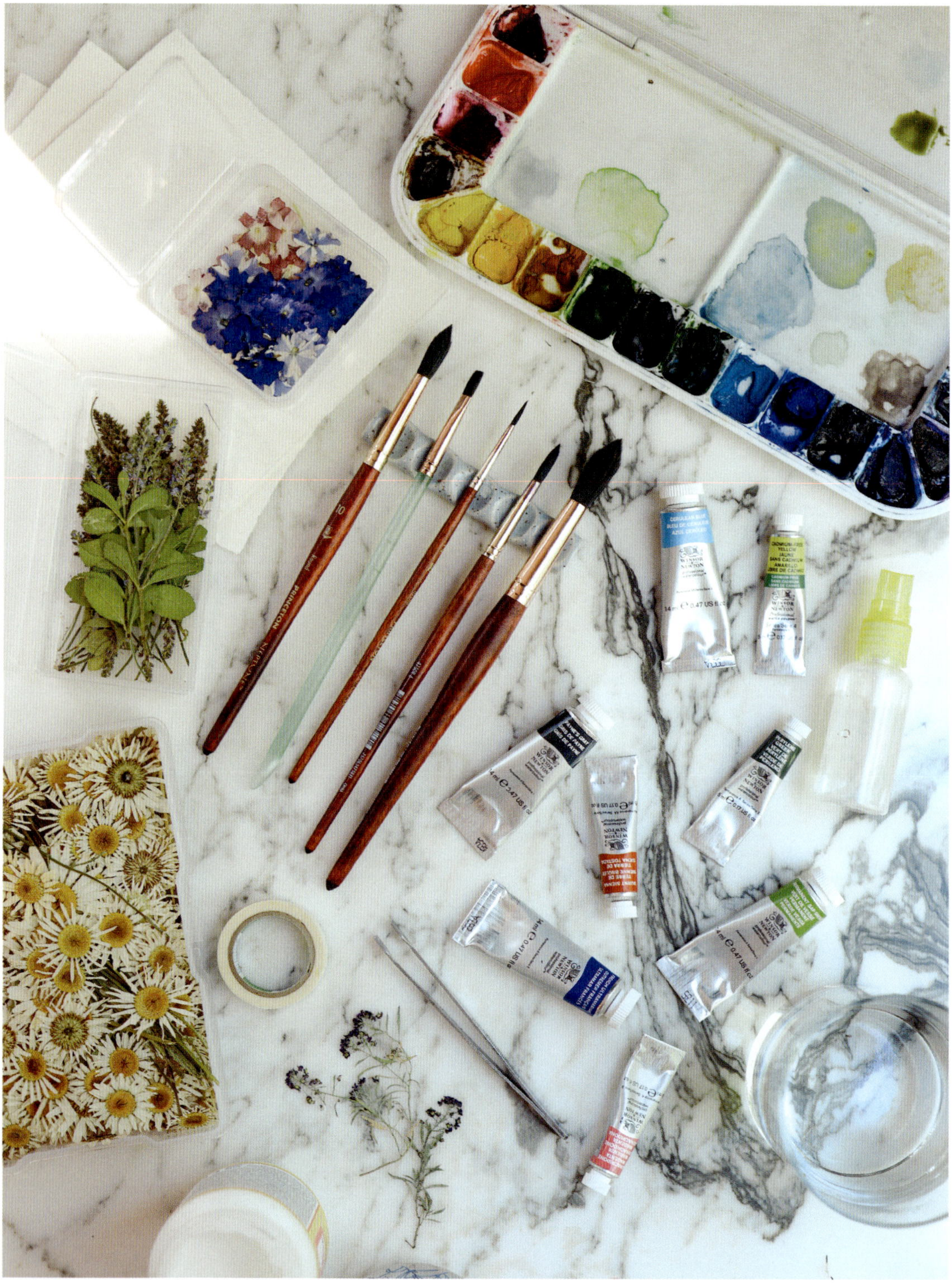

palettes

I like to squeeze my tube paints into an empty palette and let them dry for a day or two, reanimating them with a spray bottle of water before I use them. This allows me to work with tube paints while having a compact, portable palette I can use in my studio or on the go. When I need more space to mix colors, I like to use ceramic palettes, plates or glass dishes, but these are less portable. You'll need a place to mix colors for the projects in this book, whether it's in your selected palette of paints or on a separate nonporous surface.

I refer to different consistencies of paint mixtures on your palette throughout the book: watery, moderately pigmented, pigmented and "straight from the pan." These descriptions refer to the differing ratio of water to pigment, leading to different concentrations and depths of color.

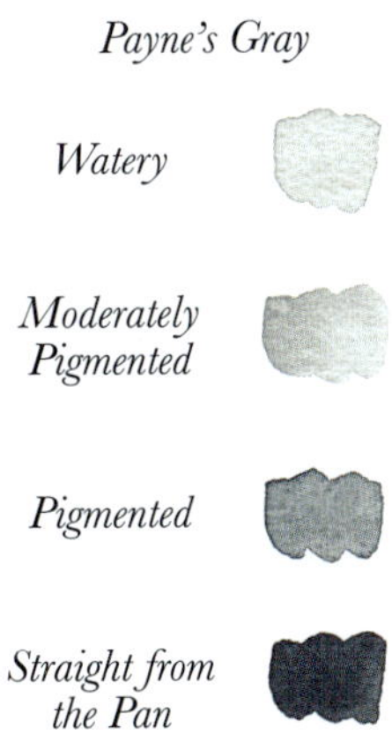

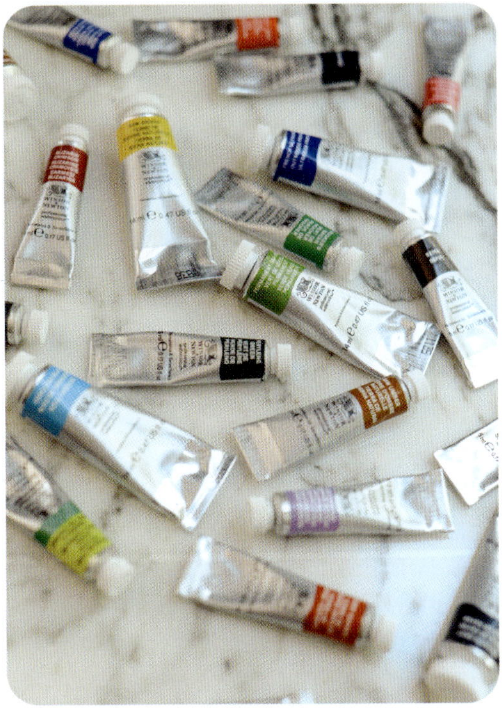

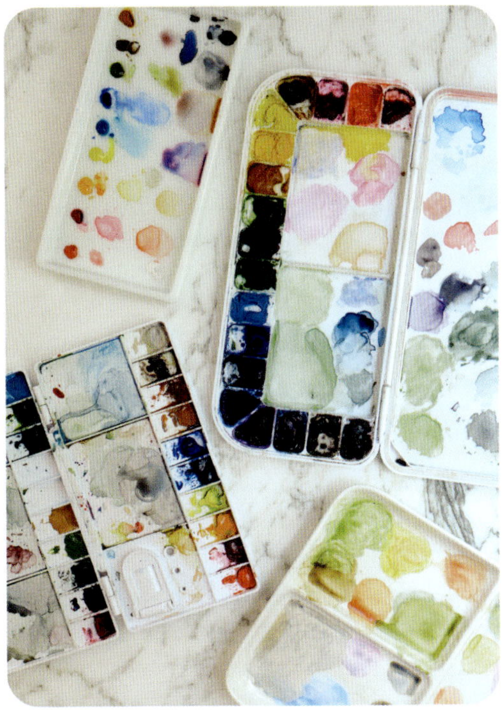

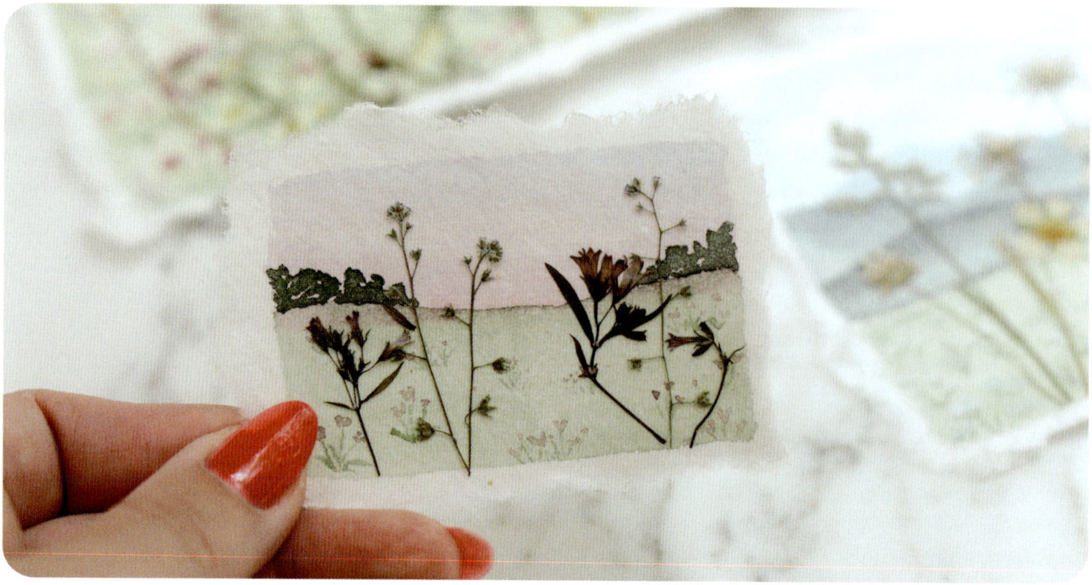

paper

When working with watercolor paints, it is important to use the right paper. Since the paint is a wet medium, and we are also planning to mount pressed florals to the paper, the paper needs to be sturdy and absorbent.

There are a few determining factors when it comes to choosing watercolor paper. The most relevant here are weight, texture and content.

Weight refers to how much the paper weighs, either in a ream (lbs) or by the square meter (gsm). Heavier papers tend to be more expensive than lighter ones, and they can handle heavier washes without buckling. For the projects in this book, you will want to use 140 lb (300 gsm) paper at a minimum.

Texture refers to the surface of the paper. Hot press paper has a smooth texture. Cold press paper (sometimes called "not" as in "not hot press") has a semi-rough texture, and rough paper has the most pronounced texture of the three. I typically use cold press papers.

Content refers to the makeup of the paper, particularly what kind of fibers are used in manufacturing. Most papers are made from either cellulose (wood pulp) fibers, cotton fibers or sometimes a combination of both. Cotton papers are more expensive than papers made with cellulose, but I find cotton far easier and more enjoyable to work with, so the extra cost is worth it to me. If you are just starting out, I recommend experimenting with different papers to see what you prefer.

When I started painting watercolor flowerscapes, I used papers handmade by a fellow artist, and I still use those papers quite often! I've found that when I use them, the paint colors and lines appear softer (more muted), and it's easy to create great gradients for skies. Plus, the deckled-edge texture from the papermaking process can't be beat.

brushes

The world of paintbrushes can be really overwhelming, with seemingly infinite options on the market, but I like to keep it really simple. I use primarily round brushes, which are versatile and can manage basically everything in this book! A good round brush has a nice pointed end, which you can use to achieve a thinner line, as well as a rounded belly that you can use to create a thicker line.

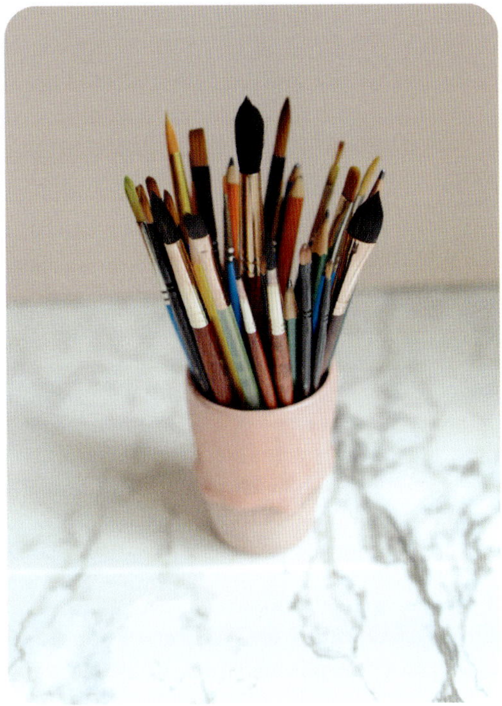

Round brushes come in many sizes, and I find it useful to have a mix. For this book, I used size 2, 6, 10 and 14 round brushes, as well as a ¼-inch (6-mm) square wash brush for just a few things. You may also find it helpful to have a rigger brush, which is a small thin brush with long bristles that's good for painting delicate lines. A filbert brush (a brush with a thick ferrule and oval-shaped bristles) will be useful too, especially for floral work.

You don't need to spend a fortune on brushes, but you should take care of the ones you get so they last a long time. Don't leave the brushes resting in your jar of water; carefully clean them in running water after each use and lay them flat to dry (although it's fine to store dried brushes with the bristles pointed up).

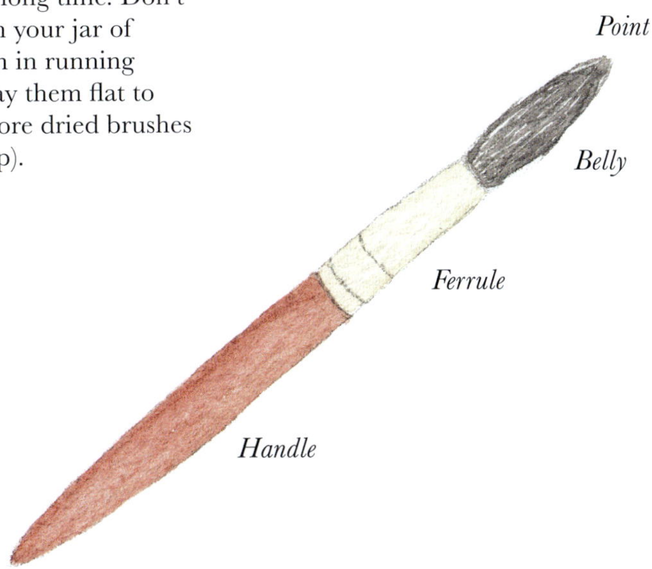

other helpful tools

Aside from paint and a palette, paper and brushes, there are a few other materials you'll need to gather before you start painting, plus a few more items that aren't necessary but are helpful to have:

A jar of clean water. I like to use a clear glass jar of clean water to clean my brush and create color mixes. As you paint and dip your brush in your jar, the water will start to get dirty, so if you keep using it, your color mixes won't be as pure. I simply replace the water once it gets too cloudy or muddy, but some people like to set up more than one jar, keeping one clean and clear, and using the other for rinsing.

A small spray bottle filled with clean water. This is a great little tool to keep in your kit so you can spray your paints. Rehydrating them with a little bit of water before you go in with your brush makes it easier for you to pick up pigment, especially if you need concentrated paint straight from the pan.

A ruler. This is helpful for drawing straight lines for horizons—and more!

A roll of tape. Tape is a great way to keep your painting flat and secure while you are working. I like to use Holbein® soft tape to tape the edges of my paper down to a piece of cardboard or other work surface. Once your painting is dry, you can carefully peel the tape away to reveal a crisp white border around your painting.

Paper towels. It can be helpful to have a paper towel or two handy while you work, for removing excess moisture from your brush or for lifting paint for different effects on your project. You can also use an old kitchen towel or rag, or some plain white paper napkins.

Opaque white paint. For instances where you want to add white back into an area that's already been painted, having some white paint on hand is helpful. I use Dr. Ph. Martin's® Bleedproof White™ for a few of the projects in this book, but you can use a white gouache if you have it.

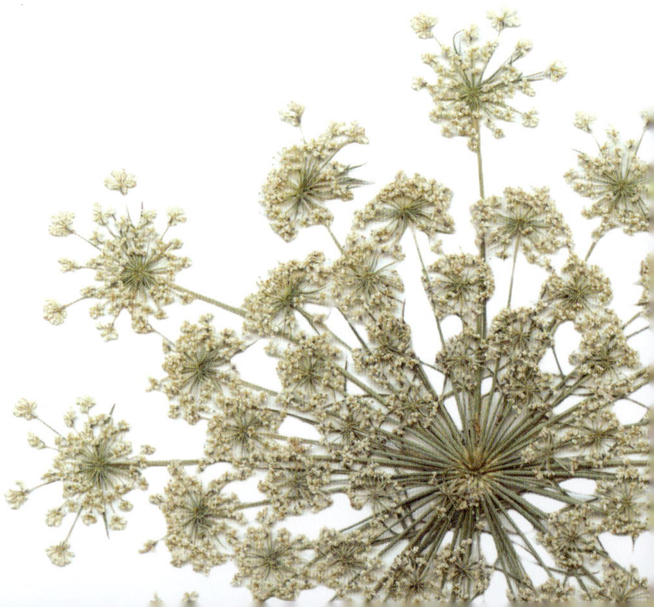

FUNDAMENTALS AND TECHNIQUES

There are a few phrases, techniques and processes that are repeated throughout this book, so if you are new to the art of watercolor painting, it is helpful to review and practice them here.

A *thirsty brush* is a paintbrush whose bristles have been cleaned and dried, or almost dried, so it is ready to absorb a lot of paint.

A *loaded brush* is a paintbrush whose bristles are already saturated with water or paint, so it is ready to apply paint or clean water to your painting.

Wet-into-dry is a technique of painting on dry paper, whether the paper has already been painted and dried, or it has not yet been painted. This technique generally yields hard lines and edges and is good for adding detail.

Wet-into-wet is a technique of painting on wet paper, whether the paper is wet with just clean water, or it has a layer of pigment already applied. This technique yields a lot of blending and softening of edges, depending on how much moisture is on the paper and on the brush (more moisture = more blending).

A *wash* is an even, thin layer of color across an area of your painting. We will use this technique often when we are painting skies and sometimes when we are creating the base layer of meadows and fields. A wash can be done on dry paper (wet-into-dry) or paper that has been dampened with clean water (wet-into-wet).

A *graduated wash* is a wash with a color transition, whether it is with a single color from pigmented to watery, or a group of two or more colors seamlessly blending together.

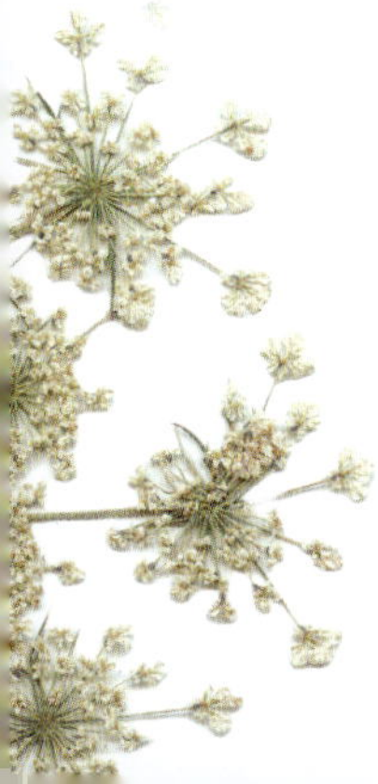

implying perspective

Many of the projects in this book involve painting a broad, sweeping landscape and superimposing pressed flowers in the foreground. To make an effective painting, it helps to imply some perspective, adding depth and dimension to a flat artwork. This can be done a few ways:

Objects in the distance are lighter and cooler-toned. This is an atmospheric effect; the more atmosphere (space) between the viewer and subject, the more atmospheric haze. You can achieve this look in your paintings by adding more water and adding a bit of blue or purple to your pigments.

Distant objects are smaller and closer together. For example, when you are painting flowers within the meadow, the flowers toward the bottom of the page (closest to the viewer) should be larger and more spaced apart than the flowers higher up on the page, nearing the horizon. These distant flowers should be smaller, with shorter stems, and they can be positioned more closely together. This approach also applies to trees; closer trees are larger, whereas distant trees are shorter and thinner.

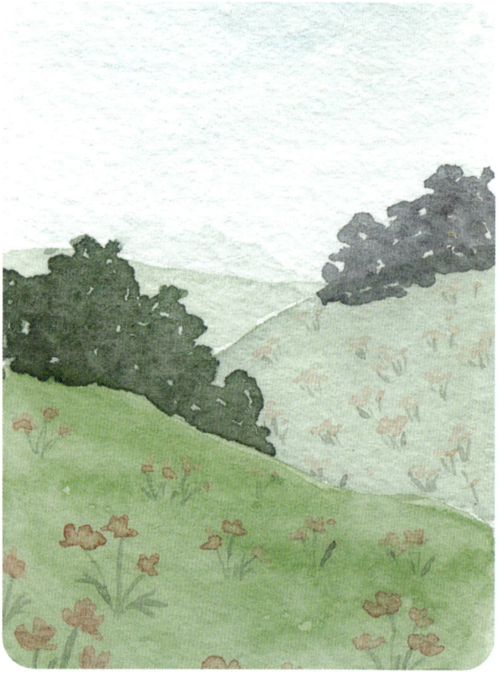

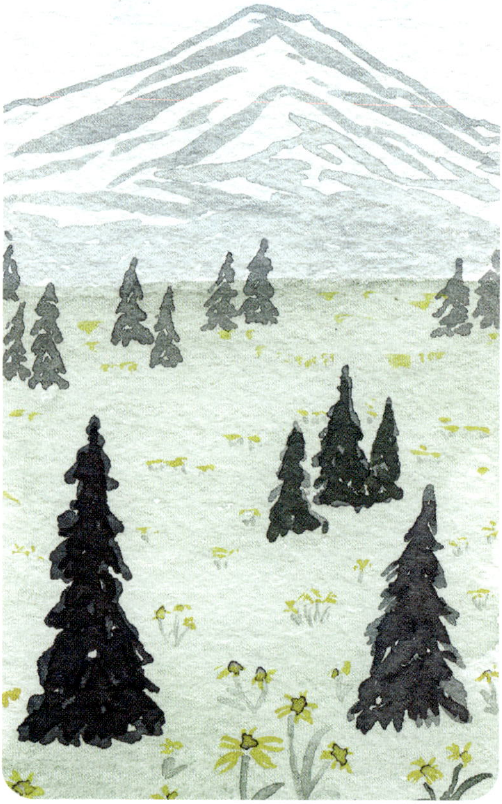

Details fall away in the distance. This technique is related to the previous point, but it still bears mentioning. Distant flowers or clumps of trees don't always need to be defined individuals. We can use strategically placed blobs and patches of color to suggest these elements. If you are standing in a meadow, the flowers closest to you are defined and sharp, but those near the horizon appear simply as swaths of color.

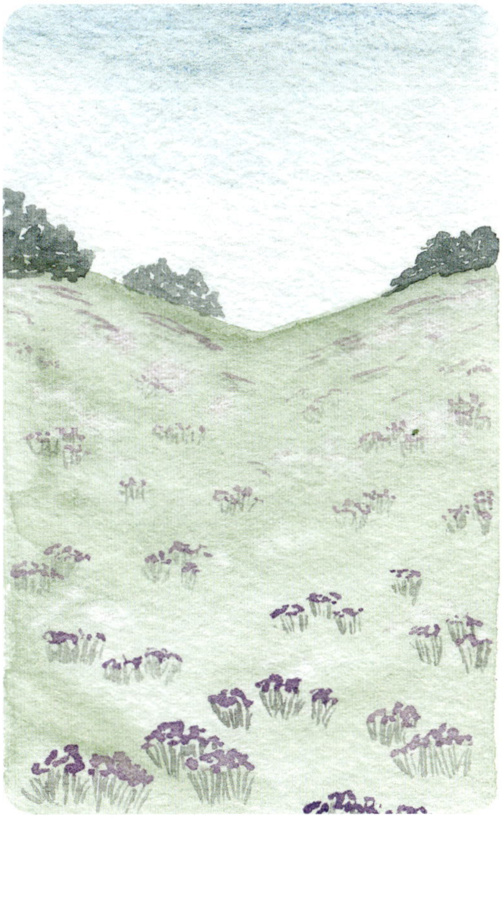

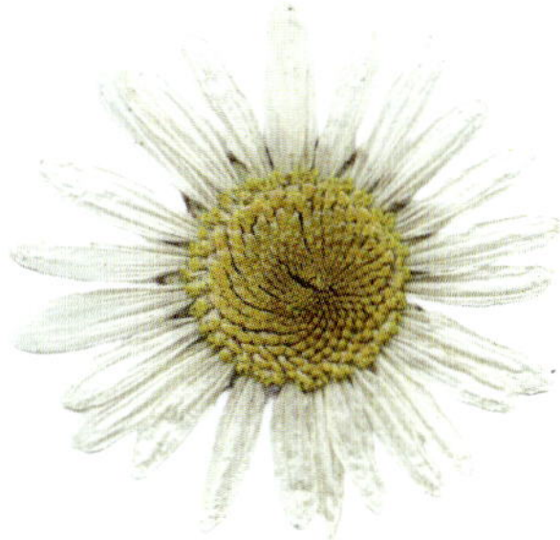

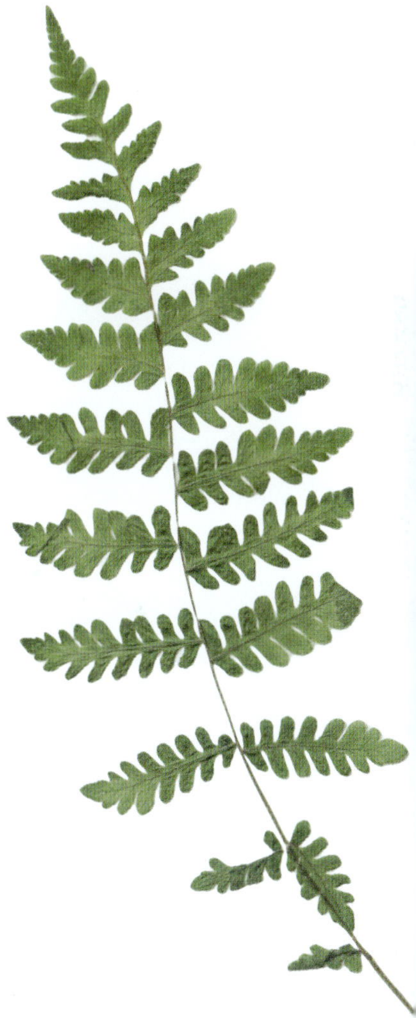

PRACTICE EXERCISES

There are some common elements that are used in many different projects in this book. Let's review some techniques before we jump into full projects.

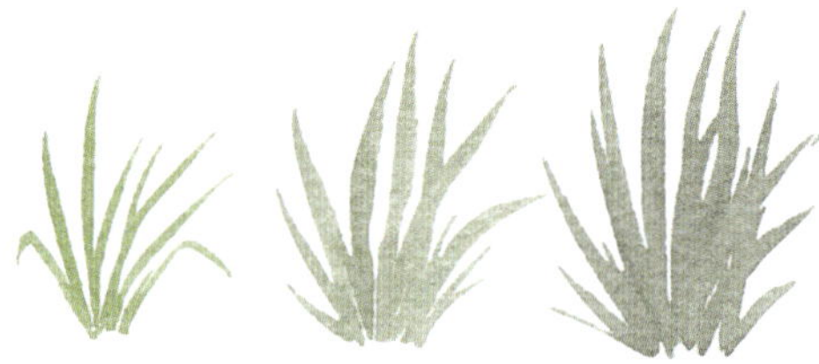

Grasses

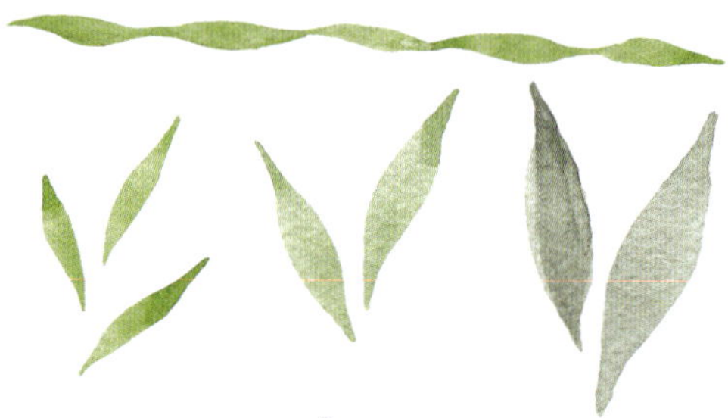

Leaves

painting grasses

Grasses play an important role in the meadows, fields and shoreline scenes in this book. The brushstrokes used to create grasses are similar to those used for flower stems, too.

To practice the brushstroke needed to paint grasses, select one of your round brushes. Smaller is typically better here, but if your round brushes have a sharp point, you can achieve great results with a larger brush too. Dip the brush in some moderately pigmented green or brown paint. Then, holding the brush perpendicular to the paper, place the brush point lightly on the paper and swipe a quick vertical line upward, lifting the brush with a flicking motion to create a wispy, tapered end to the brushstroke. This single mark could be a blade of grass. To create a clump of grasses, make lots of these brushstrokes, all originating from roughly the same point on the page. Vary the angles of the marks for an organic mass of feathery grasses.

You can add some interest to your grasses by painting little dots and dashes around the tops of some of the blades, to give the effect of seed heads.

painting leaves

Leaves are a simple but important component to the flowers we will paint in our watercolor flowerscapes. We will focus on one main leaf type: the simple ovate leaf.

To practice the brushstroke needed to paint leaves, pick up one of your round brushes and some green paint. Hold the brush almost perpendicular to the paper, but at a slight angle. Then place the point of the brush to the paper, starting your leaf with a thin mark. Next, press through the belly of the brush to create a wider mark. Pull the point of the brush through the wider mark made by the belly, lifting pressure gradually until only the point of the brush remains on the opposite end of the leaf. Then lift it off to create a tapered end.

These leaves can vary in length and width, depending on your brush size and the amount of pressure you place through the belly as you paint. You can practice this brushstroke by repeating the steps outlined previously, but keep your brush in contact with the paper to create a line of thick and thin marks. This will help you get a feel for the amount of pressure needed to create one of these simple tapered leaves.

painting tiny flowers

linear flowers (e.g., lavender, salvia, larkspur, lupine, etc.)

Pick up some moderately pigmented paint with your size 2 round brush. Using the brush point, paint a vertical line of five to seven little dots and dabs, making them slightly smaller toward the top. Paint another line the same way, next to the first, varying the overall height and angle. Add two or three more lines of dots in the same way.

Once these have dried, use a size 2 round brush to pick up a moderately pigmented green color for the stems and leaves. Using light pressure through the brush point, drag a thin line downward from the bottom of one of the linear flowers. The length of the stem below the flower should be about half of the total plant length (e.g., flower 50 percent, stem 50 percent). You can add a few short green lines or marks within the flower itself to fill in any gaps, but it doesn't need to be super exact or realistic. These are loose flowers.

Then, add stems and leaves to the remaining flowers in the cluster, allowing the stems to meet at the bottom in the same general area.

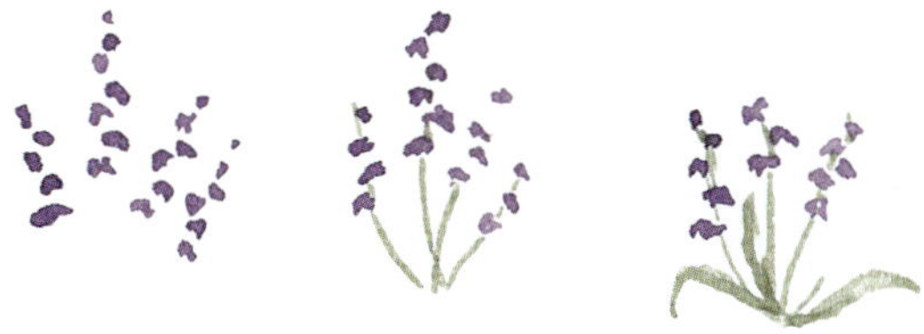

Linear Flowers

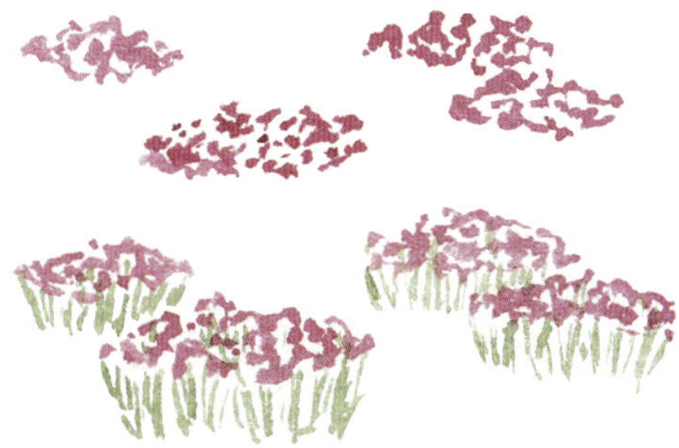

Cluster Flowers

cluster flowers (i.e., sweet alyssum)

Cluster flowers are low-growing flowers with countless individual blossoms in large masses. To begin, pick up some moderately pigmented paint with your size 2 round brush. Using the brush point, paint a bunch of little dots and dabs in an oval-shaped horizontal cluster, leaving gaps between some of the dots but allowing a few to touch and run together. Add more oval-shaped clusters of dots nearby at different heights and shapes.

Once these have dried, pick up a moderately pigmented green color for the stems. Using many short, quick vertical brushstrokes, paint stems beneath the flower dots. They don't need to line up perfectly, and they can intersect with each other—the goal is simply to illustrate dense, low-growing flora. These plants don't necessarily need any leaves added to them.

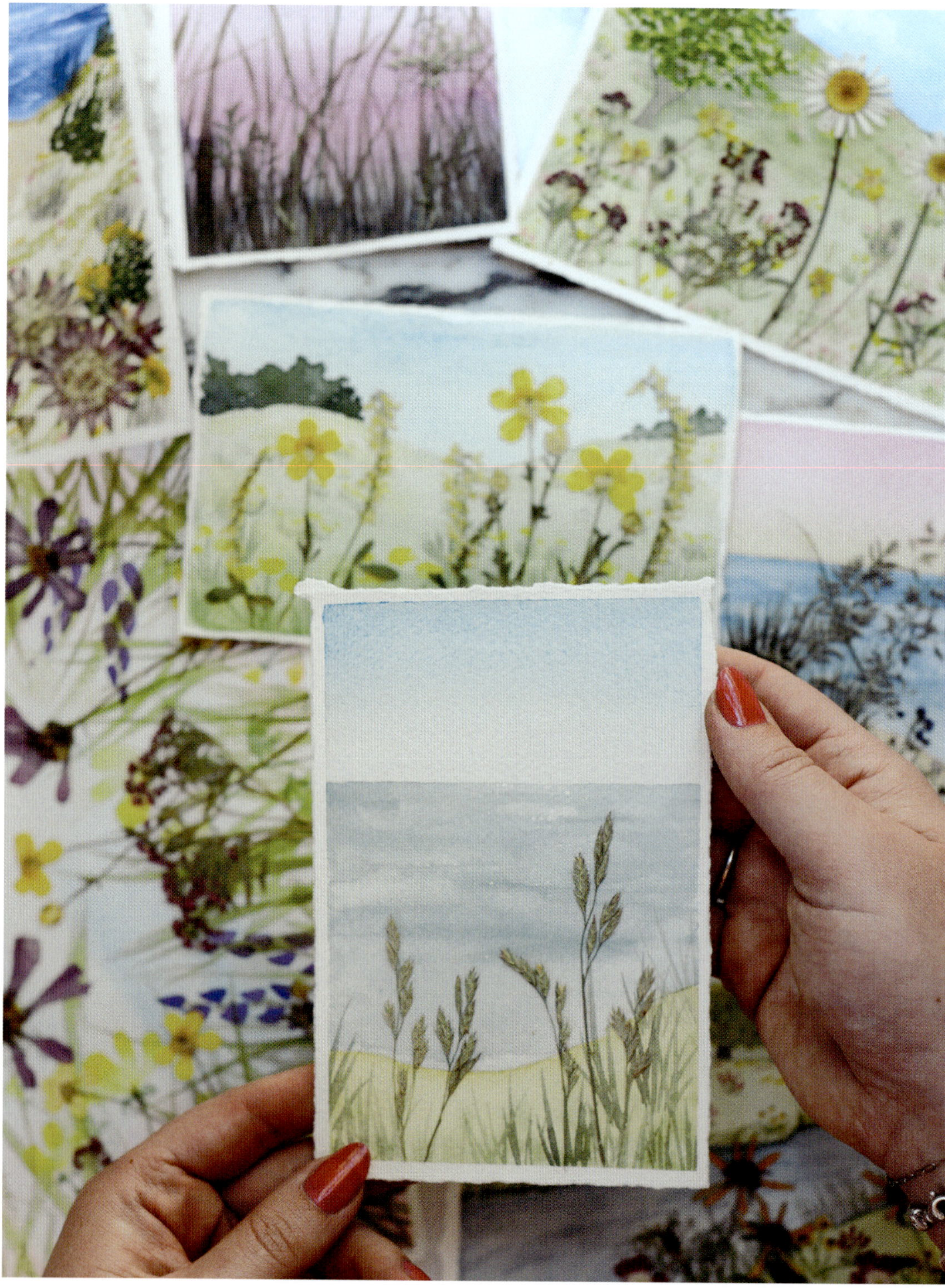

cup-shaped or "V-shaped" flowers (e.g., buttercups, tulips, poppies, etc.)

Using a filbert brush, pick up some moderately pigmented paint. Using the broad side of the brush, paint two small brushstrokes to create a *V* shape. Then add a thinner petal or two by using the side of the brush. It should look like the side (profile) view of a round flower, or sort of like a small tulip. Paint a few more of these flowers nearby, as though they could all be branching from the same plant.

You can also use a small round brush for this, but you may need to add additional brushstrokes to get the same effect. In other words, rather than using two broad brushstrokes to create the *V* or cup shape, you may need to use four or five.

Once the flowers have dried, add stems. Using moderately pigmented green paint and your size 2 round brush, lightly paint a thin, gracefully curved line from the base of one flower downward. The length of the stem can vary, but for this type of flower, I like to make it three or four times the length of the flower head, so the flower appears tall and wispy. Add stems to the other flowers nearby, connecting all the stems at their bases to create one main plant.

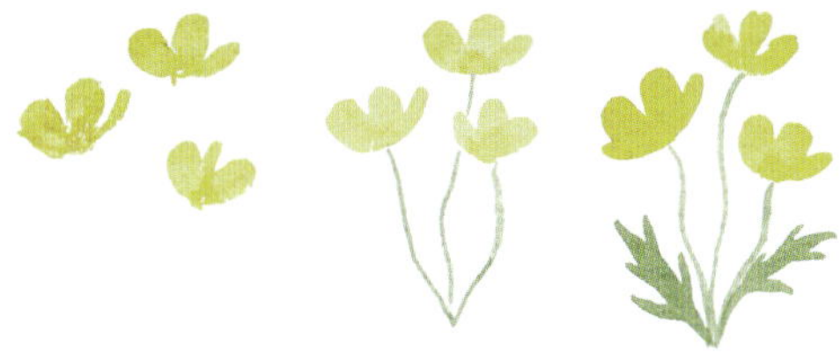

Cup-Shaped Flowers

The leaves for these flowers will be more detailed in nature than ones we have painted so far. Using the same paint mixture and brush as before, paint another stem on the outer side of the flower stems, placing more pressure through the brush for a broader line, and connect it with the same base point as the other stems. Next, pick up the brush and place the point just below the top of the leaf and to the left. Then make another small mark, dragging the brush into the leaf. Move to the right-hand side of the leaf and repeat. Finally, create two more marks, one on either side, below the first two. You should have a leaf with five unique points. You can practice with this leaf shape, changing the length, width and spacing to create different effects.

star-shaped/radial flowers (e.g., daisies, black-eyed Susans, etc.)

Using a small round brush (the smaller the brush, the smaller the flowers) and some moderately pigmented paint mixture, paint short lines radiating out from an imagined central point in a circle, like a firework or starburst. This will be a face view of the flower. You can paint a profile (side) view of the flower by painting similar lines radiating from an imagined central point, but in a half circle or less. Paint a few examples of each type in a small group.

Once these flower petals are dry, use a pigmented mixture of another color of paint and the same brush to tap little dots in a vague circle in the imagined central point. For black-eyed Susans, use yellow paint for the petals and a darker brown-black color for the center; for daisies, use white gouache for the petals and a sunny yellow color for the center. For the face-view flowers, this center is in the middle; for the profile-view flowers, this center is at the top where the petals meet.

To paint the stems, use the same process we used for the linear flowers: Using a small round brush and moderately pigmented green paint, lightly paint a line down from one of the flowers (nestling the brush between two petals to start). Paint similar stems on the other flowers in the grouping, allowing the bases of the stems to meet in roughly the same area. Paint a few small simple leaves on alternating sides along the stems (page 36).

umbel flowers (e.g., Queen Anne's lace, fennel, cow parsley, etc.)

To practice painting these flowers in white, create a watery wash of color (green, ideally, since this will be the backdrop to many of our flowers). Then allow it to dry completely. Next, pick up some white opaque watercolor or gouache on your small round brush. Paint little circular and semicircular clusters of tiny dots with the brush point, making sure the clusters have the rounded side on top and the flat side on the bottom. Allow these to dry.

To complete the umbels on the semicircular flowers, pick up some pigmented green mixture (darker than the background) with your small round brush. Lightly paint a series of very small lines (flower stalks) from beneath the white dots, connecting them at a central point just below the flower. Then paint a single, slightly thicker line downward from that central point for the main stem. For the round flowers, paint the same slightly thicker line for the main stem (since we don't see the small flower stalks for these).

For the leaves, use this same brush and paint mixture, and paint a thin light line like another stem, originating from the base of the other stems. Then place your brush point within this line and paint a few quick, swiping strokes outward from either side—as if you are painting tiny blades of grass with tapered ends—up and down the central line. You should end up with a feathery leaf. Paint one or two more of these leaves on the sides of the plant.

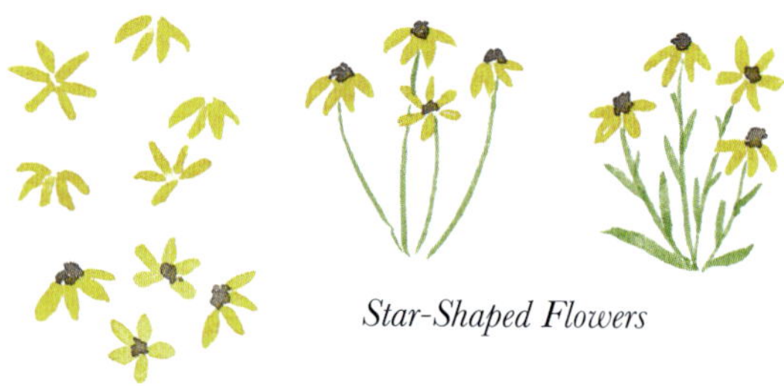

Star-Shaped Flowers

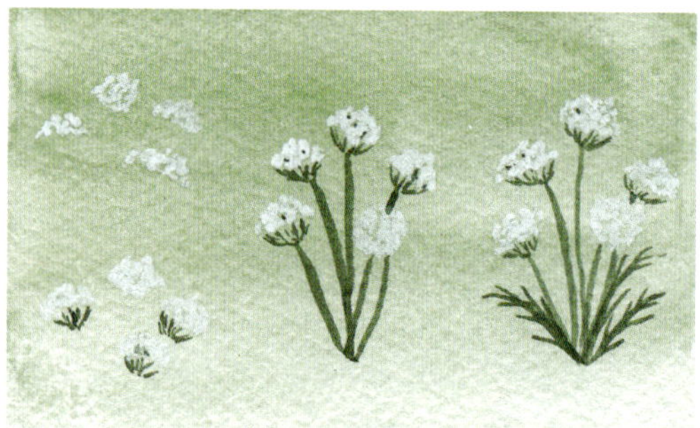

Umbel Flowers

trees

deciduous trees (distant)

For a distant group of trees, use one of your larger round brushes loaded with a dark-green pigmented paint mixture. Tap the point of the brush to the paper in a series of dots and dabs, varying the amount of pressure and the angle of the brush to make different shaped marks. You can be a bit lazy with your brush here, not picking it up fully between every mark. Allow these marks to form a cluster—with some gaps and spaces but plenty of overlap in the center—until you have an irregular blob. With a few horizontal, swiping strokes, clean up the bottom of this blob so it can rest on a distant horizon.

deciduous trees (near)

To paint closer deciduous trees, use one of your round brushes and a moderately pigmented yellow or green paint mixture. Tap the point of the brush to the paper in a series of dots and dabs, changing the angle of the brush and leaving some gaps throughout. Think about the crown shape of the tree you are painting—whether it is a tall, vertical, rectangular or oval-shaped crown or a broad, expansive, circular or horizontal oval-shaped crown—and keep your marks mostly within that shape. Keep in mind that trees aren't perfectly geometric in shape, so use these imagined shapes only as the loosest guideline.

With a darker shade of the pigment you already used, add more marks to your tree without completely covering up what is there. This helps add dimension and movement to the leaves.

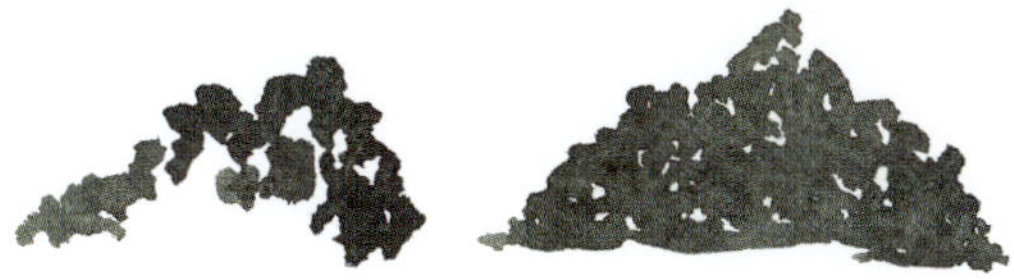

Deciduous Trees (Distant)

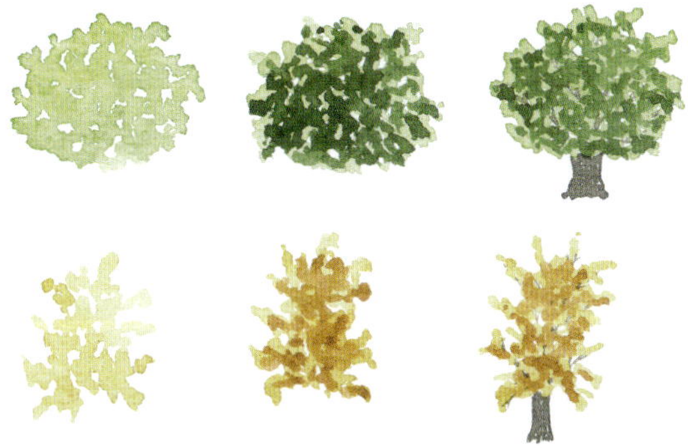

Deciduous Trees (Near)

As a final step, create a dark grayish-brown mixture on your palette to paint the trunk and branches of the tree. (Burnt Umber and Payne's Gray are my go-to combination.) First, paint a rectangle at the base of the crown, as the trunk. Try to imagine this in proportion to the crown you have painted. Imagine the limbs and branches fanning out from the trunk up through the crown. Most of these will be hidden by the leaves, but you can use the point of your brush to paint short little segments using straight lines and *V* and *Y* shapes. Make sure these lines are thin.

evergreen trees

Use one of your round brushes loaded with a pigmented dark-green mixture. Holding the brush like a pencil, with the point of the brush pointed toward the top of the page, tap it on the paper to make an irregular triangular shape comprised of dots, blobs and short diagonal lines. Continue adding dots and blobs, allowing your brush to be lazy at times and not completely leave the page between brushstrokes, to lengthen the triangle and create a gently tapered shape, widening slightly as you move downward. Finish the bottom of the tree with a roughly flat bottom.

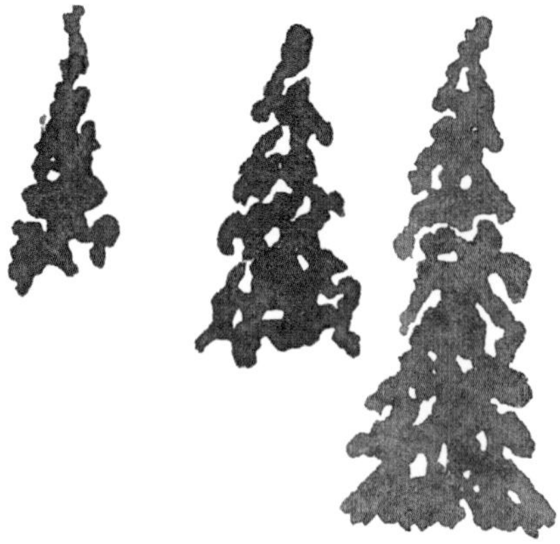

You can also paint evergreen trees by painting a straight vertical line before adding dots and blobs along this line (the trunk). Allow the tree to become wider as you move toward the bottom of the line.

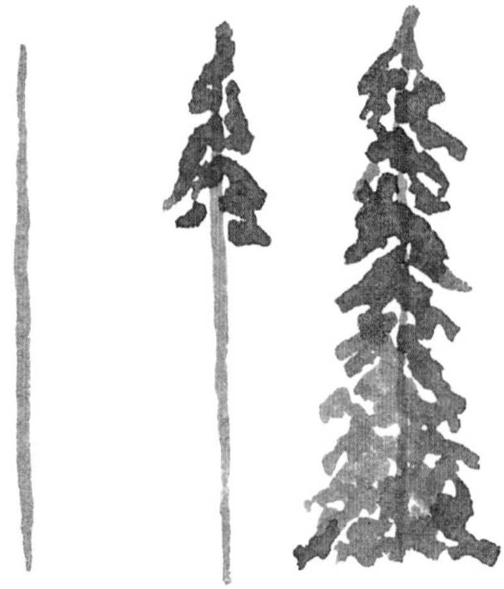

PART II

putting it all together

You can make watercolor flowerscapes in any size you would like. The dimensions of your project will depend on your comfort zone and the scale of the flowers you would like to use. Tiny wildflowers work better on small-scale pieces, while larger flowers fit better on a big page.

The majority of the projects I've painted for this book measure 5 x 7 inches (12.5 x 18 cm) and 8 x 10 inches (20 x 25 cm), with a few that are 4 x 6 inches (10 x 15 cm), but in my own work, I've also made watercolor flowerscapes as small as 2 x 2 inches (5 x 5 cm) and as large as 11 x 14 inches (28 x 36 cm). If you plan to work with different dimensions, you may need to adjust your brush selections in addition to your flower selections.

If you are unsure what size to paint but you have certain flowers you want to use, experiment first. Place the flowers on sheets of paper of various sizes to see how much space they will occupy, and then decide whether or not that will work with the landscape you plan to paint.

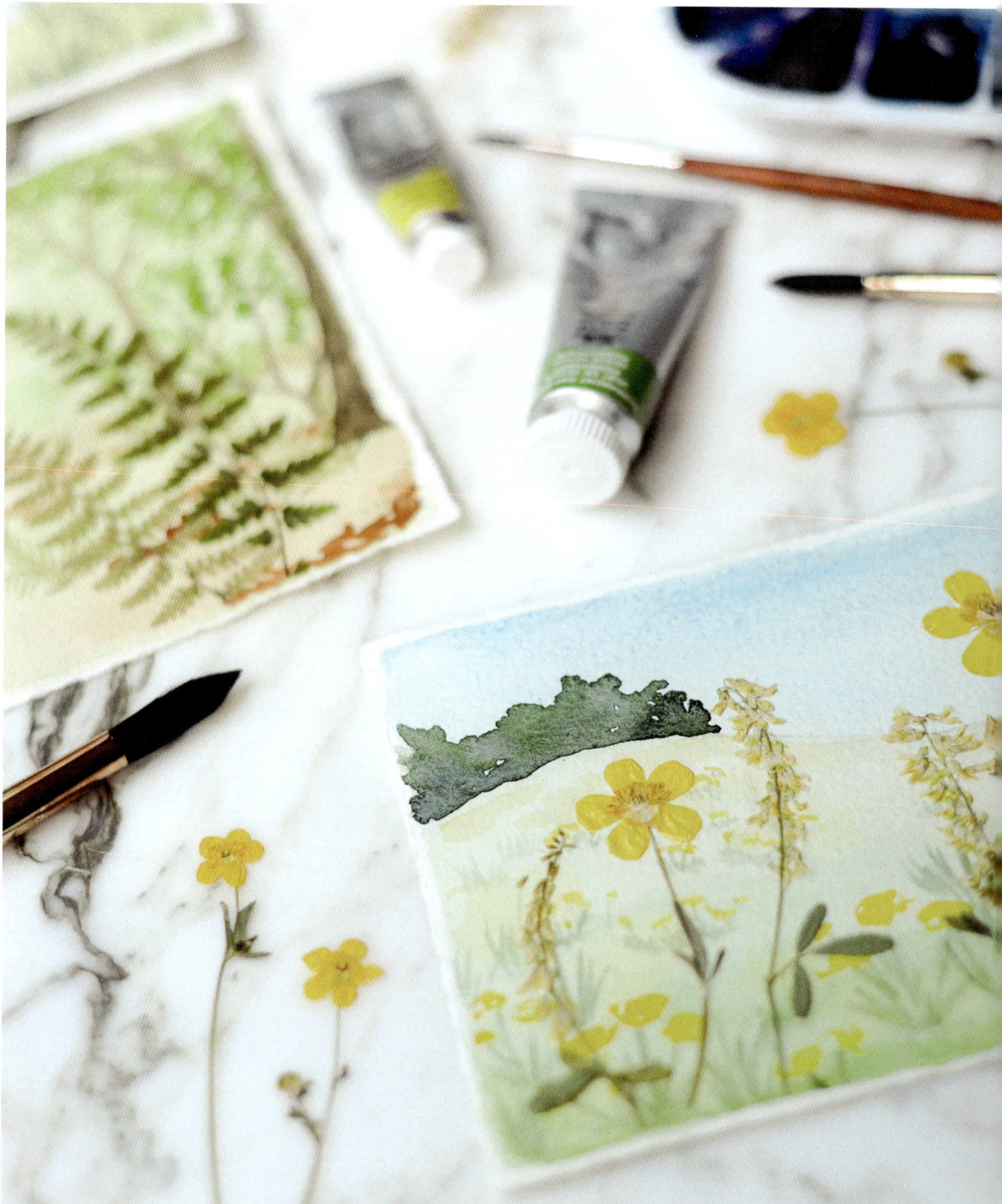

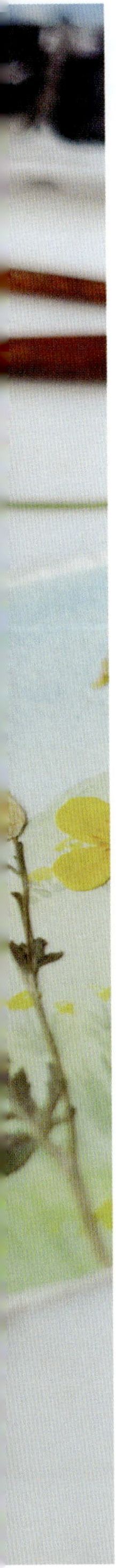

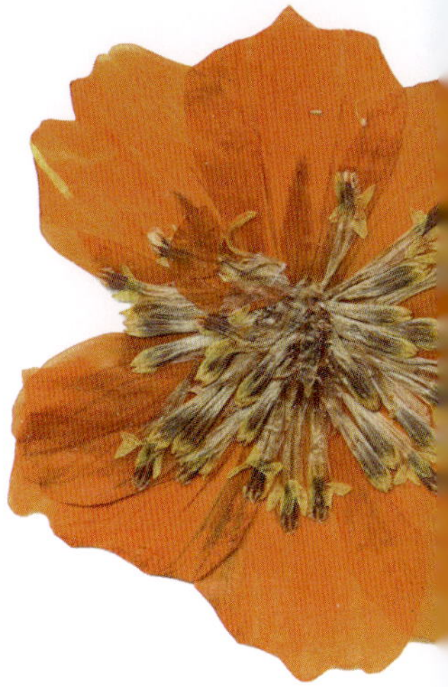

simple STARTS

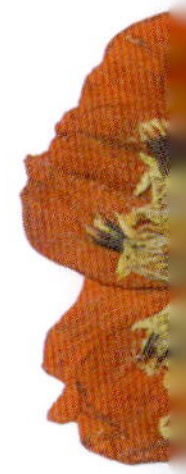

These first few projects are designed to be a gentle and fun introduction to the combination of using watercolors and pressed flowers. To practice some of the foundations we learned in the first part of this book, we will explore creating graduated washes, painting some simple tiny flowers and using other techniques. Then, we will adorn our paintings with a simple palette of pressed flowers to complete our first watercolor flowerscapes.

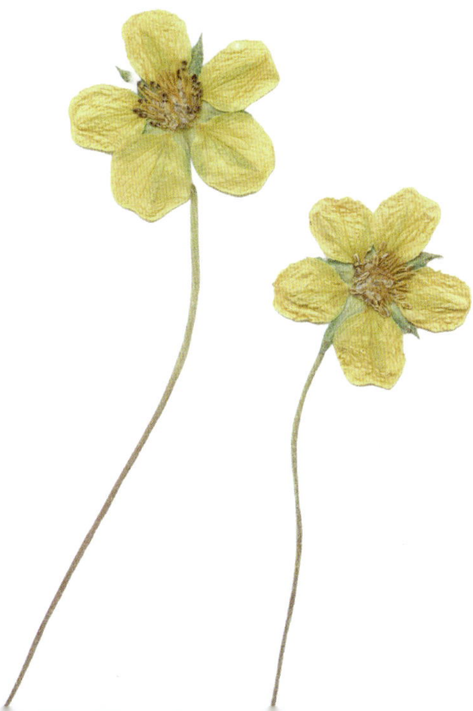

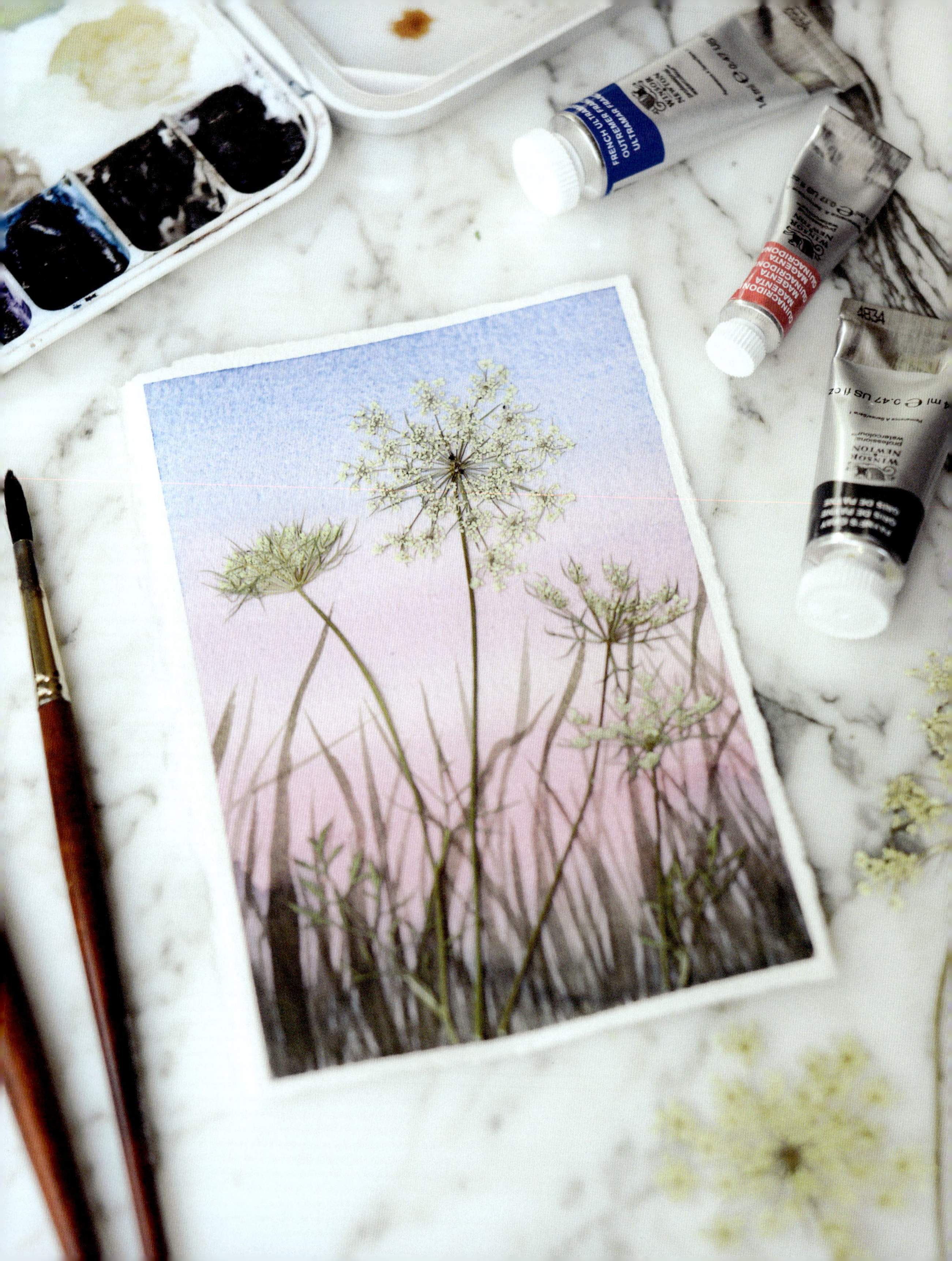

WILDFLOWER SUNSET

A sunset gradient and some grasses in silhouette are the perfect backdrop for a few delicate wildflowers in this simple—but striking—painting. We will explore blending colors with wet-into-wet technique and practice brushstrokes that will be used throughout many of the projects in this book. For this piece, I am using some Queen Anne's lace, both flowers and buds on stems. These flowers are easy to press, have tons of intricate detail without adding a lot of color and look great in a field of grasses. You could also use pressed grasses or other delicate, wispy pressed flowers if you don't have access to Queen Anne's lace.

size

4 x 6" (10 x 15 cm)

brushes

Wash brush
Size 10 round brush
Size 6 round brush
Glue brush

flower palette

Queen Anne's lace on stems, with leaves attached

materials

Tweezers (optional)
Scissors
Glue
Waxed paper
Heavy Books

color palette

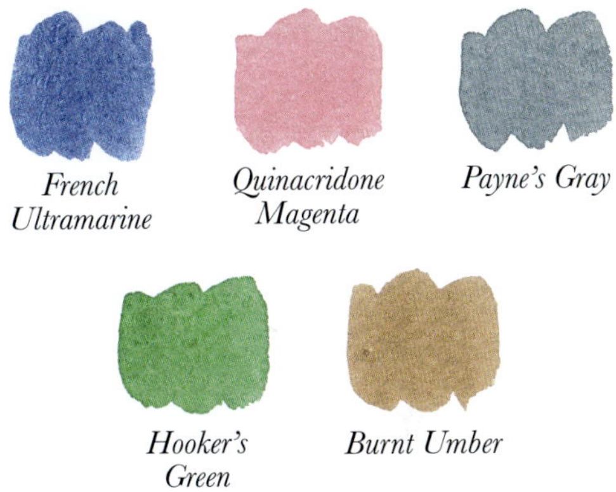

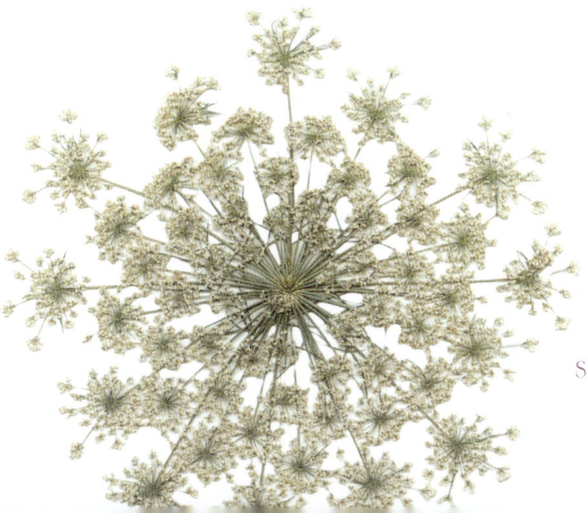

2

3

4

step 1

On your palette, create three washes: a wash of French Ultramarine with just a drop of Quinacridone Magenta; a wash with a 50/50 mix of French Ultramarine and Quinacridone Magenta; and a wash of Quinacridone Magenta with just a drop of French Ultramarine. You will end up with three puddles of color, each a different shade of purple.

step 2

Load your size 10 round brush with the first mixture (mostly blue), and begin making sweeping horizontal strokes at the top of the paper. Continue painting until you have filled the top one-fourth to one-third of the page. Dip your brush in your water cup and drag it along the edge of the cup to remove some excess water. Then, paint along the bottom of your first section to soften the edge.

step 3

Clean your brush. Then, while the previous layer is still damp, pick up some of the 50/50 mixture and paint a horizontal band right beneath the portion you just painted. Next, paint a band right above that line, so it overlaps into the bluish-purple portion, which will help the two sections start to blend. Continue painting downward until you have filled about one-half to two-thirds of the page. When you reach the end of this section, dip your brush in your water cup and drag it along the edge to remove some excess water. Then, paint along the bottom of your purple section to soften the edge.

step 4

Clean your brush. Then, while the paper is still damp, pick up some of the third mixture and repeat the same process from the previous steps until you reach the bottom. We are going for a smooth gradient of color, so if there are any hard edges, use a damp (not soaking wet) brush to soften them. Be careful not to overwork it, though! Allow the piece to dry for a bit before moving on.

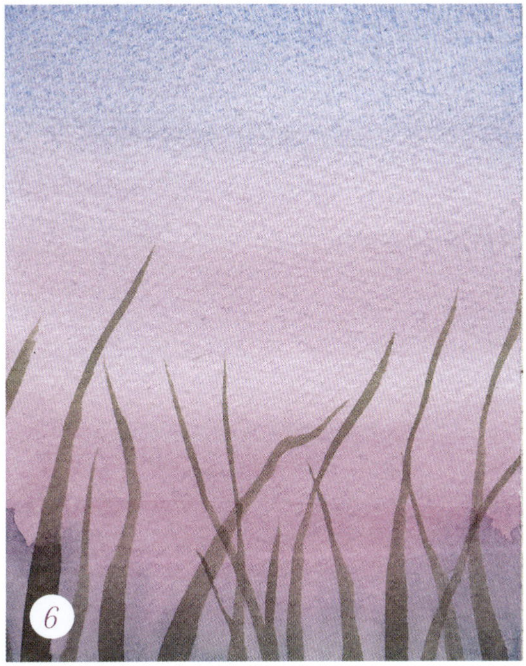

step 5

Create a watery mix of Payne's Gray on your palette. Then, dampen the bottom quarter of the page with clean water and your wash brush. (If preferred, you can use a large round brush for this instead.) Load your size 6 brush with the Payne's Gray mixture, and paint a stripe across the very bottom of the page. The damp paper should allow this paint to bleed and bloom upward. Use the point of the brush to tap the paper to add in some more pigment in clusters right above the stripe you just laid down, making sure everything connects. (If there are gaps, fill them in with more pigment.) We want to end up with a dark, hazy area at the bottom of the page. Allow the painting to dry.

step 6

Create a pigmented mix of Hooker's Green and Burnt Umber on your palette for a dark earthy-green color. Then add a drop or two of Payne's Gray to darken it further. Using your size 6 brush, pick up some of this paint, and begin painting blades of grass. Starting with the point of your brush pointing downward at the bottom of the page, apply pressure through the belly of the brush while swiping the brush upward. Lift the brush while still dragging it upward on the paper so it forms a tapered end on the blade of grass. For this step, we want the blades of grass to end somewhere within the bottom half of the page. Paint more blades of grass, moving across the page and varying the angle of each blade, allowing some to cross. You can also shake your hand a little bit while dragging the brush upward to give the grasses some bend and shape.

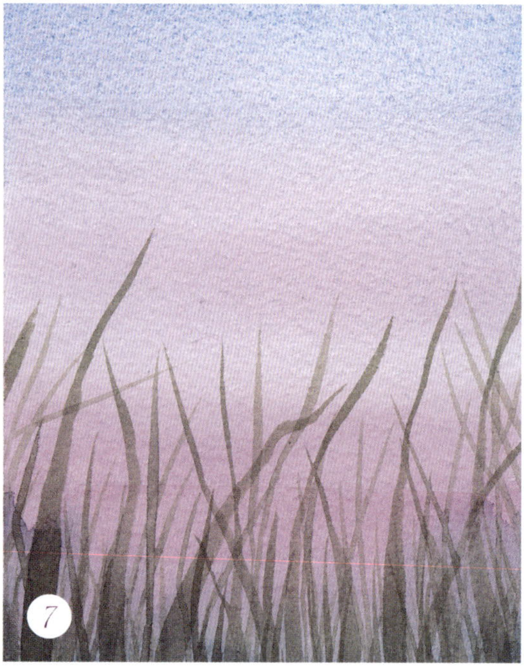

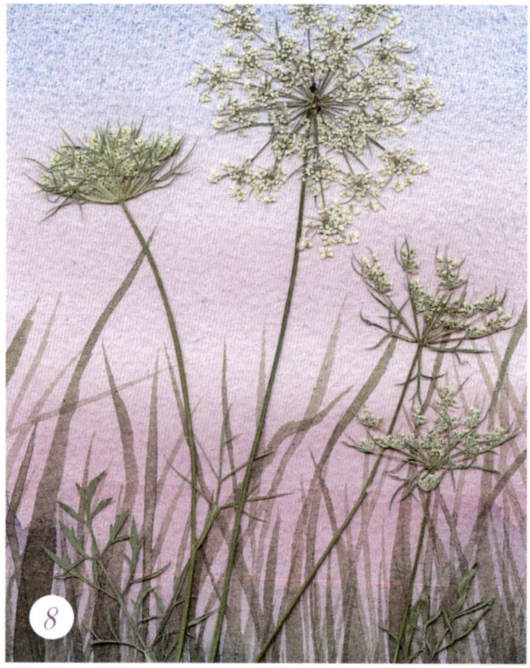

step 7

Load your brush with more paint, as needed, and continue filling in the lower portion of the page with more blades of the grass. Use lighter pressure on the brush so just the brush point makes contact with the page, but keep the rest of your technique consistent. This will make thinner blades of grass. Continue painting grasses until you are happy with the look! Allow it to dry completely. The painting portion is complete!

step 8

It is now time to add our pressed flowers. Position your flowers on top of your painting carefully, using your fingers or tweezers. I like to vary the heights of the flowers and keep the overall look asymmetrical, so I am using one full, round Queen Anne's lace as the tallest flower, rising above the tallest grasses and placed just to the right of center. Then I am surrounding it with buds and foliage at shorter heights and at varying angles from the bottom of the page.

Once you are happy with your layout, trim the stems to length and begin picking up the flowers one by one. Using your glue brush, carefully paint the back of each flower with a thin layer of glue and press them onto the paper using your fingers or tweezers. Once they are all mounted, set a piece of waxed paper on top of your piece and weigh it down with a few heavy books. Allow it to dry for at least 15 to 20 minutes before carefully peeling away the waxed paper. If you do this too quickly, you can peel your flowers off your page or break them. (See Mounting Flowers on page 22 for more details.) Your piece is now complete!

SEA BREEZE

The sight of beach grasses gently swaying in the breeze on a clear day, while the sound of the ocean fills the air, is a recipe for instant tranquility. This simple painting employs a serene color palette of blues and greens, and the addition of a few sprigs of pressed grass add texture and depth to complement the calm atmosphere. It comes together quickly, and in just a few steps, making it a great place to start. Grass seed heads are nice to harvest and press in late spring. If you don't have access to these, you could make this into a flowery scene by adding some small pressed flowers among the painted grasses.

size

4 x 6" (10 x 15 cm)

brushes

Size 10 round brush
Size 6 round brush
Glue brush

flower palette

Grass seed heads on stems

materials

Tweezers (optional)
Scissors
Glue
Waxed paper
Heavy Books

color palette

Cerulean Blue

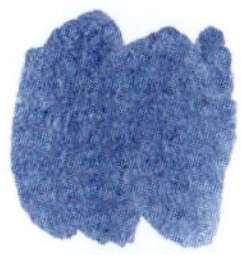
French Ultramarine

Hooker's Green

*Raw Sienna**

Cadmium-Free Yellow

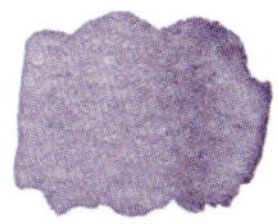
Winsor Violet

Burnt Umber

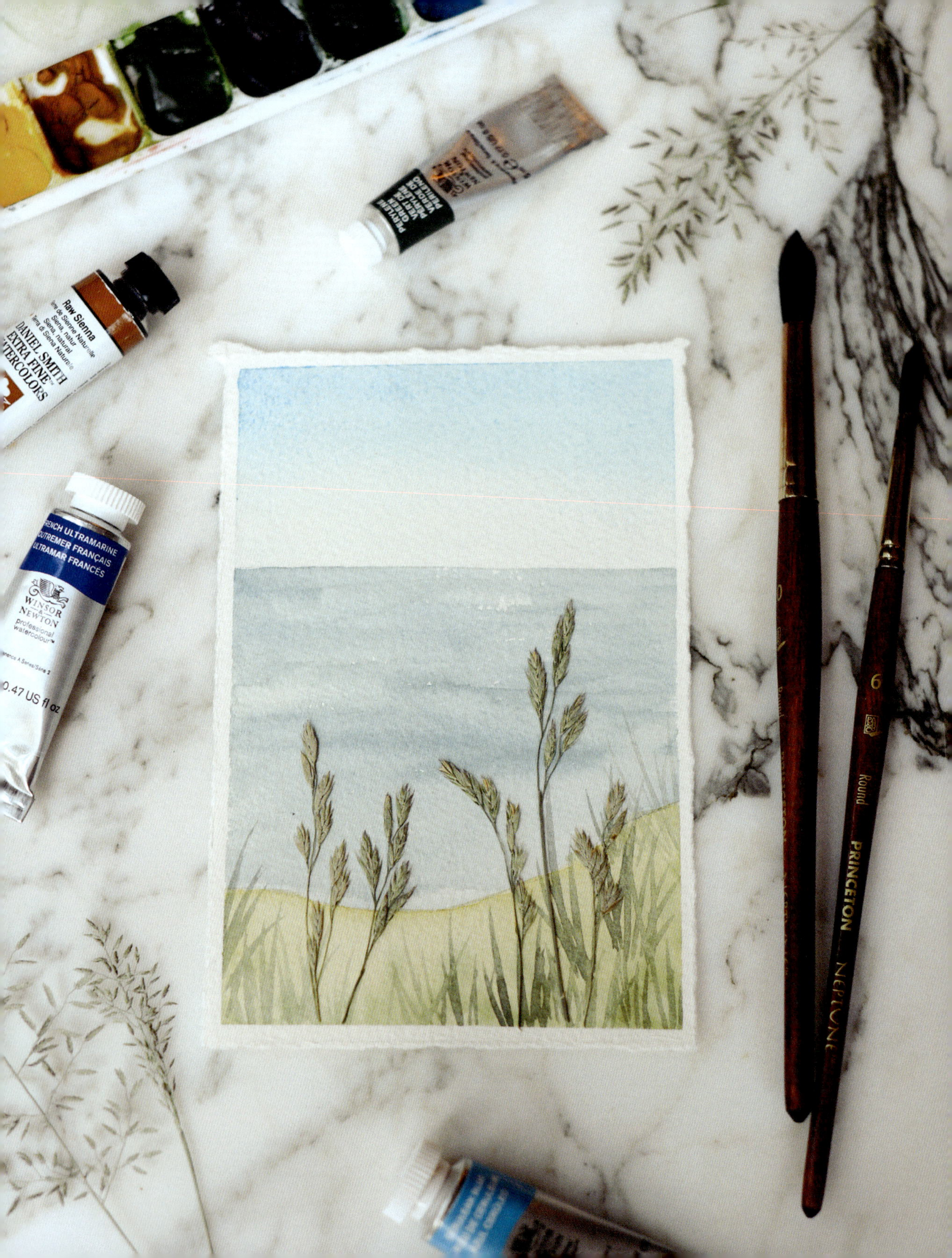
Raw Sienna
DANIEL SMITH
EXTRA FINE
FRENCH ULTRAMARINE
OUTREMER FRANÇAIS
ULTRAMAR FRANCES
WINSOR
NEWTON
professional
watercolour
0.47 US fl oz
6
Round
PRINCETON
NEPTUNE

1

2

step 1

Lightly draw a horizon line a third of the way from the top of the page. Next, lightly draw an uneven line across the bottom of the page, making it higher on one side. This will be our sand dune.

Make a watery mix of Cerulean Blue on your palette. Pick up some of this mixture with your size 10 round brush, and start making sweeping horizontal brushstrokes at the very top of the page. Continue making these brushstrokes as you move down to the horizon line. If the brush begins to dry, dip it in your water cup and drag it along the edge of the cup lightly to squeeze out a little bit of the water. You should get a nice graduated wash from darker to lighter. Allow the painting to dry.

step 2

When the piece is dry, create a mix of French Ultramarine with just a little bit of Hooker's Green on your palette. Load your size 10 round brush with this mixture, and carefully paint a straight line along the horizon, right beneath the first pencil line. Continue making horizontal strokes as you work down the page toward the second pencil line, picking up more paint from your palette as necessary. It's okay if a little bit of the paper texture shows through—and it's okay if it doesn't! Once you reach the sand dune line, carefully drag your paint brush along it. It's also fine if you see some irregular paint blooms or marks here. The ocean isn't still, and this is a simple, loose painting. Allow the painting to dry.

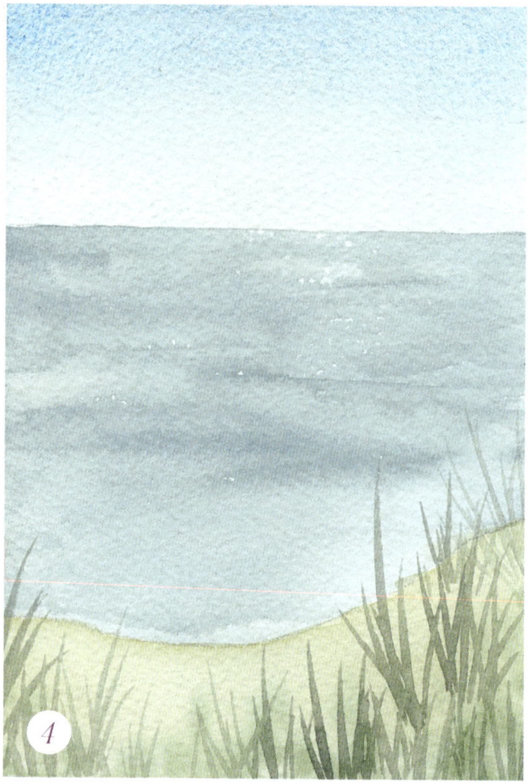

step 3

Create two paint mixes on your palette: Raw Sienna mixed with Cadmium-Free Yellow and a dash of Winsor Violet (for sand); and Hooker's Green with Burnt Umber (for earthy-green beach grass). Using your size 10 round brush, pick up some of the yellowish mixture, carefully paint along the sand dune line and fill in the rest of the white space beneath it. Then, while it is still damp, switch to your size 6 round brush and pick up some of the green mixture. Lightly tap the point of the brush along the bottom of the page in irregular clusters, using more paint in the area where the sand dune is taller. Because the paper is damp, these marks will soften and bleed into the sand. Allow the painting to dry.

step 4

Add a little bit of French Ultramarine to the greenish mixture on your palette to give it a slightly cooler tone. This will be for our beach grasses. Pick up some of this mixture with your size 6 brush, and hold the brush so it is perpendicular to the page. With light pressure on the point of the brush, quickly make sweeping upward brushstrokes. Lift the brush while swiping upward in order to create a tapered end on each brushstroke. Vary the direction and length of these strokes as you add more, allowing them to cross each other and "grow" from different places on the sand dune, but be careful not to cover up the sand completely. Allow the painting to dry. The painting portion is now complete!

step 5

In this step, we will add the pressed grass seeds heads or flowers. Carefully arrange the grass stems across the bottom of the page using your tweezers or your fingers. You will likely need to trim the stems for them to fit, but don't do this until you are sure of your final arrangement. (I like to leave the longer stem sticking off the bottom of the paper; then I come back in and break it or cut it when I am ready to finalize the design.) To keep things looking natural, vary the heights of the grasses, and look at your materials to see if you can break any side shoots off at the lower portion of the seed head. Often, one grass stem can be broken down into several usable parts, which will look a bit more natural on a smaller watercolor, rather than using one big clump.

Once you are happy with your layout, trim the stems to length and begin picking up the flowers one by one. Using your glue brush, carefully paint the back of each flower with a thin layer of glue, and press them onto the paper using your fingers or tweezers. Once they are all mounted, set a piece of waxed paper on top of your piece, and weigh it down with a few heavy books. Allow the piece to dry for at least 15 to 20 minutes before carefully peeling away the waxed paper. If you do this too quickly, you can peel your flowers off your page or break them. (See Mounting Flowers on page 22 for more details.) Your piece is now complete!

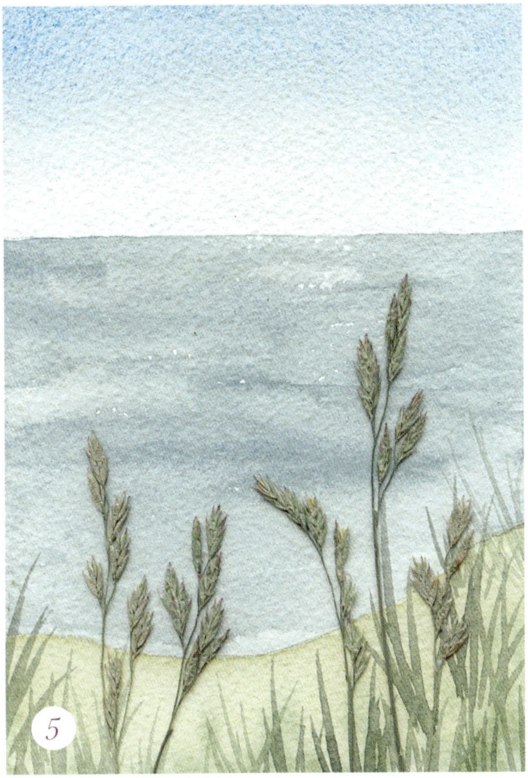

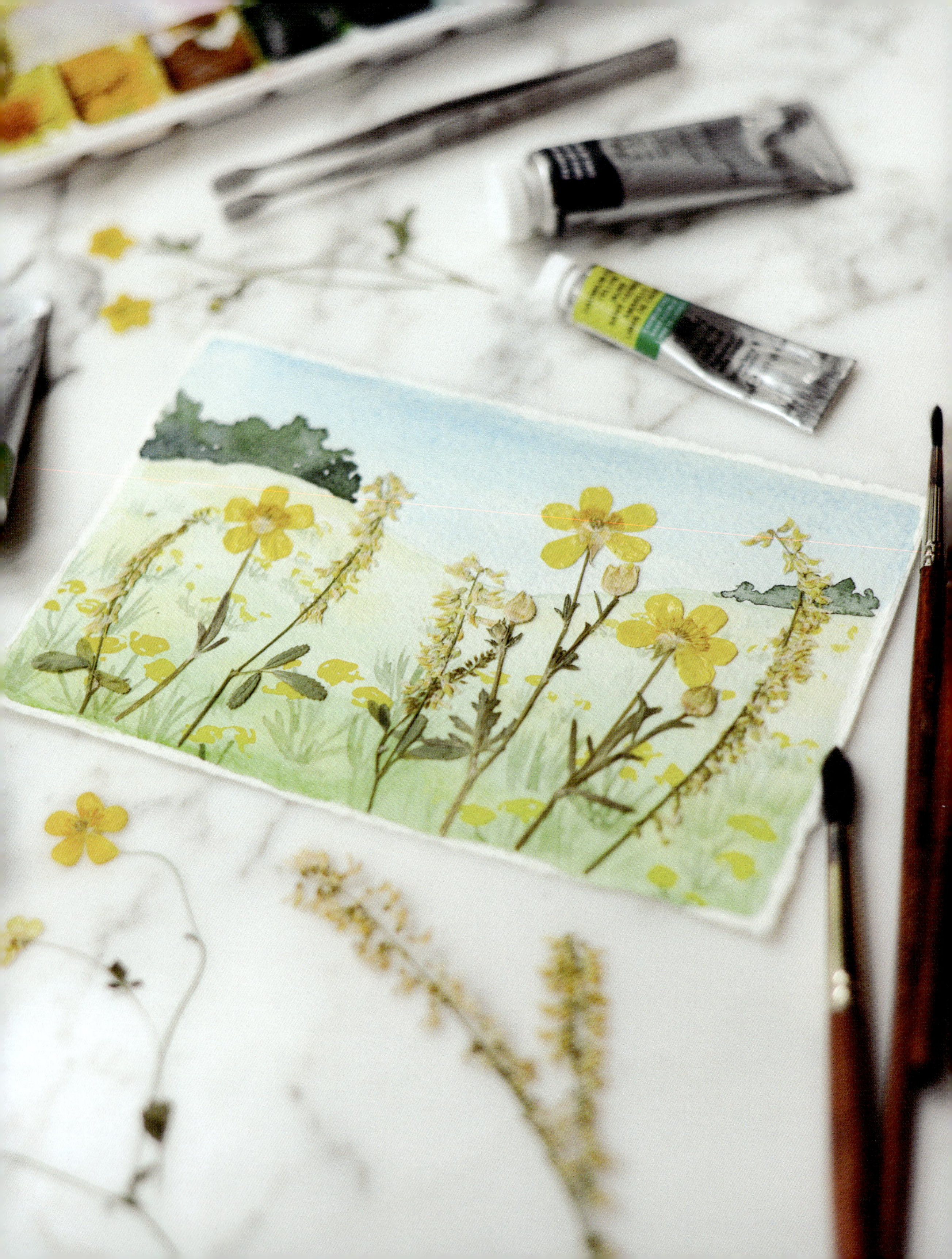

EARLY SPRING

After a long, cold winter, there is nothing quite like seeing bits of color return to the landscape in the form of greening grass and tiny wildflowers. Capturing the feeling of those first warm days in spring, we will paint gentle green hills beneath a bluebird sky and give the impression of some grasses and small yellow flowers. The addition of a few bright-yellow pressed flowers in the foreground and a darker line of trees in the distance will add depth and contrast to the finished project. You can experiment with scaling this scene up or down; I am using a smaller sheet of watercolor paper.

size

4 x 6" (10 x 15 cm)

brushes

Size 10 round brush
Size 6 round brush
Size 2 round brush
Glue brush

flower palette

Buttercups
Yellow clovers

materials

Tweezers (optional)
Scissors
Glue
Waxed paper
Heavy Books

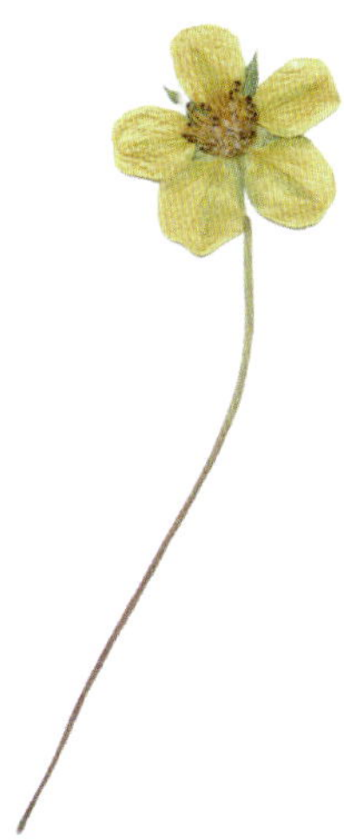

color palette

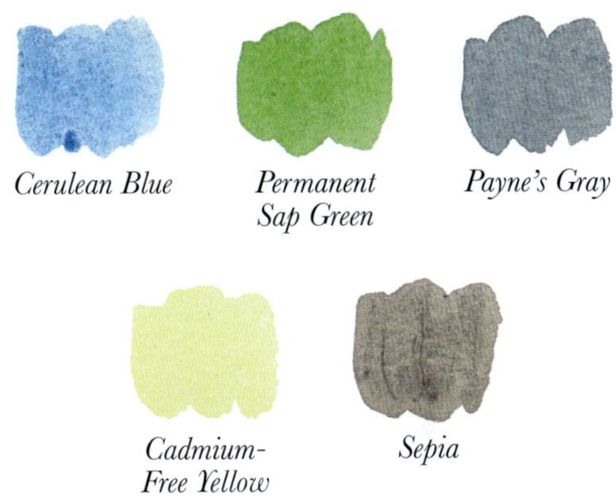

step 1

Lightly sketch some hills about one-third of the way down your paper. Then, on your palette, create a lightly pigmented mix of Cerulean Blue paint and water, and load up your size 10 round brush. Starting at the top of the page, use sweeping horizontal brushstrokes to paint in the sky, filling in the space above your pencil line. Allow the painting to dry.

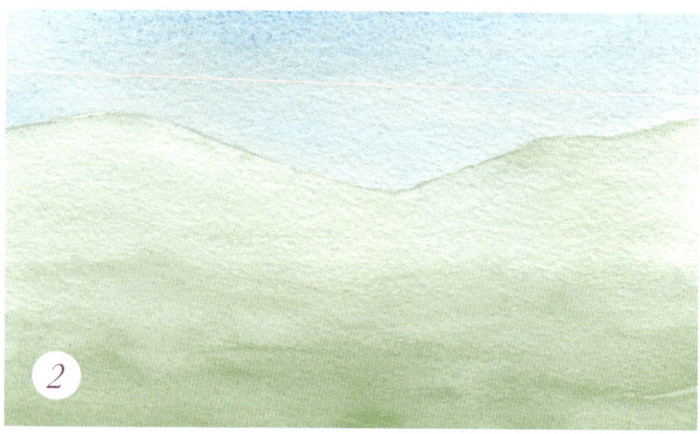

step 2

Once your sky has dried, erase your pencil marks. Create a moderately pigmented mix of Permanent Sap Green and water on your palette. Starting at the bottom of the paper this time, use your size 10 brush to paint similar broad, sweeping brushstrokes as we did in step 1. Paint upward to the established hill line, allowing your paint to become a bit less pigmented (by adding more water) as you work upward. Allow the painting to dry.

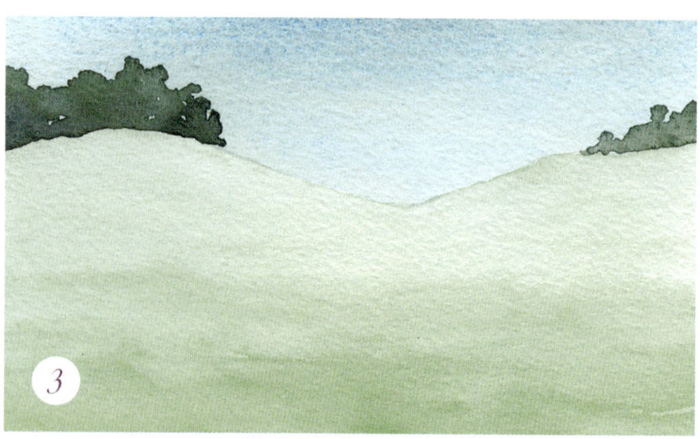

step 3

Create a pigmented mixture of Permanent Sap Green with a little bit of Payne's Gray on your palette for a cool-toned dark-green color. Using the size 10 round brush, grab some of this paint, and use the point of the brush to tap in some irregular dots and marks along the hilltops. These will become distant trees. Continue tapping these dots next to one another, leaving some gaps here and there for skylight to come through.

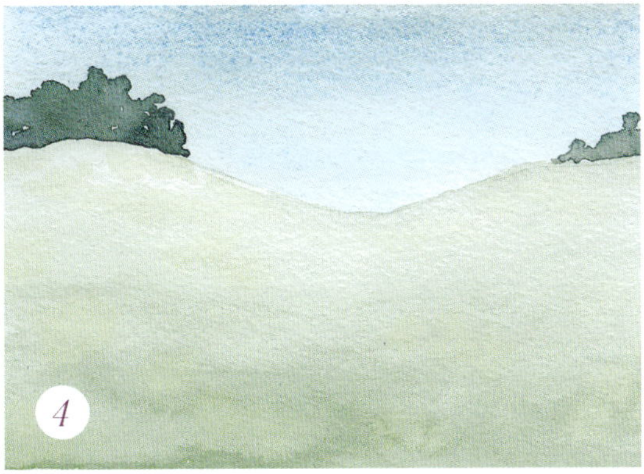

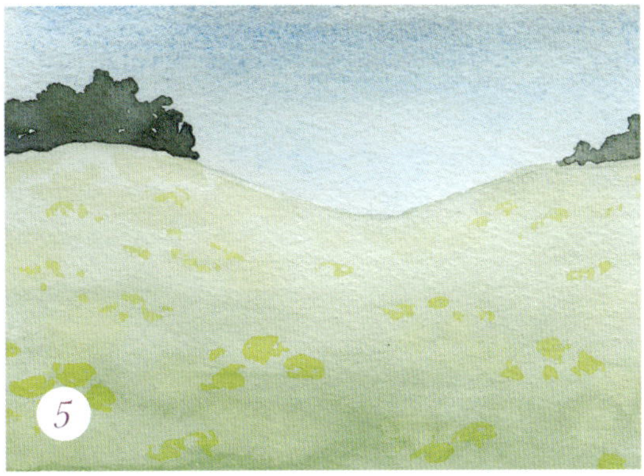

step 4

Using clean water and your size 10 brush, rewet your grassy hills with a thin layer of water, being careful not to disturb the trees you have just created. (Alternatively, you can wait for the trees to dry completely before you move on to this step.) Once the entire grass field is wet, use the tip of your size 6 round brush to lightly tap in dots of Cadmium-Free Yellow paint, straight from the pan. The wet paper will cause these dots to "bloom." In the foreground, toward the bottom of the paper, make the dots farther apart. As you move up the paper and toward the hilltops, the dots can cluster closer together or become larger swaths of yellow. Since the paper is wet, these yellow patches will blend and become subtle spots of color rather than distinct marks. Allow the painting to dry.

step 5

Once the paper is fully dry, use your size 6 brush and a concentrated Cadmium-Free Yellow paint from the pan to create a few more yellow marks, which will be more defined this time. Somewhere in the bottom third of the page, use light pressure and the tip of the brush to move the bristles in a circular motion to create a small, irregular oval shape. Continue to paint these shapes, clustering them together in groups of two to five, varying their spacing and size. You can also vary the pressure to allow some thinner lines and gaps to imply an organic bloom. As you move up the hillside, make the marks smaller and closer together until they resemble tiny dots in close groups. Allow the painting to dry.

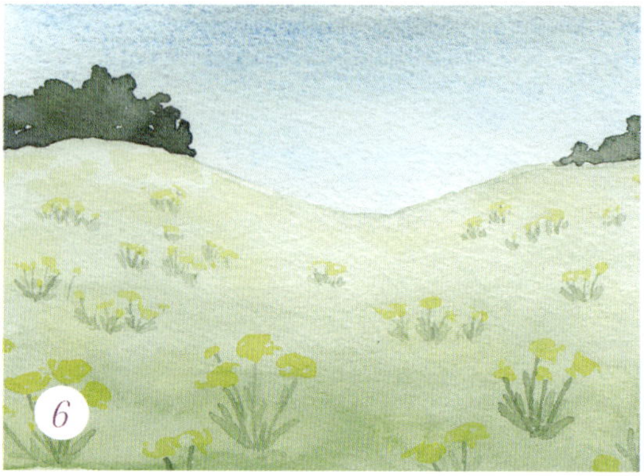

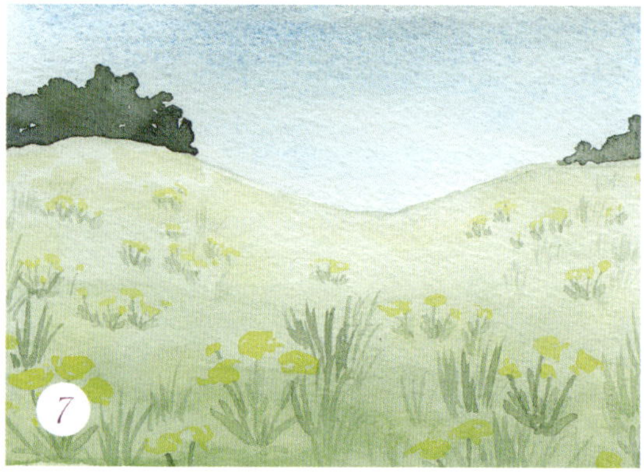

step 6

Mix together some Permanent Sap Green and Sepia paint on your palette to create a dark-green mix. This will be for our flower stems. Using the size 2 round brush and light pressure, start at the bottom of each flower and drag a delicate line of paint downward for its stem. Since the flowers are growing in clusters, you may connect your lines (or nearly connect them) beneath the flowers to show they are growing from one plant. The larger flowers toward the bottom of the page should have slightly thicker and longer stems, while the smaller ones as you move up the page should be thinner, shorter and closer together to imply they are farther away. Once your stems are finished, pick up your size 6 brush again and load it with the same dark-green paint so we can add some leaves. Paint simple leaves along the stems or at the bottom of each cluster by placing the tip of the brush to the page, then pressing lightly toward the belly of the brush as you drag downward. Gently lift the pressure to finish the leaf with just the brush point. Vary the size of the leaves per plant, and make them smaller as you move up the page, just as we did with the stems.

step 7

Using the same dark-green stem mixture and size 2 round brush, we can now add some taller grasses around the yellow flowers. Using a light touch and starting at the ground, paint each blade of grass by lightly dragging the brush upward and lifting it off the paper to create a thin tapered end. Cluster these grass blades together in clumps and scatter them across the page, once again making them smaller (and with less pigment and an even lighter touch) as you move up the paper. Do not fill in all the space, and keep it quick and loose so the lines are organic and natural. Set it aside to dry completely. The painting portion is now complete!

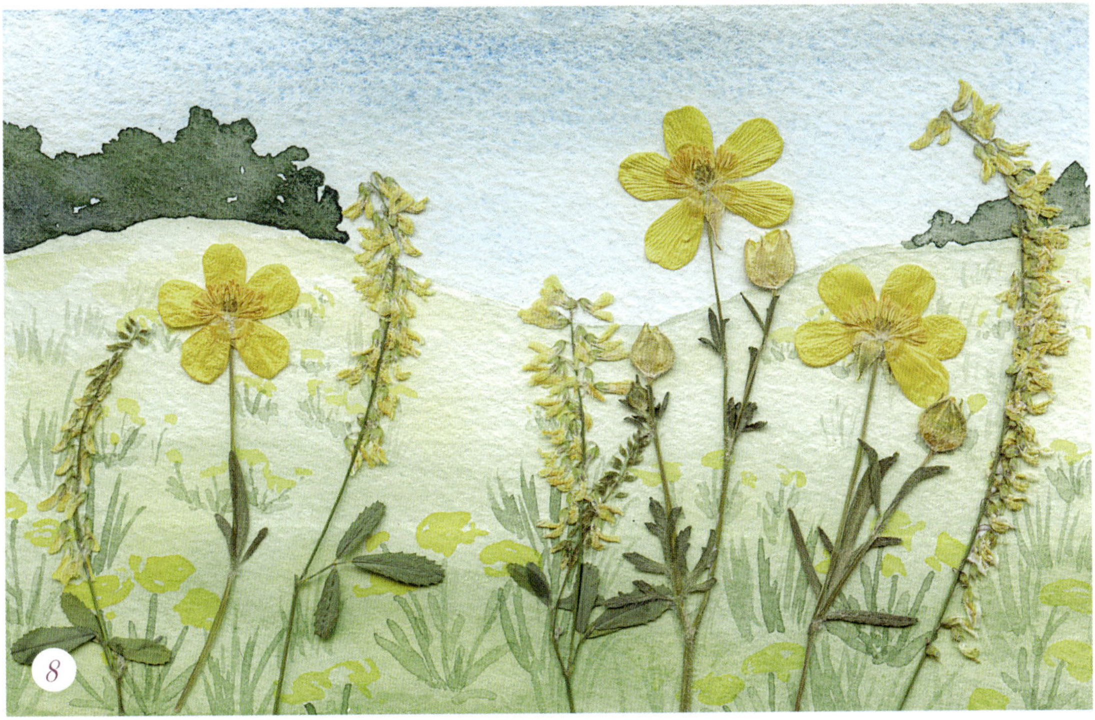

step 8

Now, we will finish our artwork with pressed flowers. Using your tweezers or fingers, gently arrange your selected pressed flowers so their stems meet the bottom of the page (as if they are growing up from the ground there). Test different arrangements to find one you are happy with. I am using some buttercups and wild yellow clovers to stick with the simple yellow, blue and green color palette. Since this is a simpler project, you don't need to add too many flowers.

Once you are happy with your layout, trim the stems to length and begin picking up the flowers one by one. Using your glue brush, carefully paint the back of each flower with a thin layer of glue, and press them onto the paper using your fingers or tweezers. Once they are all mounted, set a piece of waxed paper on top of your piece and weigh it down with a few heavy books. Allow it to dry for at least 15 to 20 minutes before carefully peeling away the waxed paper. If you do this too quickly, you can peel your flowers off your page or break them. (See Mounting Flowers on page 22 for more details.) Your piece is now complete!

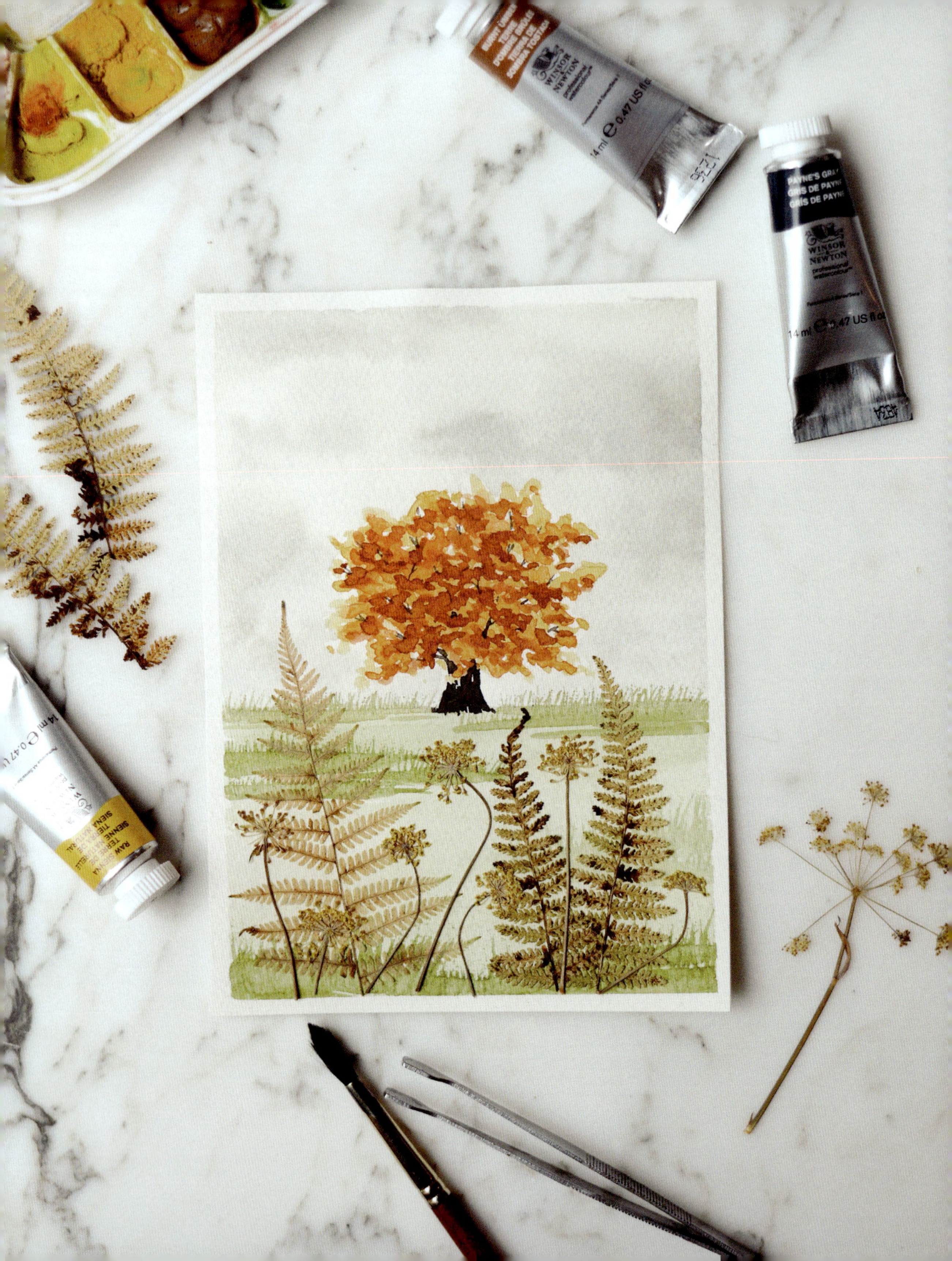
PAYNE'S GRAY
GRIS DE PAYNE
WINSOR & NEWTON
14 ml

AUTUMN OAK

When summer turns to autumn, the fields and treetops fade from green to shades of gold, crimson and brown. Even on a gray day, with skies full of heavy clouds, the autumn meadow is full of beautiful color, texture and sound. For this painting, we embrace a new color palette and mix of late-blooming pressed flowers. I've chosen some yellow ferns (collected in autumn) and parts of fennel flowers to look like small autumn wildflowers.

size

5 x 7" (12.5 x 18 cm)

brushes

Size 6 round brush
Size 2 round brush (optional)
Glue brush

flower palette

Fennel flowers
Yellow ferns

materials

Tweezers (optional)
Scissors
Glue
Waxed paper
Heavy Books

color palette

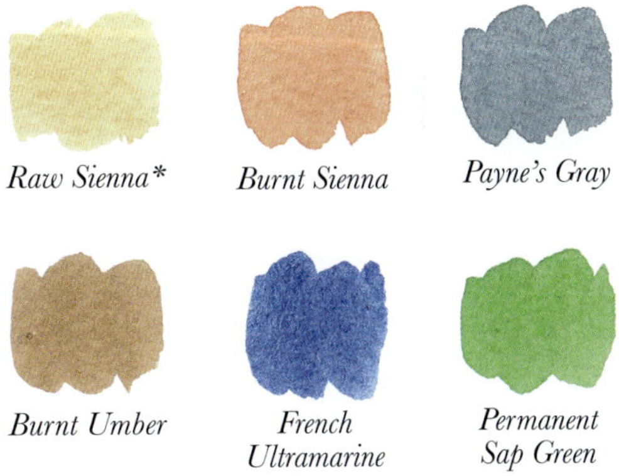

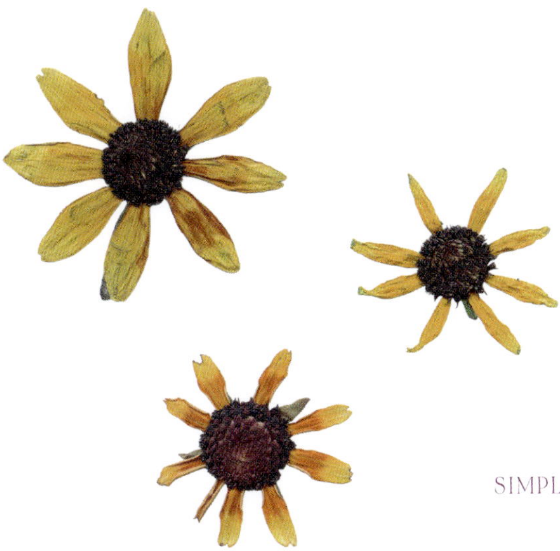

1

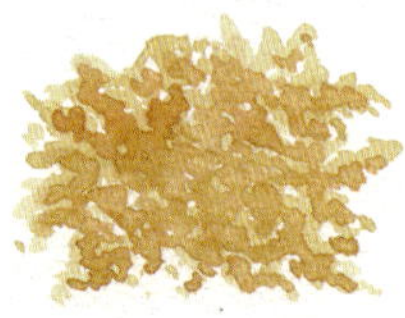

2

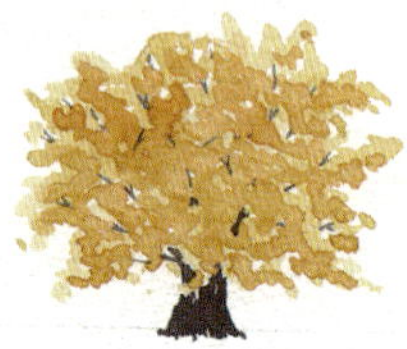

3

step 1

Draw a horizontal line across the page a little below the halfway point.

Make a watery mixture of Raw Sienna on your palette. Using a size 6 round brush, pick up some of this paint and tap dots and marks in an irregular circle above the horizon line, leaving lots of gaps. This will be the crown of a solitary oak tree, so imagine that as you paint. Leave a gap between the circular cluster and the horizon so you have a place to add a trunk later. Allow the painting to dry.

step 2

Add some Burnt Sienna to the mixture of Raw Sienna on your palette. Then, add more dots and marks to the cluster, creating a new layer but not covering up the first one. Allow the painting to dry.

step 3

Create a mixture of Payne's Gray and Burnt Umber on your palette for a dark grayish-brown. Using your size 6 round brush, paint a short trunk beneath the crown of the tree and connect it to the horizon line. The trunk should be vaguely rectangular in shape. Then, using the same brush or switching to a smaller one, paint some short, thin lines and *V* shapes within the crown to give the impression of limbs and branches peeking through the leaves. To do this, I like to imagine that the branches are fanning out from the trunk, and then I angle my marks accordingly, without making it too mathematic or perfect. You may also use a smaller brush, like a size 2, to add some of the smaller branches throughout the crown of the tree. In this painting, I chose to fill in areas that were lighter in color, or unpainted, to paint many of my branches and limbs, but you can place them where you like throughout the tree as long as their growth pattern makes sense.

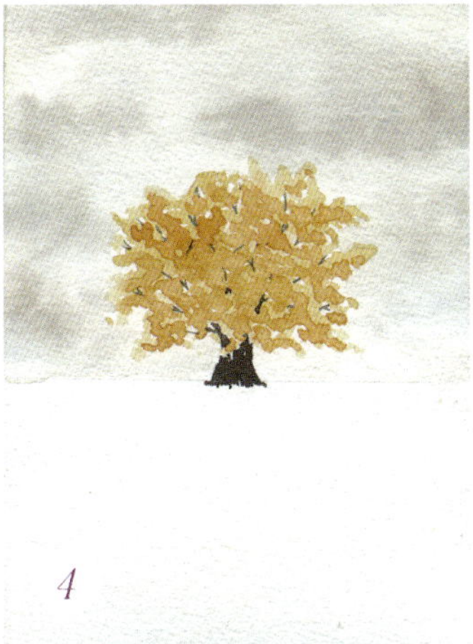

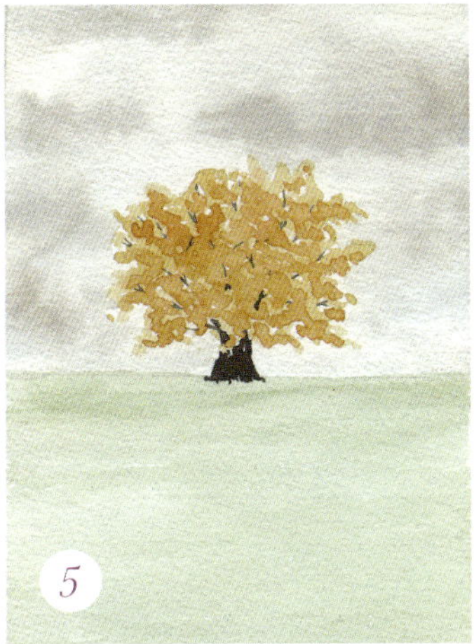

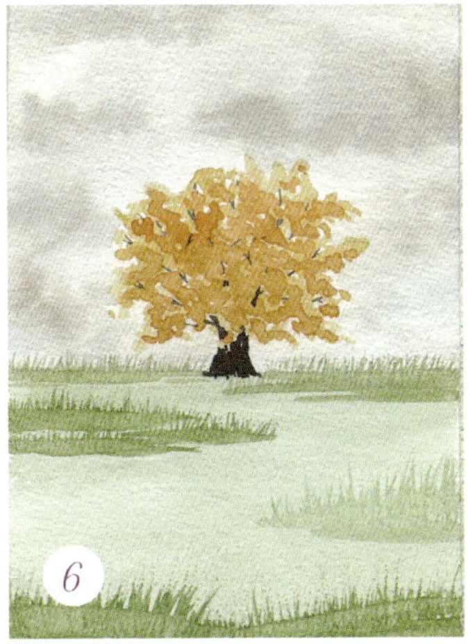

step 4

Create a watery mixture of French Ultramarine and Burnt Umber on your palette for a medium-gray color. Use your size 6 round brush and clean water to dampen the white area surrounding the tree and above the horizon line. Then, pick up some of the gray paint and make swirling marks within the dampened sky area, leaving gaps between them, to form loose clouds. The wet paper will allow the colors to soften and bleed. Push the paint around a bit until you are happy with the way the clouds look.

step 5

Create a watery mixture of Permanent Sap Green and Burnt Umber on your palette. Load your size 6 round brush with this paint, and make sweeping horizontal brushstrokes in the remaining white portion of the page below the horizon line, covering the entire area.

step 6

Then, add some more Burnt Umber to the mixture on your palette and load your brush with this darker pigment. Swipe a few lines horizontally right where the meadow meets the sky. Then, flip your brush upside down and hold it like a pencil. Press the non-bristle end into the wet paint on the paper to scratch small vertical lines upward, dragging the pigment upward in a little grass-like mark. Be sure to use pressure that is firm enough to move the paint but not firm enough to rip through the paper. Quickly work your way across the paper, making lots of these little vertical marks.

Create a few more patches of this darker color throughout the meadow, and repeat the process of scratching lines into each. You may find it more effective to work one patch at a time, first painting one horizontal strip, then making the scratch marks in it, before moving on to paint another horizontal strip.

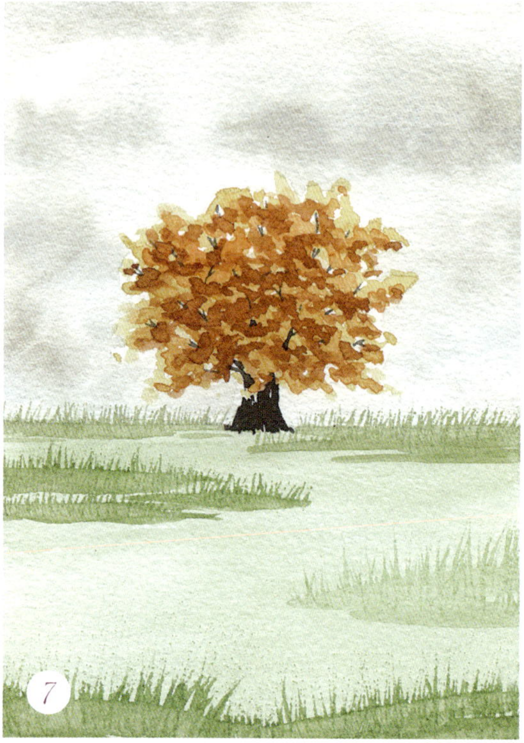

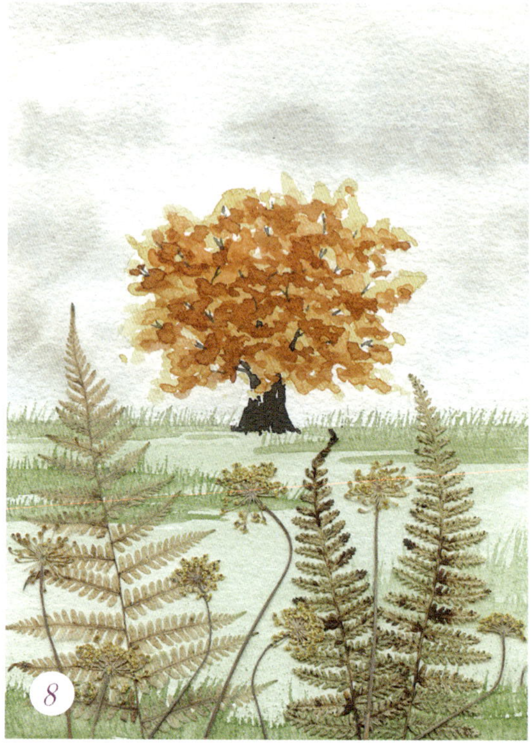

step 7

Combine some Burnt Sienna and Burnt Umber on your palette. Then, load your size 6 brush with it. Returning to the oak tree, use the brush point to tap more marks into the crown of the tree, adding shadows selectively but not completely covering the existing lighter colors. Allow the painting to dry. The painting portion is now complete!

step 8

Select your pressed flowers, and begin placing them on your paper. They will appear to be growing from the bottom of the page, in the foreground.

Once you are happy with your layout, trim the stems to length and begin picking up the flowers one by one. Using your glue brush, carefully paint the back of each flower with a thin layer of glue and press them onto the paper using your fingers or tweezers. Once they are all mounted, set a piece of waxed paper on top of your piece and weigh it down with a few heavy books. Allow it to dry for at least 15 to 20 minutes before carefully peeling away the waxed paper. If you do this too quickly, you can peel your flowers off your page or break them. (See Mounting Flowers on page 22 for more details.) Your piece is now complete!

FERN FOREST

A walk through the woods in spring can be a wonderful grounding experience. The earth is waking up as new plants begin to emerge from below. New leaves catch the sunlight in the canopy above, and birds happily chirp in the warming air. For this painting, we will create a greening forest scene accented with spring ferns to capture the tranquil magic of the forest. I am using small ferns, pressed in spring.

size

5 x 7" (12.5 x 18 cm)

brushes

Size 10 round brush
Size 6 round brush
Size 2 round brush
Glue brush

flower palette

Small ferns in various sizes

materials

Tweezers (optional)
Scissors
Glue
Waxed paper
Heavy Books

color palette

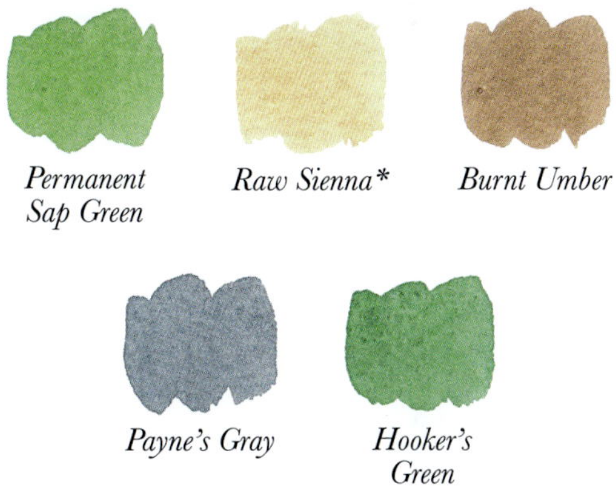

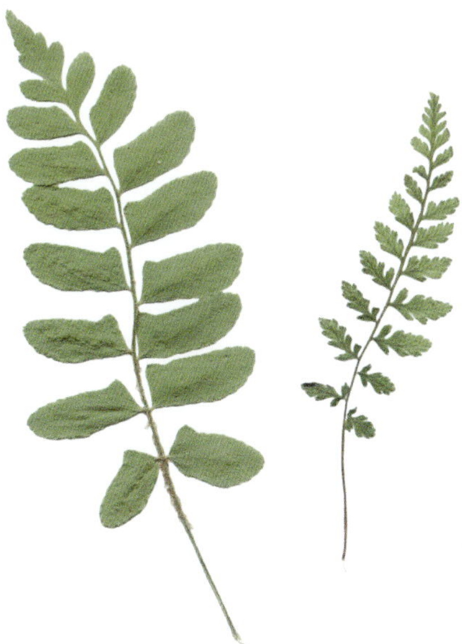

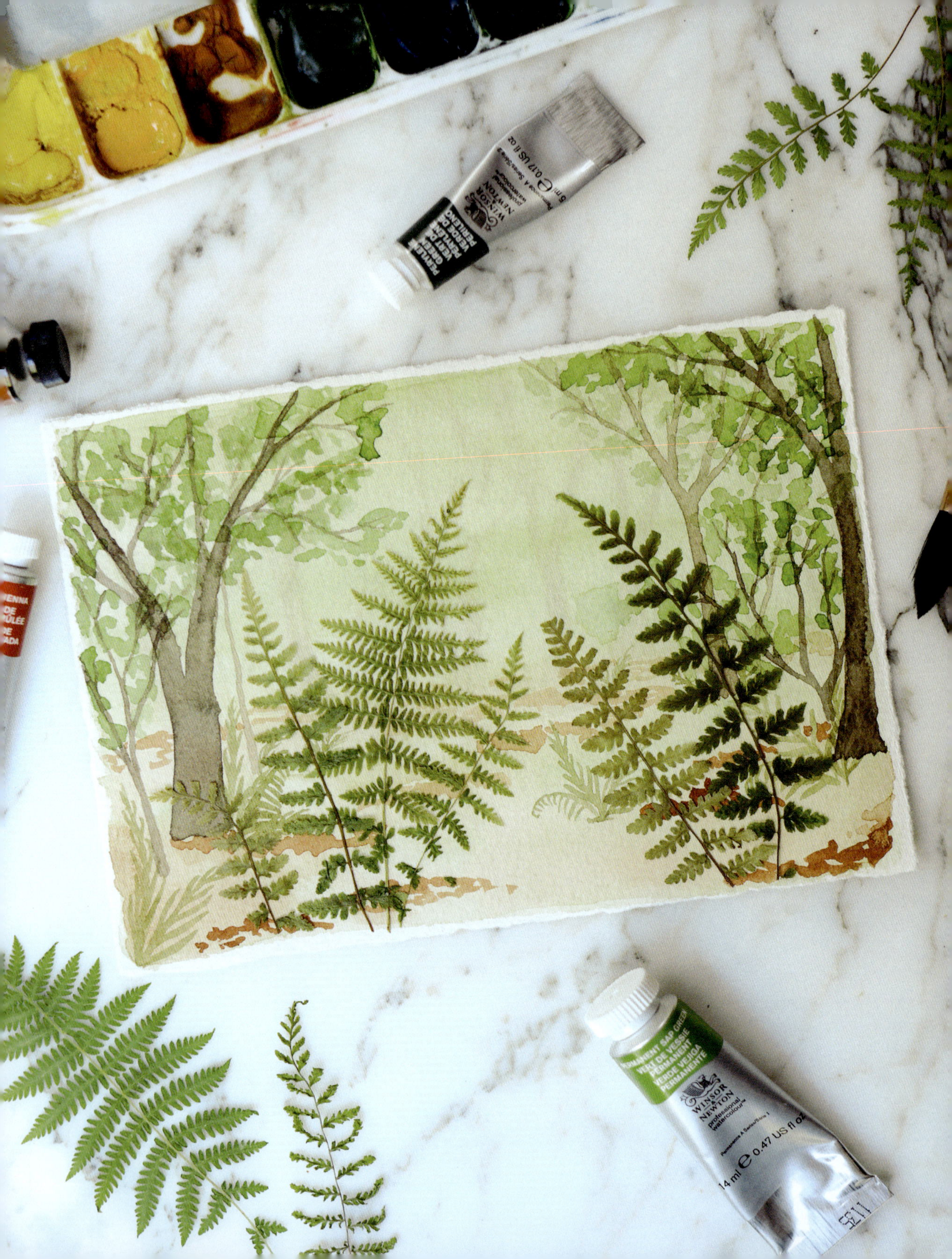
VERT DE VESSIE
PERMANENT
VERDE VEJIGA
PERMANENTE
WINSOR & NEWTON
professional
watercolour
14 ml 0.47 US fl oz

step 1

Create a very watery mix of Permanent Sap Green and Raw Sienna on your palette. Using your size 10 brush, paint the entire paper with random strokes to cover it in a pale green.

step 2

While your paper is still damp, load your size 10 brush with a watery mix of Burnt Umber paint, and touch the tip of the brush to the paper along the bottom third of the paper. Create groups of these marks so they bloom and bleed together to create soft patches of color among the green. This will give the impression of leaf litter on the forest floor. Continue to make random marks across this bottom third to half of the paper, while leaving some patches to show the green layer.

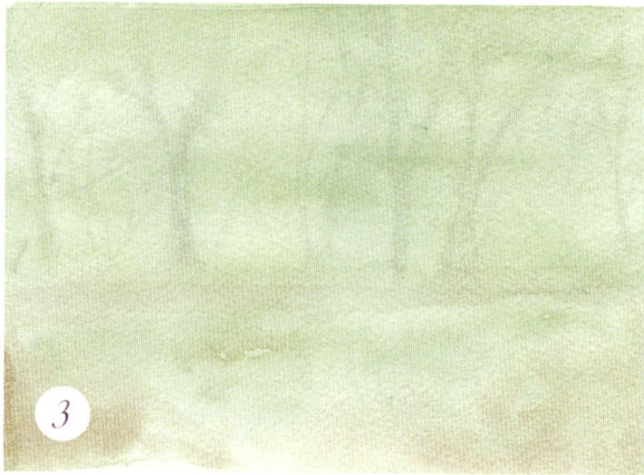

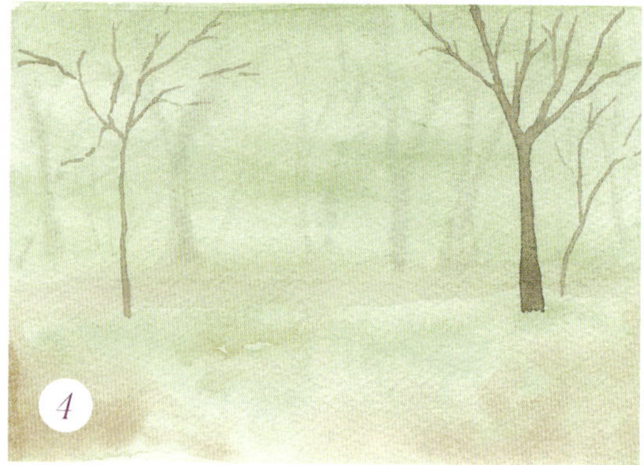

step 3

Check if your paper is still damp on the upper (still green) portion. If it has dried, use your size 10 brush and clean water to brush over that area to dampen it again. Then, create a watery mix of Payne's Gray and Burnt Umber paint to achieve a light-gray color. Load your size 6 brush with the light gray, and begin painting distant trees with their trunks starting around the horizontal midline of the page. With your brush pointing toward the bottom of the page, place its tip to the paper, and then drag upward to create the trunks. Add trunks of varying thicknesses and spacing across the page, including some very thin, shorter ones as young trees on the forest floor. For some of the trees, you can add a fork or multiple forks by splitting the main trunk into two at an angle (like a *Y*, but don't make it symmetrical). Continue forking the branches as you move up the tree to create an expanding canopy, using less pressure on the brush the higher you go to create smaller branches. Since the paper is damp, these will bleed and bloom a bit, which is what we want since they are far into the background. Allow the painting to dry.

step 4

Create a slightly more pigmented mix of Burnt Umber and Payne's Gray, and paint a few more trees with their trunks starting slightly lower on the page than the previous step. This, along with the darker color and crisp edges, will make them seem closer to the viewer. Use the same techniques for creating the trees as in step 3. You can leave gaps on some of the upper branches, because we will be adding leaves next.

step 5

Using the tip of your size 6 brush and a moderately pigmented mix of Permanent Sap Green, tap marks along the branches of the newest set of trees. Slightly vary the size and shape of the leaves by changing the angle of the brush and the amount of pressure you use. Allow the painting to dry.

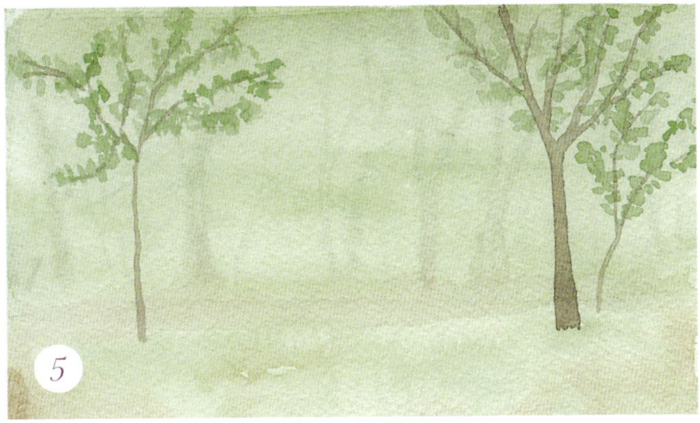

step 6

Mix up a very pigmented mix of Burnt Umber and Payne's Gray. Load your size 6 brush with this paint, and create the last layer of trees on both sides of the page, starting the trunks closer to the bottom of the page than the previous layers. As before, you will want to use the same techniques and vary the thickness of the trunks. This will be the darkest layer of the painting. Feel free to spend a bit more time on these trees since they are the most prominent. Allow the painting to dry completely.

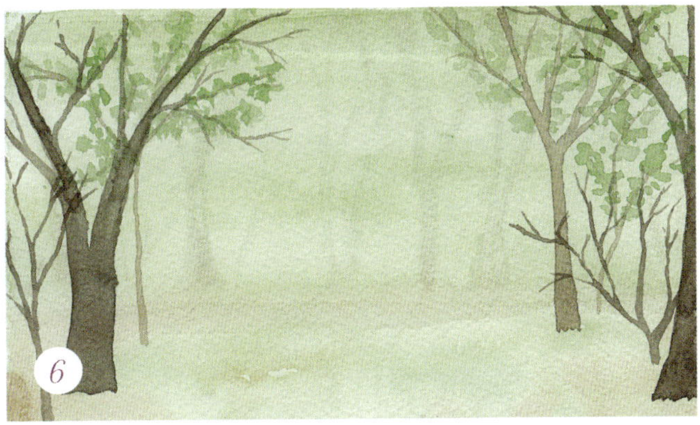

step 7

With a moderately pigmented mix of Permanent Sap Green and your size 6 brush, add leaves to this latest layer of trees, just as we did in step 5.

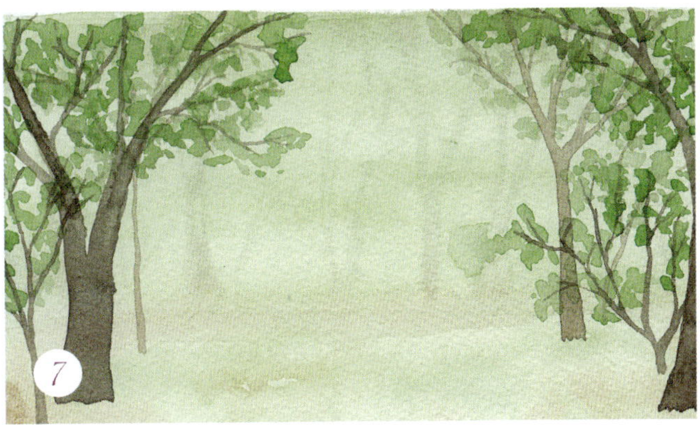

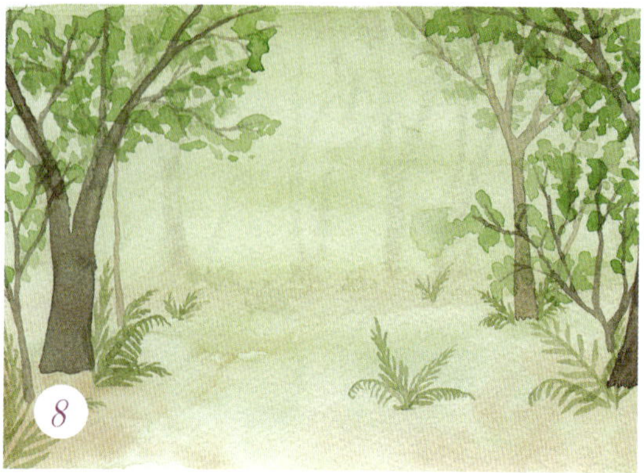

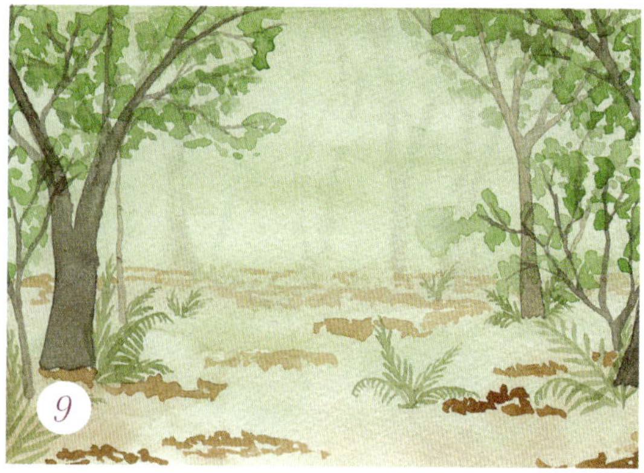

step 8

Create a mix of Hooker's Green and Burnt Umber to create a dark green. Load your size 2 brush with this mix, and begin to paint ferns along the forest floor. To paint a fern frond, choose where you'd like your ferns to grow and place the tip of your brush (pointing toward the bottom of the page) where the frond would be growing out of the earth. Using light pressure, drag the brush upward while lifting it off the page to create a tapered end. Then, starting at the bottom of the stem, use a similar dragging motion to paint each leaflet branching off at an angle, lifting the brush at the end of each leaflet to again create a tapered end (point).

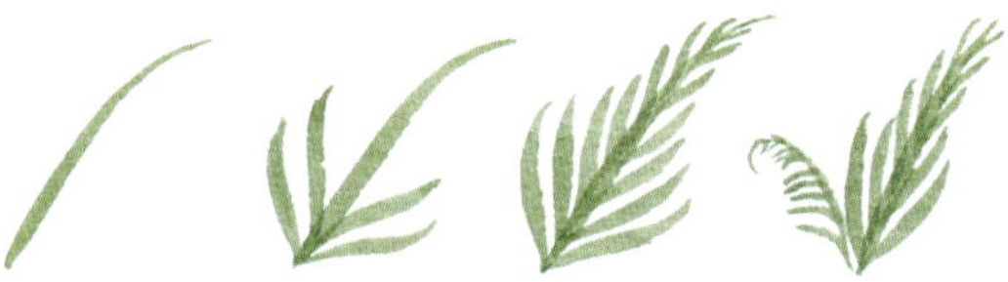

Repeat this process to create corresponding leaves on either side of the stem, reducing the size of these leaves as you move upward toward the tip of the stem. For each fern plant, paint a few fronds growing from the same spot, varying the angle of the stem. The base of the trees is a good spot for ferns! You can also space some around the foreground and midground, away from the trees. Ferns higher up the page (farther into the distance) should be smaller. For stems laying perpendicular to the ground, only paint one set of fronds, as if you are viewing it from the side.

step 9

Create a pigmented mix of Burnt Umber on your palette, and fill your size 2 brush with it. Using the tip of the brush and starting in the foreground, tap in irregular blobs to create patches of dark brown, randomly spaced across the forest floor. As you move up the page and toward the background, add more water to your paint to make the marks more subdued. Add marks and irregular lines all the way up to the place where your very first tree trunks begin, to connect those to the ground and establish a horizon. Allow it to dry completely. The painting portion is now complete!

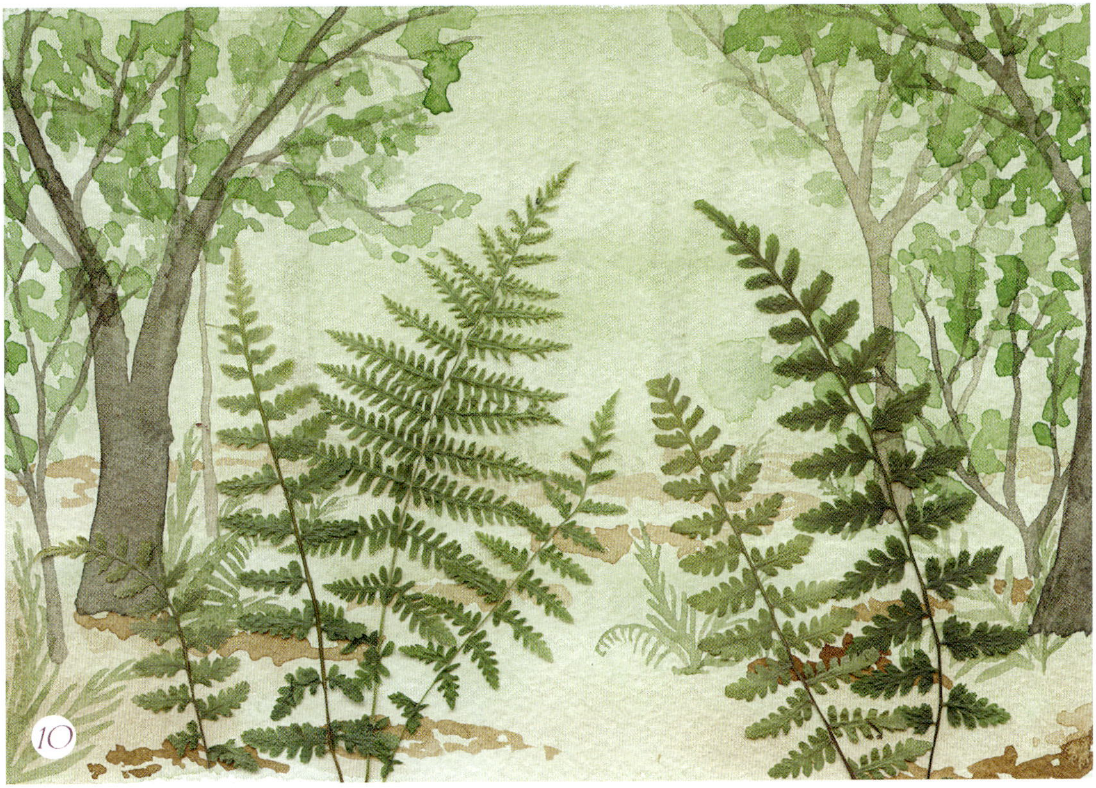

step 10

Ferns can be a bit tricky to mount at first, since there are so many little places to apply the glue, which tends to dry quickly and can also start to stick to your scrap paper. As you follow the instructions below, try to work quickly but carefully. Also, try to shift your fern around on the scrap paper while you are applying the glue, so it doesn't become stuck before you are ready to apply it to your painting. This might take a bit of practice.

Carefully arrange your pressed plant material across the bottom edge of your painting. Once you have decided on a layout and are ready to use the glue, carefully pick up one fern with your tweezers and flip it over on some scrap paper. Then, using your glue brush, gently paint the back of each leaflet and the center stem with a thin layer of glue.

Once it has been coated, carefully pick it up from the scrap paper, and lay it down in its place on the painting to mount it. Gently press down on each leaflet and the stem with your fingers or tweezers to stick the fern to the paper. Repeat with the rest of the ferns. Once they are all mounted, set a piece of waxed paper on top of your piece and weigh it down with a few heavy books. Allow it to dry for at least 15 to 20 minutes before carefully peeling away the waxed paper. (See Mounting Flowers on page 22 for more details.) Your piece is now complete!

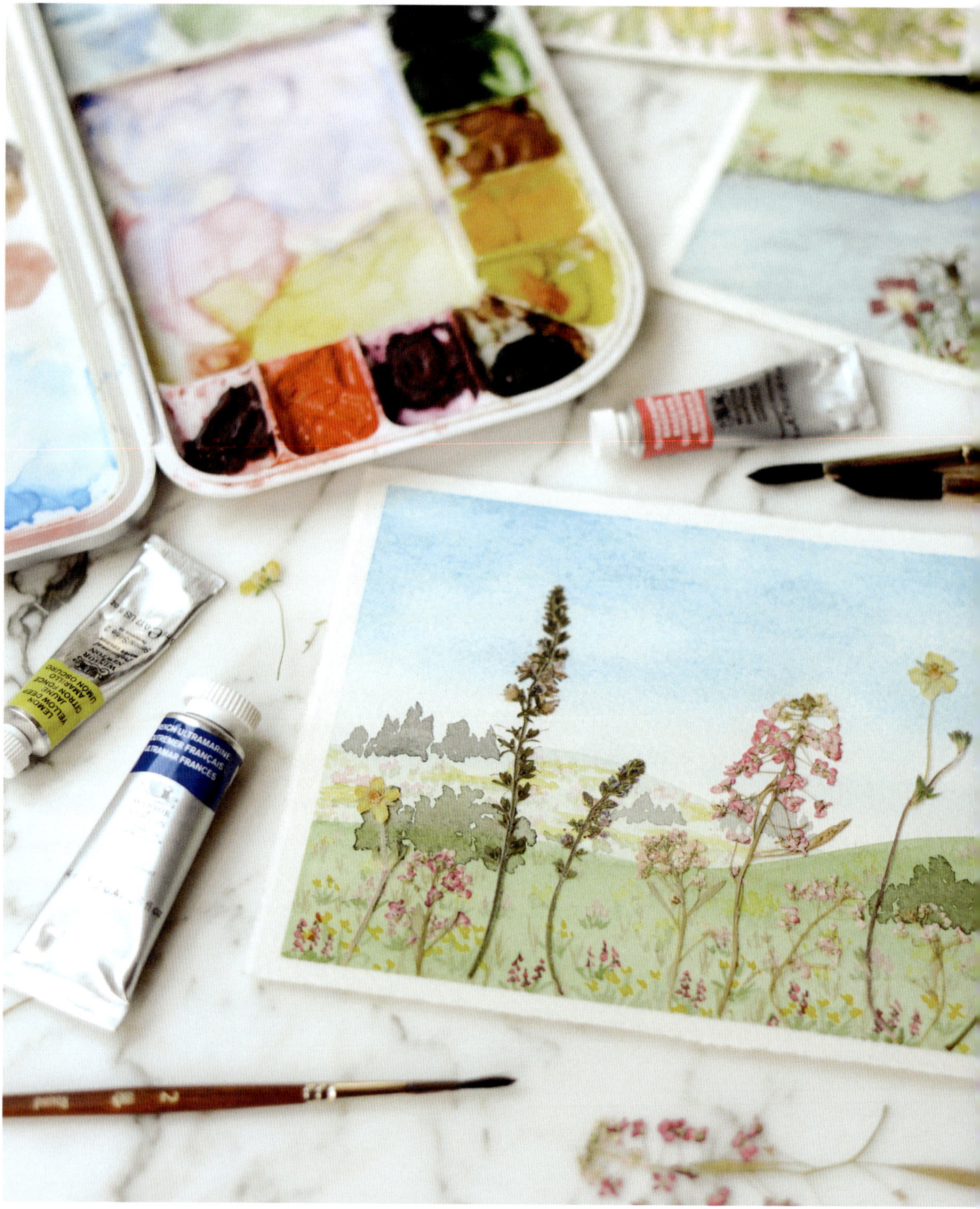

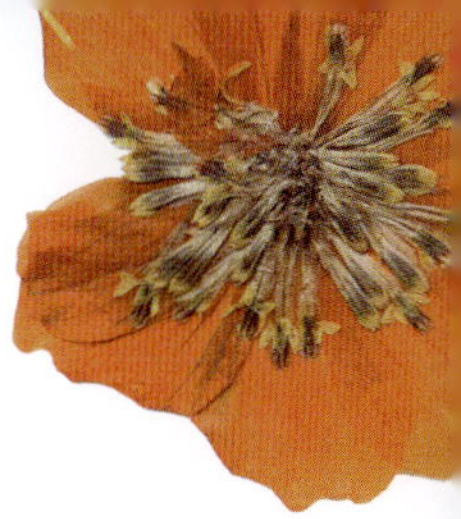

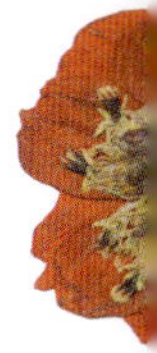

wildflower VISTAS

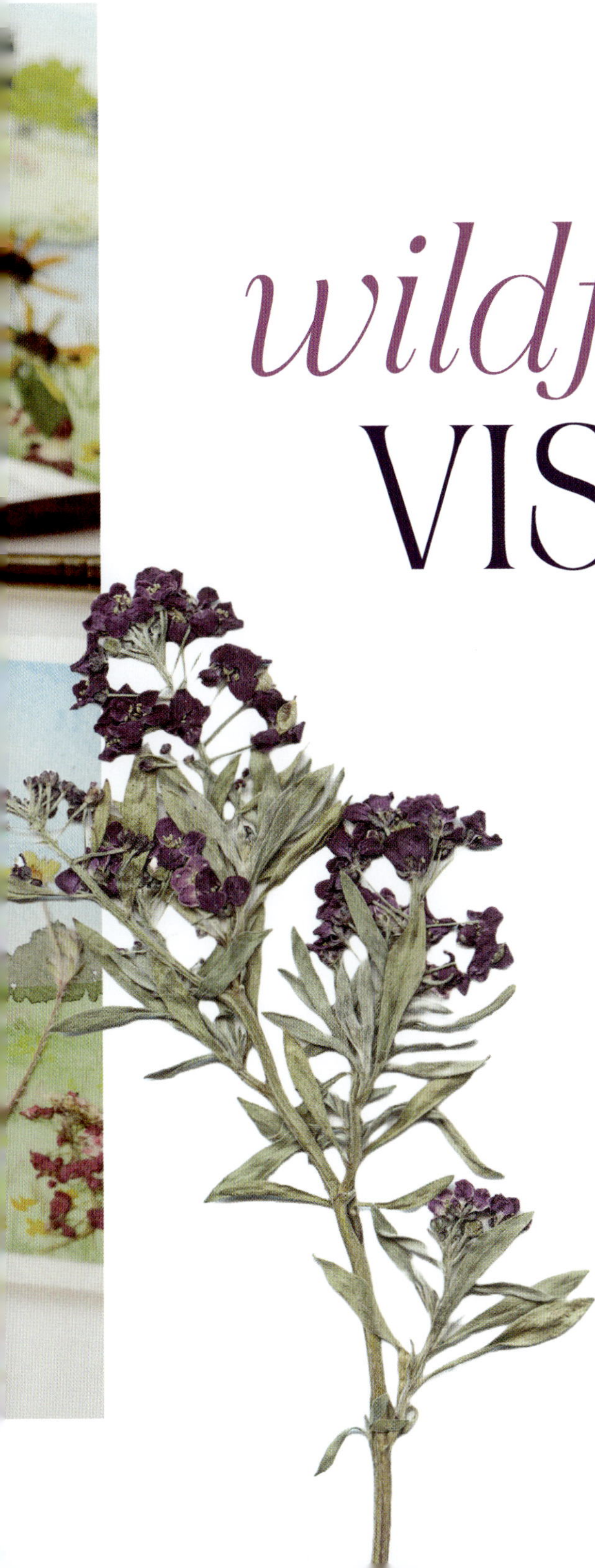

A meadow full of wildflowers is one of my favorite subjects. In this chapter, we will explore more complex pieces featuring detailed painting techniques and a diverse palette of pressed flowers. The landscapes and perspectives will vary, from a densely flowered hillside in Superbloom (page 77) to a ground-level perspective of a wild spring meadow against the blue sky in Looking Up (page 101).

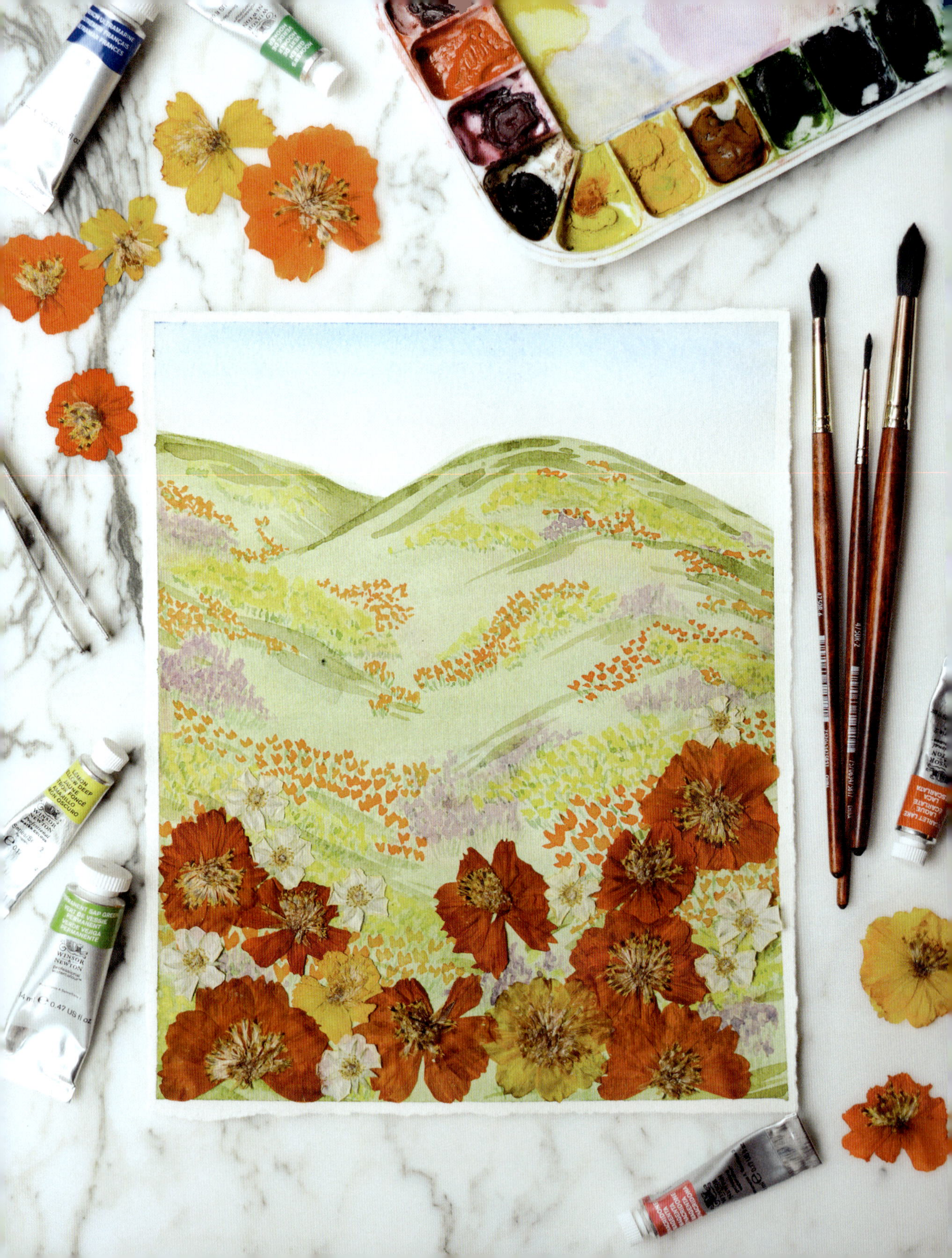
LEMON YELLOW DEEP
PERMANENT SAP GREEN

SUPERBLOOM

Superbloom is a rare phenomenon when dormant wildflower seeds all germinate and bloom at once. It occurs in the deserts of California and Arizona under special conditions, after an unusually rainy season. To highlight the superbloom character of the landscape, I mounted the flowers to the artwork without their stems. I chose sulfur cosmos, which grow in vibrant shades of orange and yellow and are relatively easy to press. I also added some smaller, paler yellow wildflowers (cinquefoils) for contrast.

size

8 x 10" (20 x 25 cm)

brushes

Wash brush
Size 10 round brush
Size 14 round brush
Size 6 round brush
Size 2 round brush
Glue brush

flower palette

Sulfur cosmos
Cinquefoil

materials

Tweezers (optional)
Scissors
Glue
Waxed paper
Heavy Books

color palette

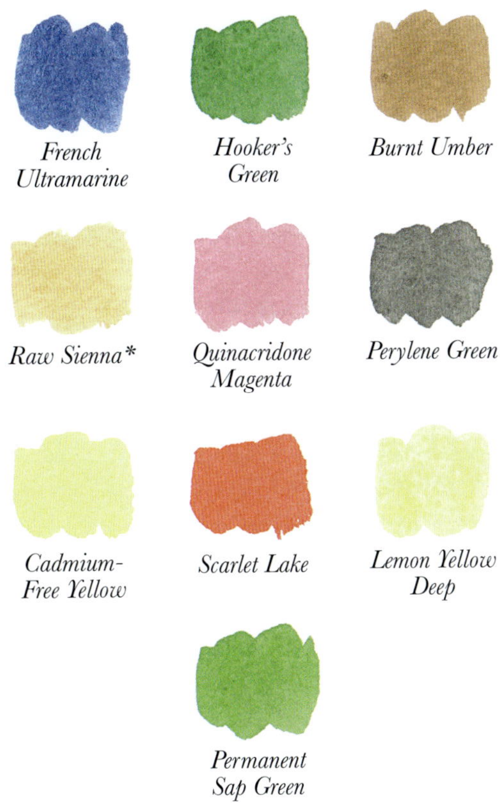

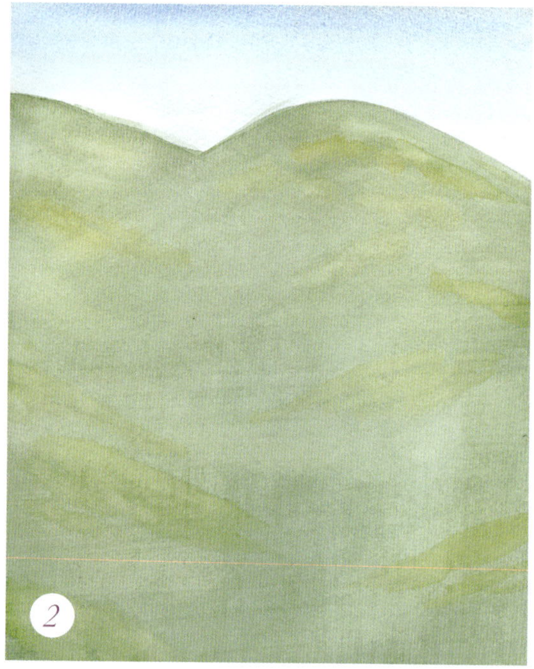

step 1

With a pencil, lightly draw in some rounded hilltops about a quarter of the way from the top of your page. I chose to draw one and a half hilltops for my painting.

Using a large wash brush and clean water, dampen the top of your paper above the pencil line. Then, create a watery wash of French Ultramarine on your palette. Using a size 10 round brush, pick up some of the French Ultramarine wash. Starting at the top of the page and working downward, paint broad horizontal strokes. We are creating a sky gradient with the most color right at the top, and smoothly transitioning to a clear colorless sky around the hilltops drawn in pencil. Lightly blend the sky with a little more water if you need to, but be careful not to add too much. Allow the painting to dry.

step 2

On your palette, create a very watery mix of Hooker's Green and Burnt Umber and a separate mix of water and Raw Sienna. Then, load your size 14 round brush with the watery greenish paint, and begin making sweeping, curved brushstrokes below the pencil line to fill in the hillside, all the way to the bottom of the page.

While the paper is damp, pick up your size 10 brush and load it with the Raw Sienna mixture. Then, make a few small horizontal brushstrokes across the hilltops, and a few larger marks at a downward angle from the edge of the page toward the center of the page. The damp paper will allow these golden marks to bleed into the green. Allow the painting to dry.

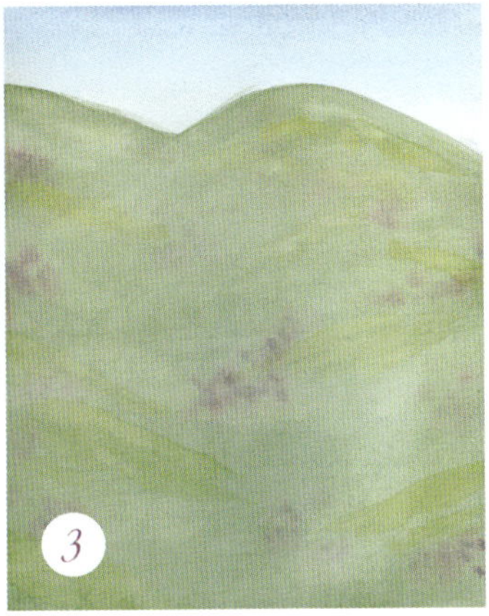

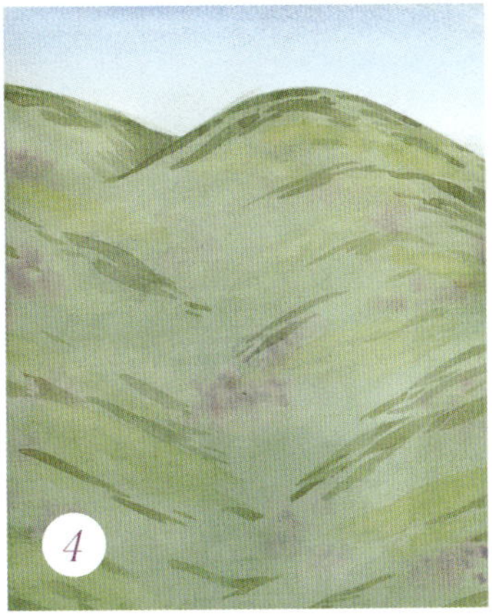

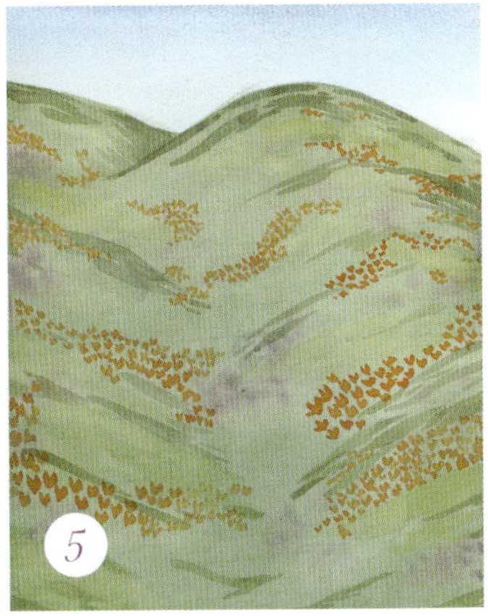

step 3

Create a mix of Quinacridone Magenta and French Ultramarine on your palette for a nice shade of purple. Spray your paper with a spray bottle (or use your wash brush and clean water) to dampen the page again. Then, pick up some of this paint with your size 6 brush and tap small dots into the hillside. Make small groupings of these dots across the bottom half of the page, with just a few placed higher up on the hills. Allow the painting to dry.

step 4

Mix up some Perylene Green and Raw Sienna paint on your palette. Then, load your size 6 brush with it. Use the point of the brush to paint broken, uneven lines along the edge of the hilltop, matching its shape. Bring one line down to cross the imaginary line of the second hill where the two meet, indicating that one is in front of the other. Then, add some more lines perpendicular to this dividing line to indicate shadow on the hillside behind. Continue adding broken lines as you move down the page, painting them at a downward angle originating from either side of the page but slightly varying the angle and length as you go.

step 5

Mix up some Cadmium-Free Yellow with a little bit of Scarlet Lake on your palette to create a bright-orange color. Then, take some of this paint on your size 6 round brush and use the point to paint little orange *V* shapes in the foreground of your painting. Paint clusters of these *V* shapes, adding some dots and other marks and allowing them to overlap a bit. I like to fit them in around some of the other shapes already in the painting, such as the yellow and purple blobs or the dark-green lines, to give it a more organic look. You can leave the bottom quarter to third of the page alone if you want, since we will be adding flowers there and covering up most of the painting anyway, or you can paint all the way down.

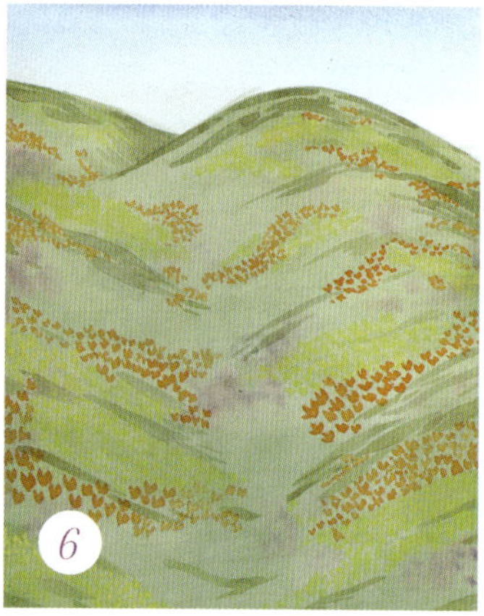

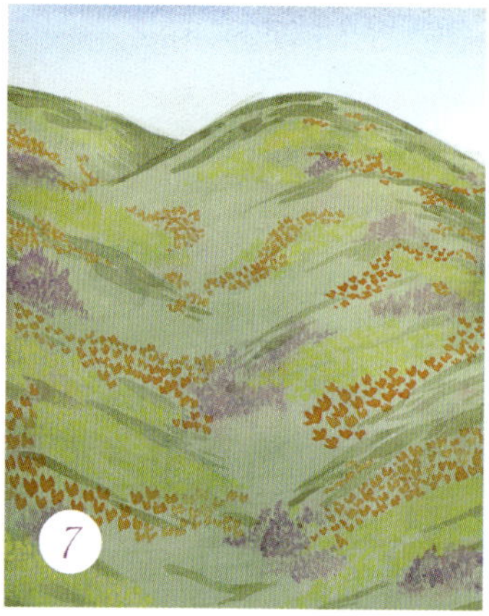

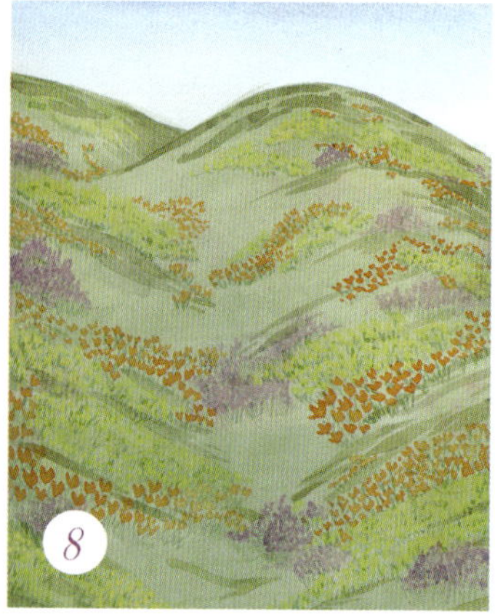

step 6

Clean your brush. Then, dip it straight into your pan of Lemon Yellow Deep, and use the brush point to lightly paint dots into the soft-yellow portions of the painting. Make lots of dots close together, following the rough shape of the yellow already on the page and working around existing orange or green marks.

step 7

Using your size 2 round brush, create a watery mix of Quinacridone Magenta and French Ultramarine on your palette for a pale bluish-purple color. Then, load your brush with this color and hold it at an angle in a pencil grip. Tap the point onto the paper on or near one of the purple areas on the hillside, with the brush point roughly pointed toward the top of the page, and make a small vertical mark. Lift the brush slightly, and use a tapping motion to continue creating these small marks in clusters on and around the existing purple areas. (See Painting Tiny Flowers on page 37 for examples of these three marks.) Allow the painting to dry.

step 8

Create a watery mix of Perylene Green and Permanent Sap Green on your palette. Then, load your size 2 brush with this mixture. Holding the brush vertically, lightly and loosely paint short vertical strokes beneath each large grouping of flowers (the orange, yellow and purple marks we made in the last three steps). These are stems to connect them to the hillside. You can add a few of these stems throughout the mass of flowers, but focus mainly on the bottom side of each cluster. Allow the painting to dry. The painting portion is now complete!

step 9

With your tweezers or fingers, gently arrange your flowers on the bottom third of your page. If you painted all the way down your page, you will cover up some of your work, but that's okay! Play around with the arrangement, overlap some flowers or leave spaces and make the layout a bit asymmetrical so it looks natural. You can carefully trim your flowers with a blade or scissors if you'd like to give them a straight edge to fit at the edge of your painting, or you can choose them to fit as they are. It is up to you!

Once you have your layout finalized, carefully begin picking each flower up with your tweezers or fingers, one by one, and gently painting the backside with your glue brush and glue. If you are using the same flowers as I am, I would recommend using the tweezers to grab at the flower's center—and be extra gentle with the glue brush, because the petals of these cosmos do tend to come loose and pull away from the center. If this happens, you can scrap that petal or try to place it back in its place when you stick the flower to the artwork. Repeat until all flowers are glued down. Once they are all mounted, set a piece of waxed paper on top of your piece and weigh it down with a few heavy books. Allow it to dry for at least 15 to 20 minutes before carefully peeling away the waxed paper. If you do this too quickly, you can peel your flowers off your page or break them. (See Mounting Flowers on page 22 for more details.) Your piece is now complete!

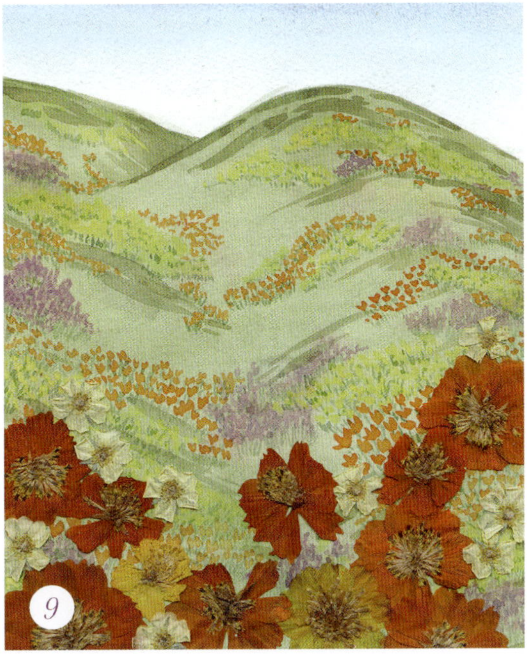

NOTE

In California and other areas, it is illegal to pick wildflowers from public lands. Grow your own flowers for pressing, or purchase similar ones from growers or florists. While I can and do grow California poppies in my garden, I chose to use orange cosmos and cinquefoil here to show other options for achieving this look.

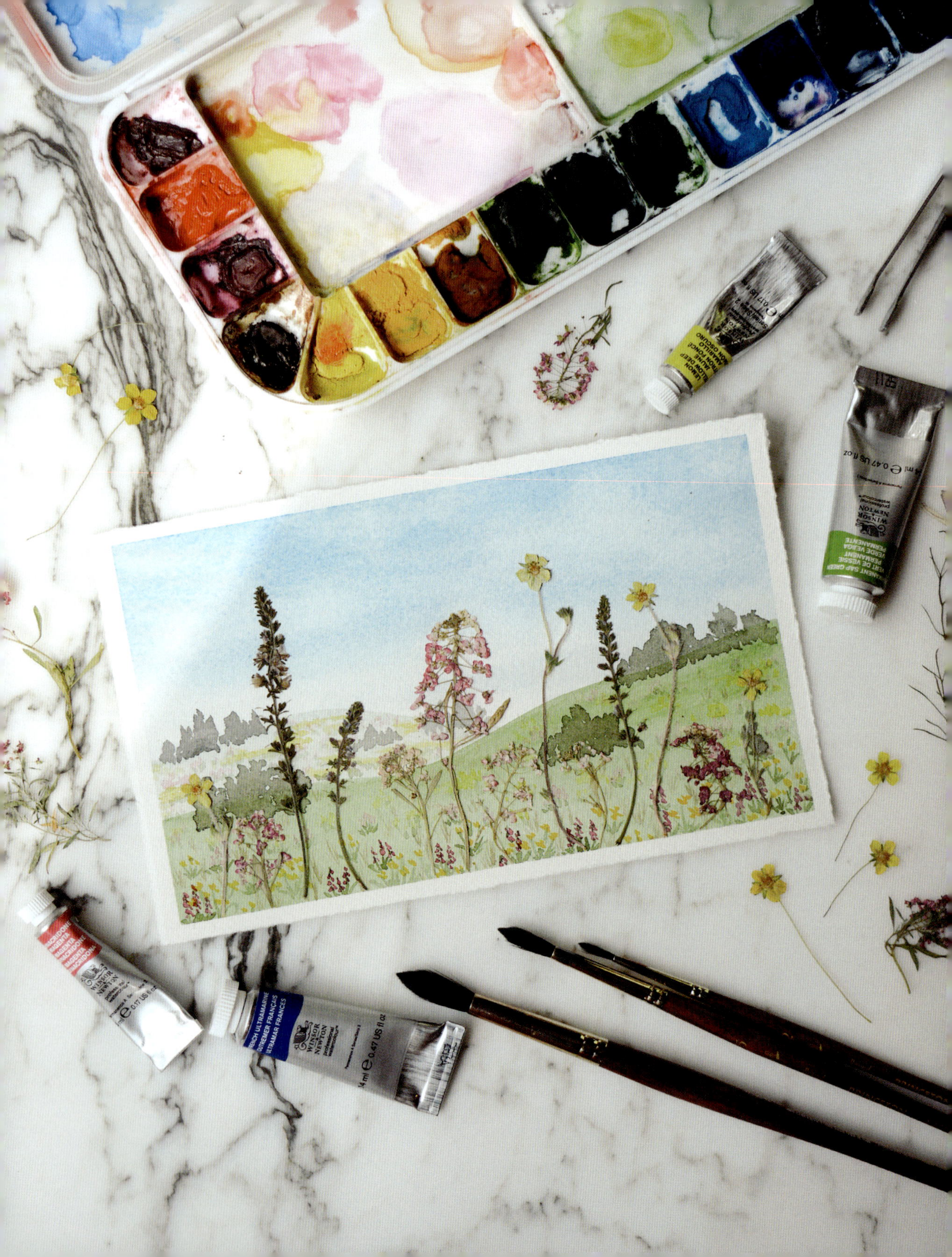
FRENCH ULTRAMARINE
OUTREMER FRANÇAIS

ABUNDANT MEADOW

The greening of the landscape and return of colorful wildflowers after a long winter is one of my favorite parts of spring. No matter where in the world you live, this painting will transport you to a vibrant and abundant meadow of blooms. In this artwork, we will paint verdant rolling hills blanketed with tiny flowers, and finish it off with a collection of pressed flowers right up front. Pink sweet alyssum, yellow cinquefoil and speedwell are the small springy flowers used in my piece.

size

5 x 7" (12.5 x 18 cm)

brushes

Size 10 round brush
Size 6 round brush
Size 2 round brush
Glue brush

flower palette

Pink sweet alyssum
Yellow cinquefoil
Speedwell

materials

Tweezers (optional)
Scissors
Glue
Waxed paper
Heavy Books

color palette

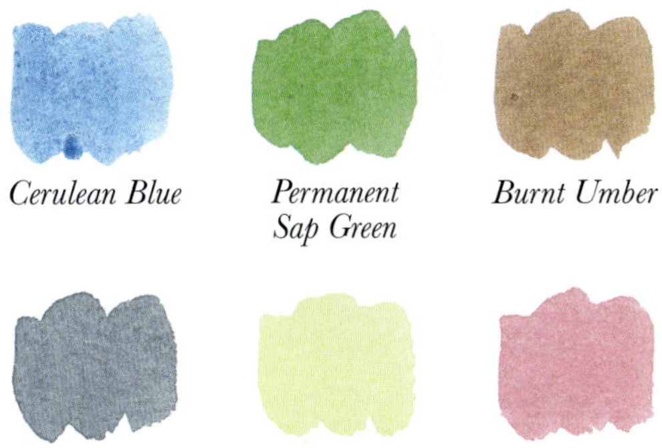

Cerulean Blue, *Permanent Sap Green*, *Burnt Umber*, *Payne's Gray*, *Cadmium-Free Yellow*, *Quinacridone Magenta*

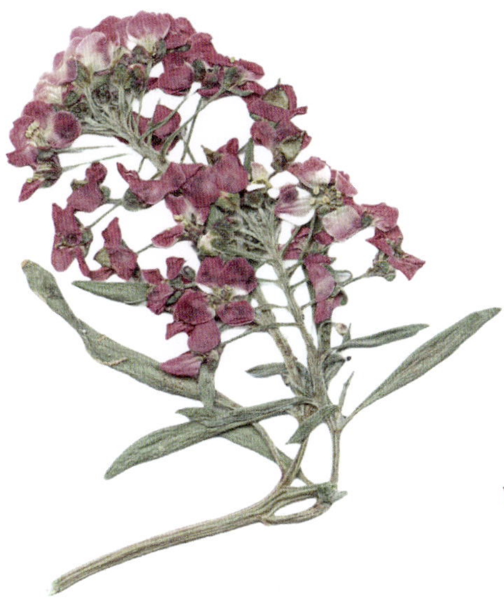

step 1

Create a lightly pigmented wash of Cerulean Blue paint on your palette. Load up your size 10 round brush, and starting at the top of your paper, use horizontal brush-strokes back and forth across the paper to create your blue sky. Fill the top third of the paper with blue, making it slightly lighter in tone as you move down the page. If you would like, you can add a slightly more pigmented mix of this blue along the top of the paper to make the top of the sky darker.

step 2

Clean off your brush in your jar of water. Then, fill your brush with clean water, and paint from the bottom of your blue wash down to the halfway point of your page. Without overworking, carefully blend to create a sky gradient, fading down toward the horizon.

step 3

While your paper is still wet, use a crumpled-up paper towel to dab at the blue sky to lift some of the pigment and create clouds. This might take some practice to get the clouds looking the way you like! After this step, allow the painting to dry.

step 4

On your palette, create a watery wash of Permanent Sap Green with a drop or two of Cerulean Blue mixed in to create a cool-green color. Using your size 10 brush, paint a gentle swooping line from one edge of your page near the bottom of your sky (around the midpoint of the page, or a little above). This will be a distant hilltop. Take the line all the way to the other edge of your paper, and then fill in below it with your cool-green wash. Allow the painting to dry.

step 5

Create a slightly more pigmented mix of Permanent Sap Green with a bit of Burnt Umber mixed in. Using your size 10 brush, paint a wavy line below your first line, and carry it from one edge of the paper to the other, varying the height to create another closer hilltop. Fill in below this line with your warmer, brighter green and allow the painting to dry.

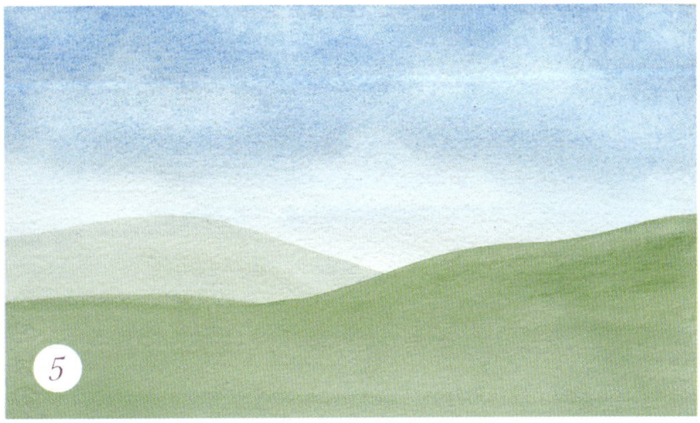

step 6

On your palette, mix a bit of Payne's Gray and Burnt Umber to create a watery-gray color. Using your size 6 brush, gently tap in some small clusters of trees or shrubs on the distant hill. Then, create a slightly more pigmented mix of Payne's Gray and Burnt Umber, with a little Permanent Sap Green added in, to paint slightly larger trees or shrubs on the closer hill.

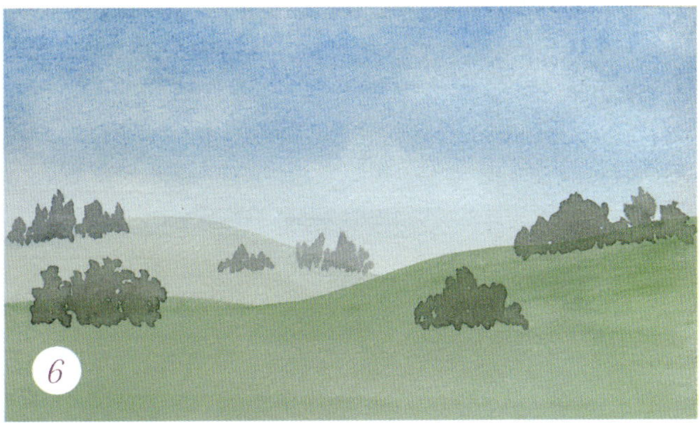

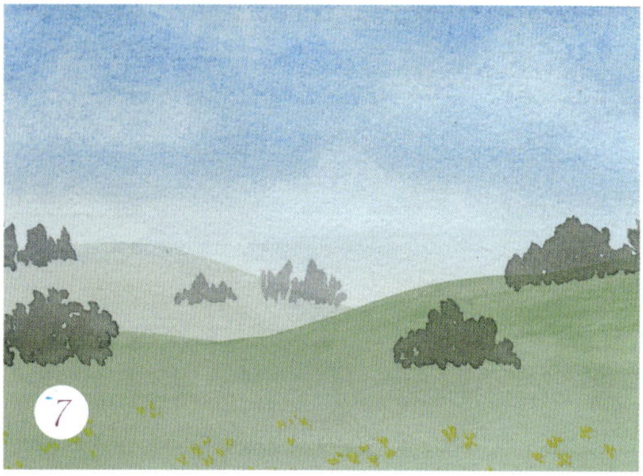

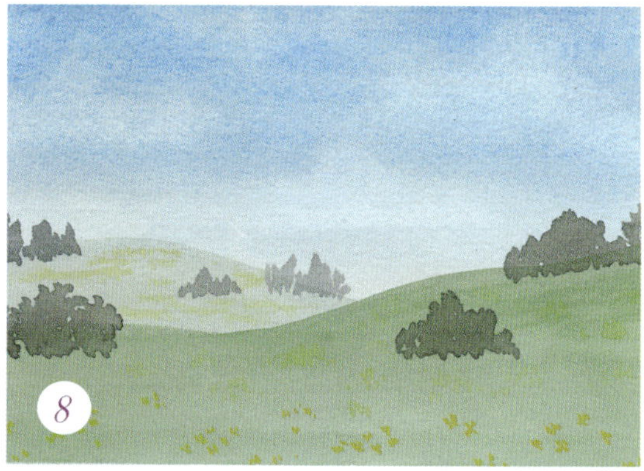

step 7

Fill your size 2 round brush with water, and dip it into your pan of Cadmium-Free Yellow. You can create a pigmented paste of this color on your palette or even use it straight from the pan. We will be using this to paint little yellow flowers in the grass. Tap in small clusters, using two to four connected dots or marks to create each flower. Since the bottom of the page is closer to the foreground, flowers here should be slightly larger, and they should become smaller and smaller as they move up the page.

step 8

Using a more watery mix of Cadmium-Free Yellow, paint smaller dots in clusters, moving up the page across the same hill. These will fade more into the green background, and they are farther away. With the same yellow, paint organic lines or blotches across the distant hill. These are faraway patches of flowers. It's okay if it looks impressionistic and loose!

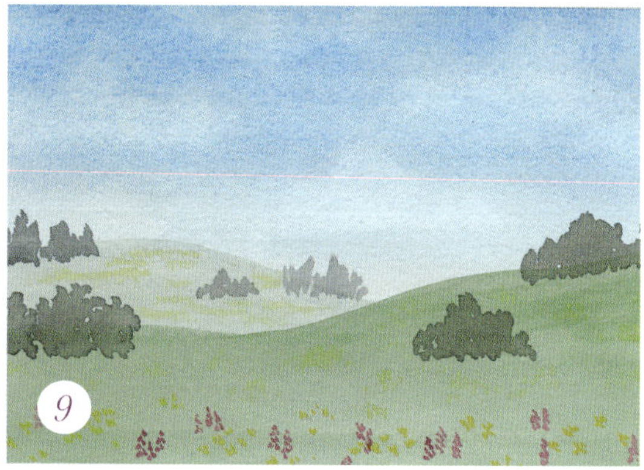

step 9

Wash your brush clean. Then, create a moderately pigmented paste of Quinacridone Magenta on your palette. Load your size 2 round brush with this pinkish color, and paint linear flowers in clusters, starting toward the bottom of the page. (For more details about painting tiny flowers, see page 37.) Add one to four more flowers on either side of your first one, close together. Starting at the bottom of the page, intersperse these clusters between the clusters of yellow flowers. I like to vary the spacing and to overlap some with the yellow flowers. Nature doesn't space things evenly, so it's best to keep your placements organic and random.

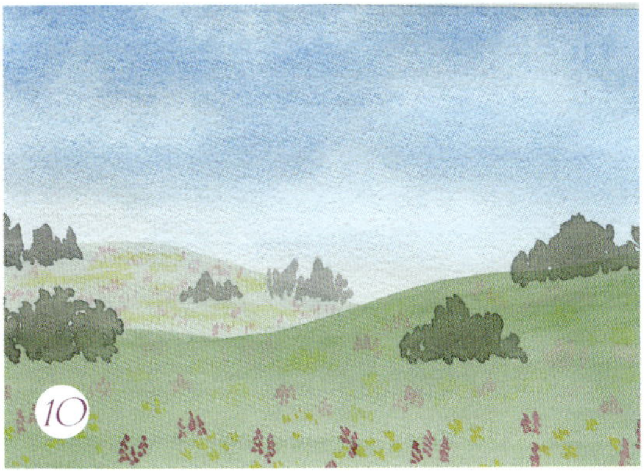

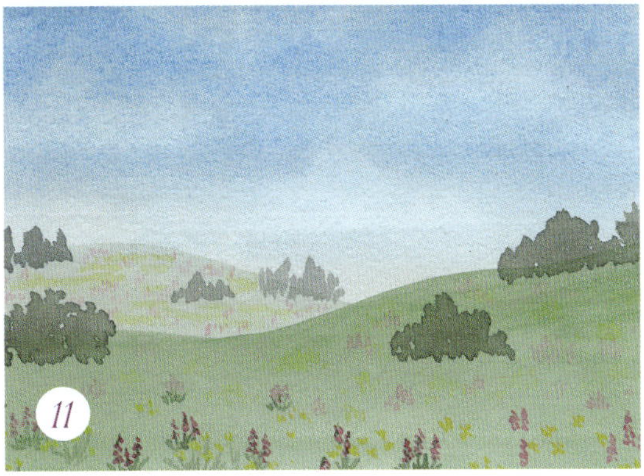

step 10

With a slightly watered-down mix of the same pink as above, continue to move up the page, painting smaller and looser versions of the pink flowers we painted in step 9. Toward the top of this first hill, the flowers could be just clusters of vertical lines. With an even more watery mix of pink, use a light hand to tap in tiny vertical dashes on the distant hill to represent faraway pink flowers.

step 11

On your palette, create a mix of Permanent Sap Green, Burnt Umber and a little Payne's Gray. You want a darker green to use for the stems of your flowers, and it needs to be darker than the green you used for the grass on the front hill so it shows up. Using your size 2 round brush, begin to paint stems connecting your flowers to the ground. The stems can be different for your two different types of flowers. For example, I went with a sturdier stem for my pink flowers, and a slightly longer, airier stem for my yellow flowers. If you are feeling ambitious, you can also add extra stems with buds or seedpods at the ends. These can be little blobs to mimic the shape of each type of flower; paint them using your stem color to differentiate between the colorful blooms. At the base of each cluster, you can also add leaves to complete each plant.

For the yellow flowers, use the same paint mixture as the stems. Start with your brush at the base of the plant, and drag it upward. Then, curve it down before it reaches the blooms, to create a graceful leaf. For the pink flowers, use the stem paint mixture. Start with the tip of your brush at the base. Next, press the belly of the brush into the paper, as you drag it upward, and then lift it off the paper. This will create a broader leaf with a pointed tip.

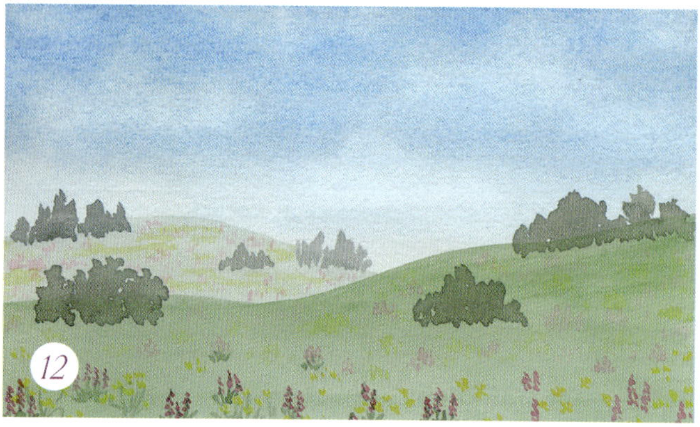

step 12

Water down the mixture you used in step 11, and continue to paint stems on your flowers receding into the background. The stems should become shorter and closer together as you move up the page, indicating that they are farther away. For the distant hill, you can just tap your watery mix of green at the base of the blobs of color, or leave the stems out if you prefer.

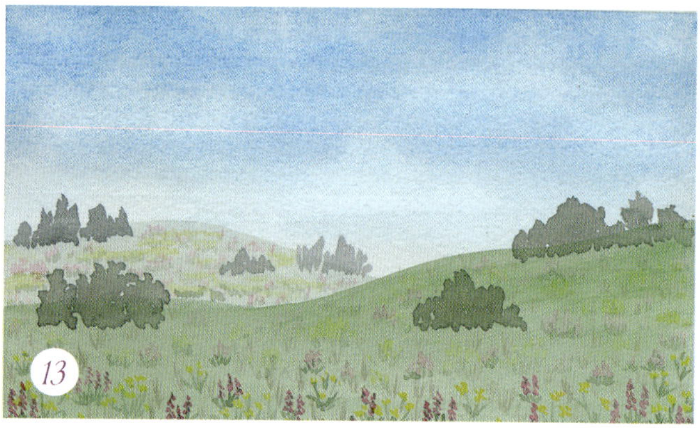

step 13

On your palette, create a watery mix of Burnt Umber with a little bit of Payne's Gray to create a medium-brown color. Using your size 2 round brush and a light hand, paint small clusters of grass by swooshing the point of the brush upward from the ground. You can scatter these randomly throughout the clusters of flowers, making the grasses shorter as you move up the page. Allow everything to dry. The painting portion is now complete!

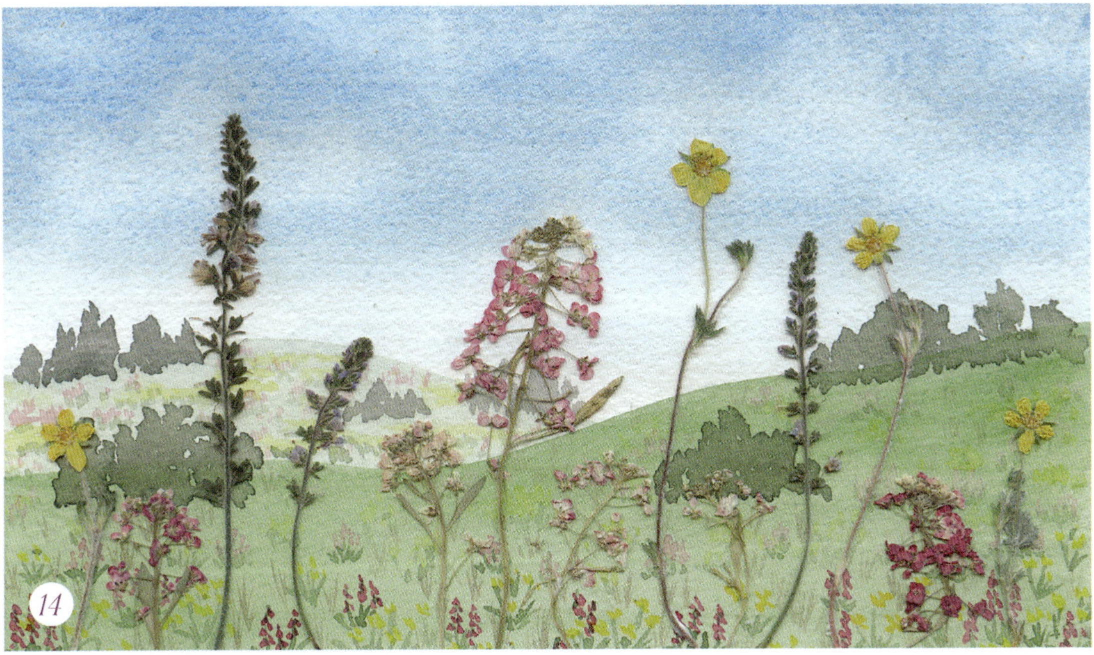

step 14

Using your tweezers or fingers, gently place your pressed flowers on your painting, moving them around until you find an arrangement you are happy with. You can clip stems shorter to make them fit your composition. I like to vary the heights and the spaces between each flower to create a mixed, organic look. If your flowers are not on their stems, you can borrow stems from other plants. (I save the bits I clip off from other projects.) Another option is to place the blooms at different heights and then paint stems in once they are glued down. I sometimes like my flowers to land above and below the horizontal halfway point on the painting, which is what I did here.

Once you have an arrangement you like, carefully pick up each flower and flip it over on a piece of scrap paper or cardboard. Using the glue brush, lightly paint the backside of the flower with glue. Then, flip it back over and place it on your painting. Very gently, use your fingers or tweezers to apply pressure to the flower and stem (if applicable) to make it stick. Repeat this process with each flower until everything is glued down.

Once everything is mounted, set a piece of waxed paper on top of your piece and weigh it down with a few heavy books. Allow it to dry for at least 15 to 20 minutes before carefully peeling away the waxed paper. If you do this too quickly, you can peel your flowers off your page or break them. (See Mounting Flowers on page 22 for more details.) Your piece is now complete!

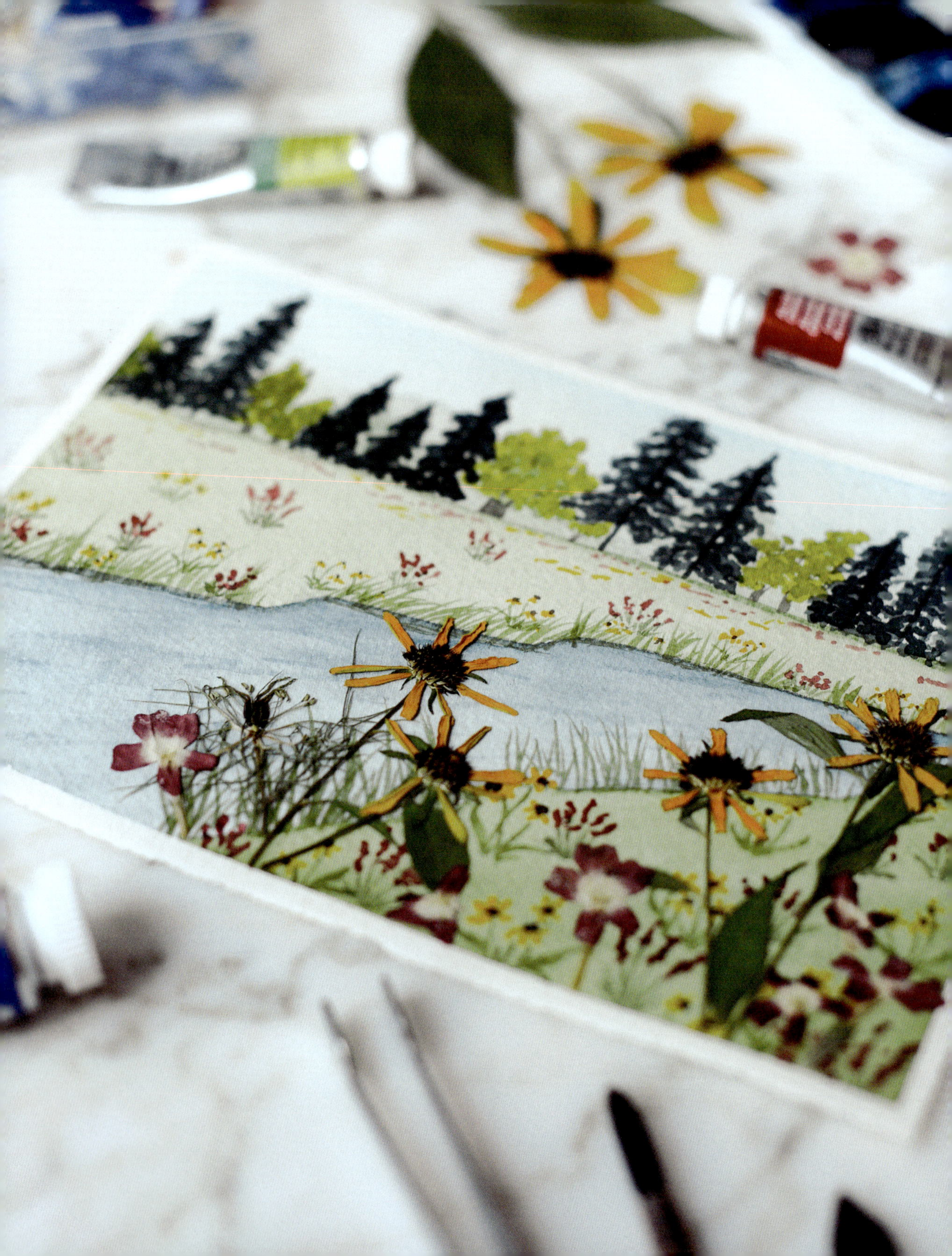

RIVERSIDE WILDFLOWERS

Imagine the sound water makes as it tumbles along, flowing over rocks and through the winding banks of the river. As you stand in a riverside meadow surrounded by trees and wildflowers, birds sing and insects busily work while you admire the peaceful landscape. You may be lucky enough to experience this type of environment in real life, but even if you're not, you can paint along and imagine yourself there through watercolor and pressed flowers. I am using small rudbeckia (black-eyed Susans) flowers from my garden and a few small red verbena blossoms.

size

5 x 7" (12.5 x 18 cm)

brushes

Size 10 round brush
Size 6 round brush
Size 2 round brush
Glue brush

flower palette

Rudbeckia
Red verbena blossoms

materials

Tweezers (optional)
Scissors
Glue
Waxed paper
Heavy Books

color palette

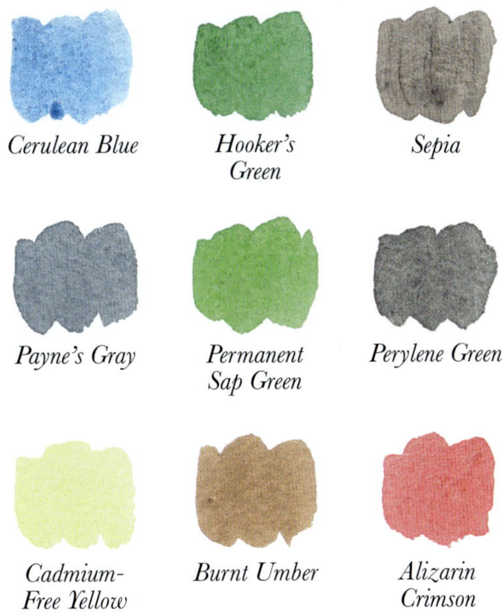

1a

1b

step 1

Using a pencil, lightly draw a horizon line straight across the paper about a third of the way from the top. Then, starting a little bit below the horizon line at the right-hand side, draw a wavy diagonal line downward across the paper, meeting the opposite edge about a third of the way up from the bottom. (This is the far bank of the river.) Draw a second line, this time starting at the bottom edge of the paper, about a quarter to a third of the way from the bottom-left corner, and draw a wavy diagonal line up to the right-hand end of the page just a little bit below the first line. (This is the near bank of the river.)

Create a very watery wash of Cerulean Blue on your palette. Load your size 10 round brush with water. Then, starting at the top of the page, use broad horizontal strokes to paint in the sky above the pencil horizon line. Most of this area is going to be covered up later with trees, so it doesn't need to be perfect.

While the paper is still damp, make a watery mix of Hooker's Green and Sepia on your palette. Pick up a little of this paint on your brush, and make a few marks here and there right above the horizon line, allowing them to bleed into the blue and connect with each other. Paint a line right along the horizon to connect these greenish marks to the ground level. They'll serve as a background to a line of trees we'll paint later.

step 2

Create a watery mix of Cerulean Blue and a little Payne's Gray on your palette. Pick up some of this paint with your size 10 round brush, and use the point of the brush to carefully paint along the edge of the river (the far-bank pencil line). Then, reloading your brush as needed, carefully follow the near-bank pencil line to fill in the rest of the river area.

While the paper is still damp (not wet), add some more Payne's Gray to your mixture to darken it. Then, paint along the far bank with this darker blue to give some shadow to the water. Allow the painting to dry.

step 3

Then, add a bit more Cerulean Blue and Payne's Gray to the wash on your palette so it is a stronger pigment mix. Pick up some of this paint with your size 6 round brush, and use the brush point to paint wavy lines on a diagonal, going in the direction of the river. Take a paper towel and blot at the river after you paint the lines, which will soften them a little bit.

(continued)

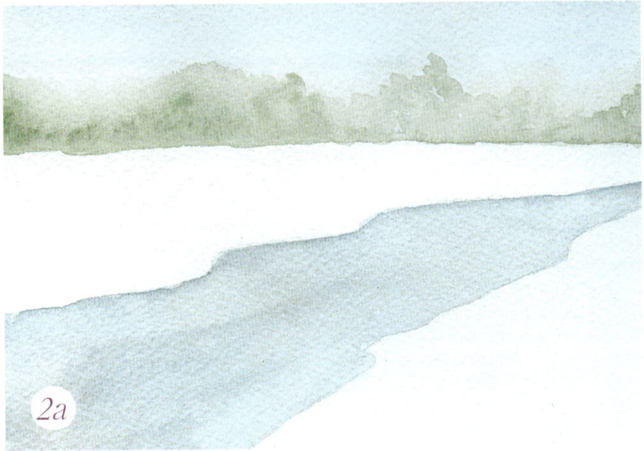

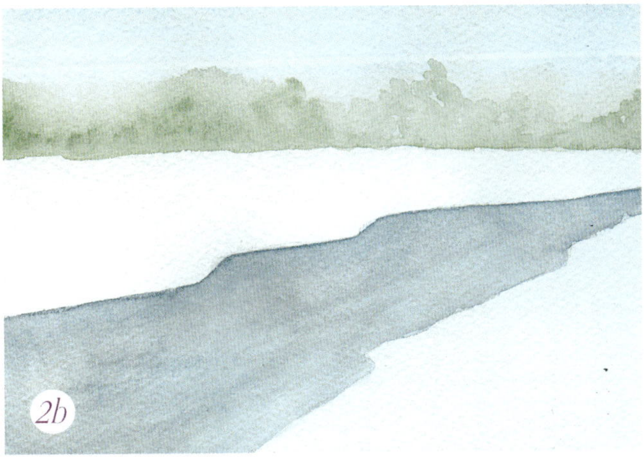

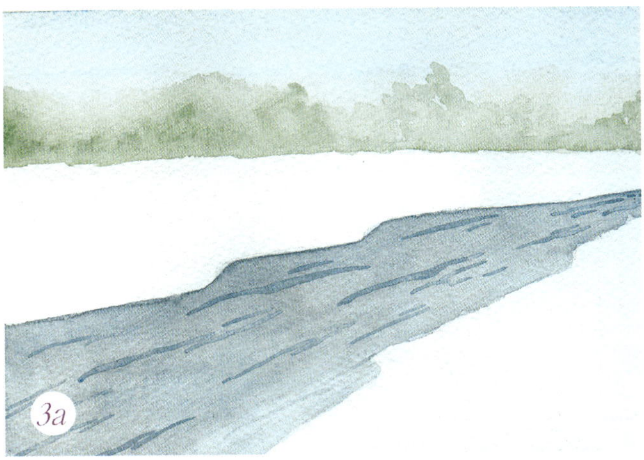

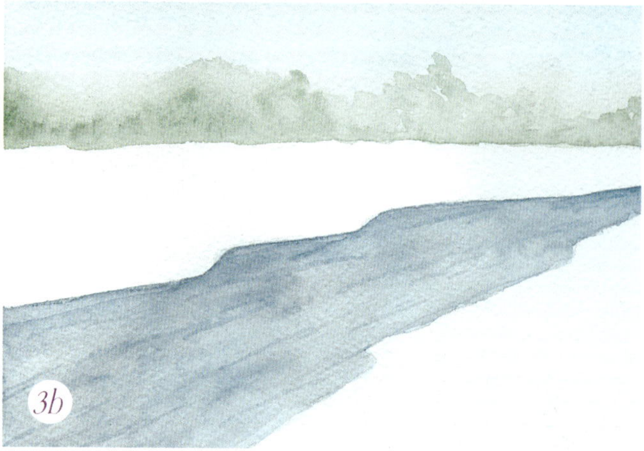

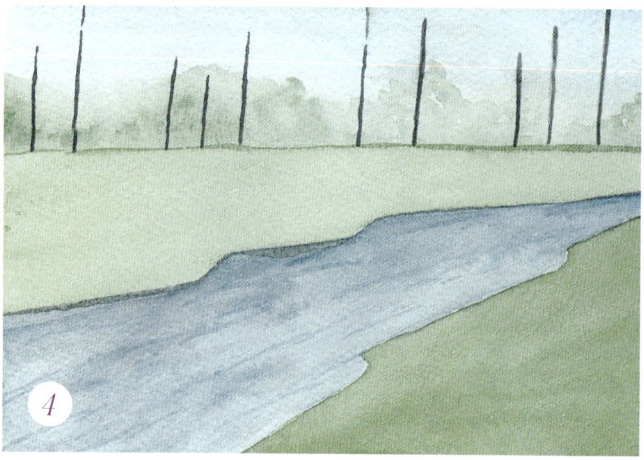

Clean off your brush, and load it with clean water. Then, paint back and forth in the direction of the river flow. This will further soften the lines. We don't want hard-edged lines in the river, but do want to give it a sense of steady movement.

step 4

Create a moderately pigmented mix of Permanent Sap Green with a little Sepia on your palette. Using your size 10 round brush, pick up some of this pigment, and carefully paint along the lower edge of the river to trace it. Then, use broad brushstrokes to fill in the remaining area in this corner of the page. Next, add a little more water to the mix on your palette and repeat this process to paint in the area above the river and below the horizon, carefully painting along the edges with the point of your brush.

Create a moderately pigmented mix of Perylene Green with a little Payne's Gray on your palette. Then, pick up some of this paint with your size 6 round brush, and use the brush point to paint vertical lines of varying heights and spacing, starting at the horizon and leading upward into the sky. Make sure to leave some larger gaps. I like to group trees in twos and threes and leave larger spaces between the groups.

step 5

Then, load your brush with more paint. Starting at the top of one of these lines, begin tapping the point of the brush to the paper to make lots of small, irregular marks (dots and dashes) on opposite sides of the line (the tree trunk). Move down the line toward the horizon, making slightly larger marks as you move down so the tree is a rough, narrow triangle in shape. Leave gaps between the marks for negative space, so the tree looks natural. Continue filling out the branches on the remaining tree trunks. As you vary the thickness of each tree, make sure the tips remain pointed. Allow the painting to dry.

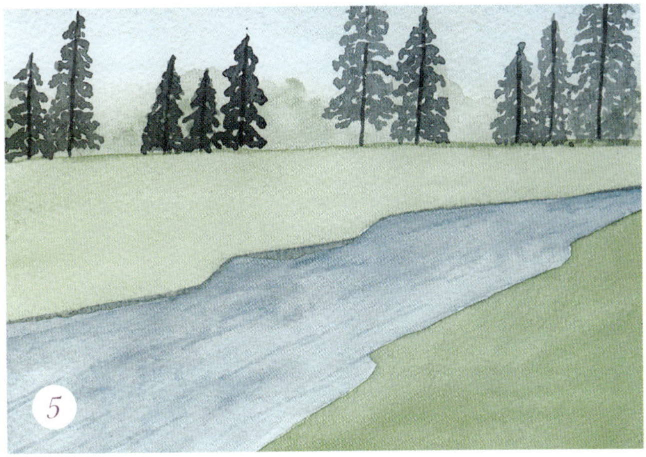

step 6

Add a little more Payne's Gray to the mixture on your palette to make it darker. (Make sure it is still a fairly pigmented mixture.) Pick up some of this paint, and loosely tap the point of the brush to make more marks on your evergreen trees. Focus on the center of the tree to create depth throughout the branches. Visualize that you are darkening the area around the trunk and on the underside of the branches, making sure to leave plenty of space for the previous layer to show through. (For details on painting evergreen trees, see page 42.) Clean your brush.

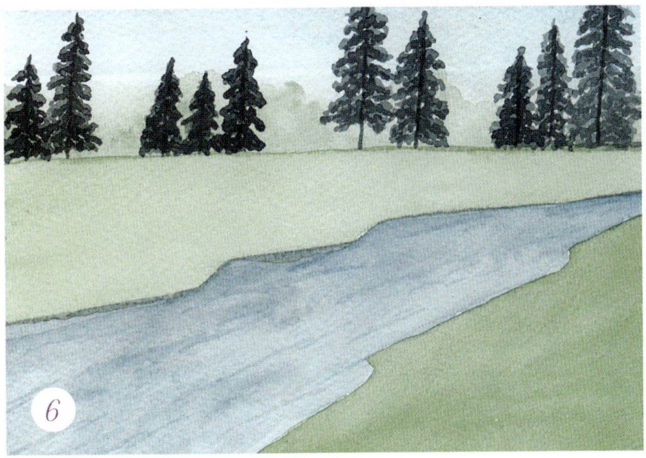

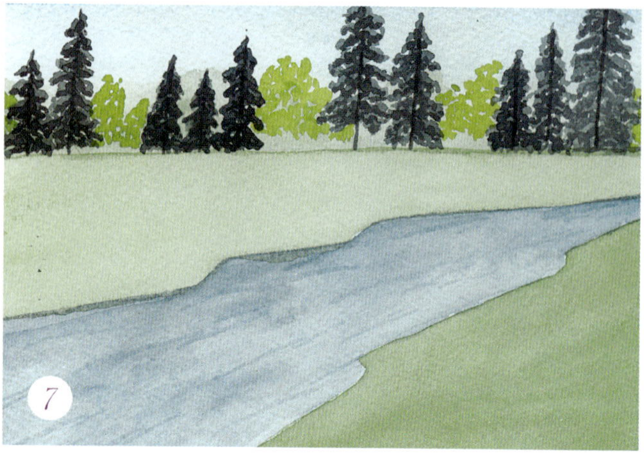

step 7

Mix up some Permanent Sap Green and Cadmium-Free Yellow on your palette for a moderately pigmented yellow-green color. Still using your size 6 round brush, pick up some of this paint and begin adding deciduous trees in between the evergreen trees. To do this, we will make similar marks as we did for the evergreen trees. However, in this case, we will connect the marks together in irregular clusters with more rounded shapes above the horizon so we can come back in and add trunks later. Allow the painting to dry.

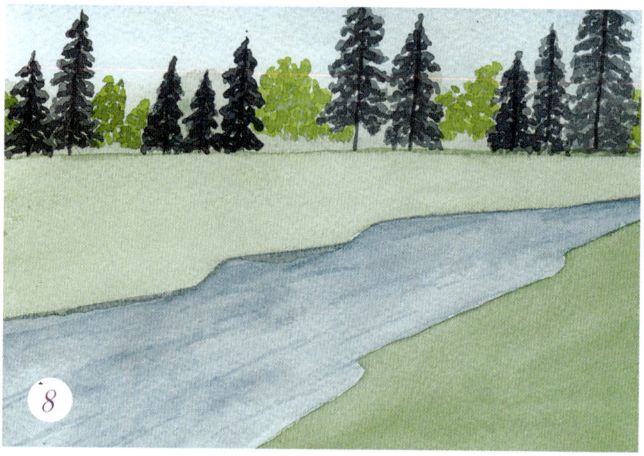

step 8

Create a mix of Hooker's Green and a little Burnt Umber on your palette. Then, as we did with the evergreen trees, add this darker color, using a light tapping motion with the point of your brush to add some shadowy areas to the deciduous trees we just painted. Don't cover up all of the lighter green!

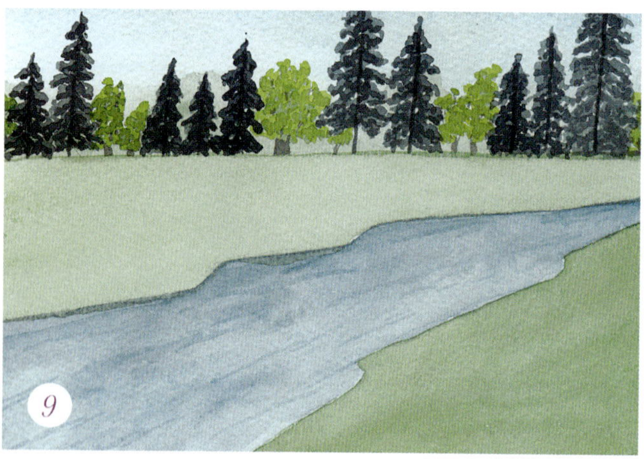

step 9

Mix up some Burnt Umber with a little bit of Payne's Gray on your palette for a dark brownish-gray color. Then, using a light hand and your size 2 round brush, pick up some of this mixture and paint trunks connecting the deciduous tree leaves to the horizon line. Next, sparingly paint tiny dashes at upward angles inside the spaces within the tree leaves. These will be branches peeking through here and there.

step 10

Pick up some Alizarin Crimson paint straight from the pan, using your size 6 round brush. Once again, make a light tapping motion with the point of your brush and create loose vertical (or slightly off vertical) lines of dots, making groupings of three to five of these lines. Paint multiple groupings of these marks across the foreground. Then, add smaller versions on the far side of the river. Add a bit more water to the paint, and then loosely paint dots in more horizontal lines across the far background, near the tree line.

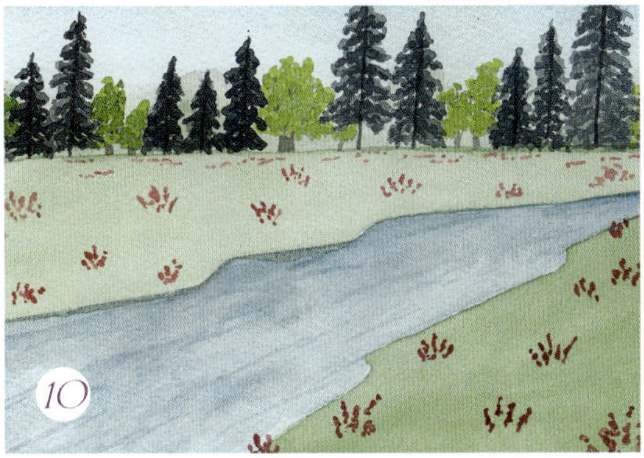

step 11

Switch to your size 2 round brush. Then, pick up some Cadmium-Free Yellow paint straight from the pan. Using the point of the brush, paint petals of yellow flowers by making small short lines in a few different configurations—a sunburst shape, an upside-down fan shape and a half-sunburst shape. (See Painting Tiny Flowers on page 37 for details.) Create groupings of these shapes, with each grouping having at least two of the shapes. These will be yellow wildflowers (rudbeckia) with their flowers facing different directions. Continue painting clusters of yellow flowers around the foreground. On the other side of the river, we'll continue creating yellow flowers, but instead of small short lines, you will make dots in similar clusters closer to the river's edge and then dots in rough horizontal lines closer to the tree line. These flowers will be impressions rather than realistic representations. Allow the painting to dry.

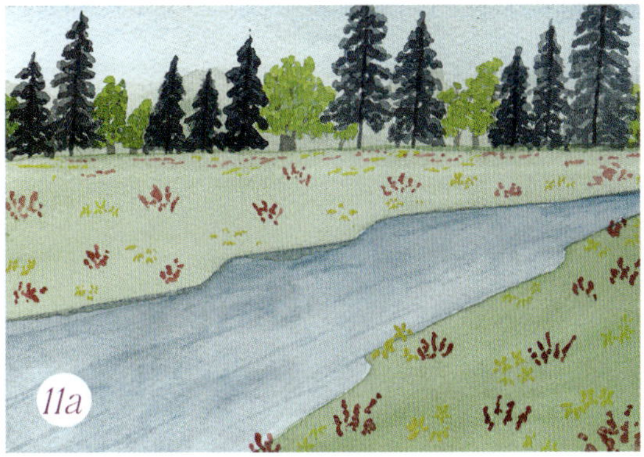

(continued)

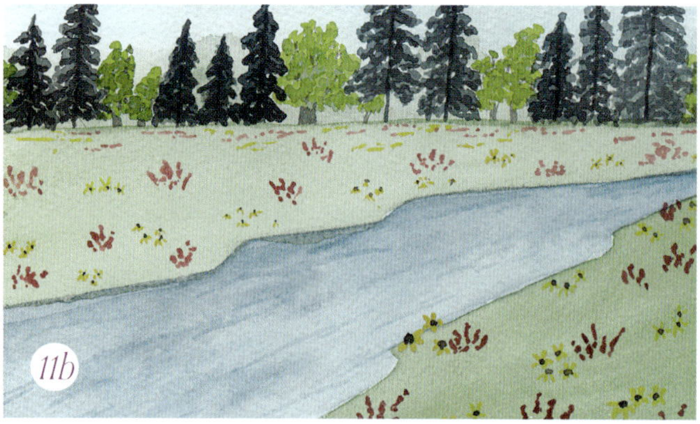

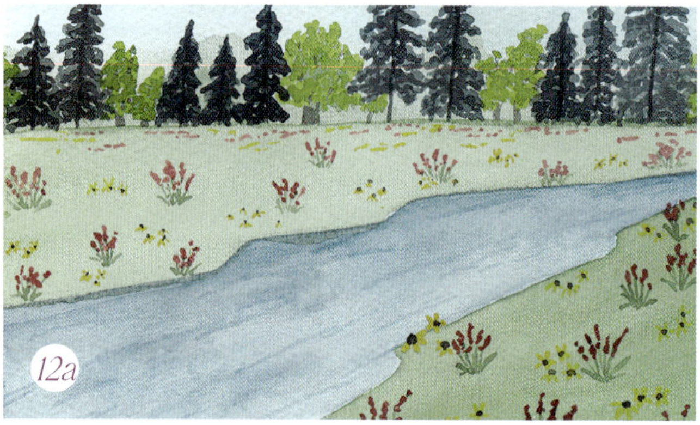

Clean your brush. Then, pick up some Sepia straight from the pan. Lightly add dark centers to the rudbeckia. For the larger flowers closer to the bottom of the page (foreground), the dark center can be a bit larger. Lightly tap the point of the brush right at the center of any sunburst shapes, at the top of any fan or half-sunburst shapes. The flowers on the far side of the river can get an even lighter touch with the brush; you don't even need to add a dark center to all of the yellow areas, especially back toward the tree line.

step 12

Create a mix of Hooker's Green and Sepia on your palette for an earthy-green color. Pick up some of this paint on your size 2 round brush. Using light pressure on the point of the brush, paint thin stems beneath each of the reddish flowers we painted in step 10. Since these flowers are painted in clusters, the stems should connect with each other at their base. Paint a few leaves at the base of the plants by dragging the point and belly of the brush upward at an angle and lifting it to create a simple, small leaf. Remember to paint shorter, smaller stems for flowers farther away.

Create a mix of Permanent Sap Green and a little Sepia on your palette for a second earthy-green color. Then, repeat the same process of adding stems to your yellow flowers. For the leaves on these flowers, you can make a slightly broader leaf by applying more pressure through the belly of the brush, and add a little wave or flourish to your brushstroke to make a curved leaf. Continue adding stems and leaves until all of the yellow flowers are complete, using smaller stems toward the background of the painting. Allow the painting to dry.

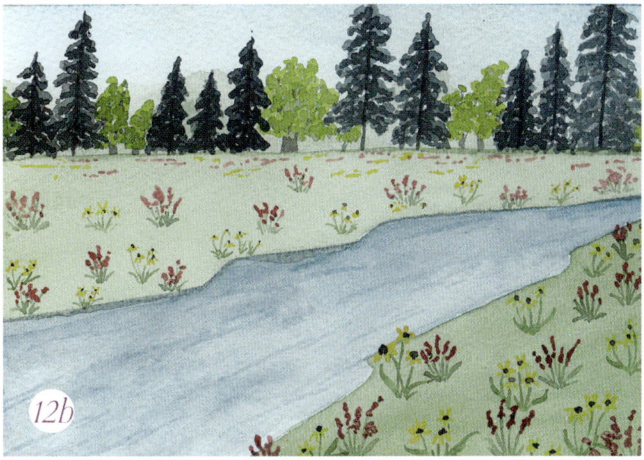

step 13

Using the same mixture of Permanent Sap Green and Sepia, load your size 2 round brush with paint and create grasses along both banks of the river (see Painting Grasses on page 36 for more details). The grasses should be a bit shorter on the farther (thinner) portion of the river and a bit taller on the wider portion toward the bottom of the page. The painting portion is now complete!

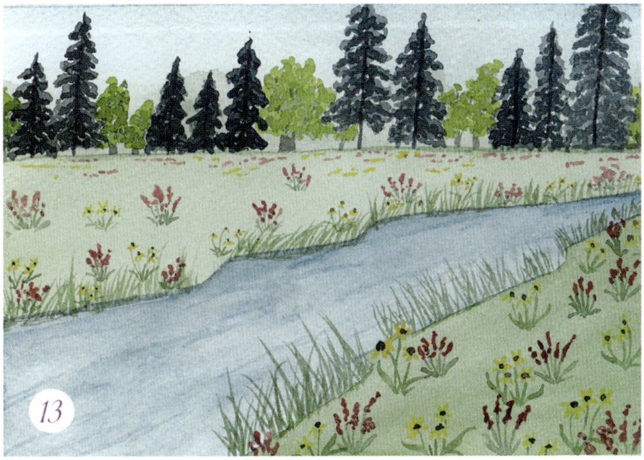

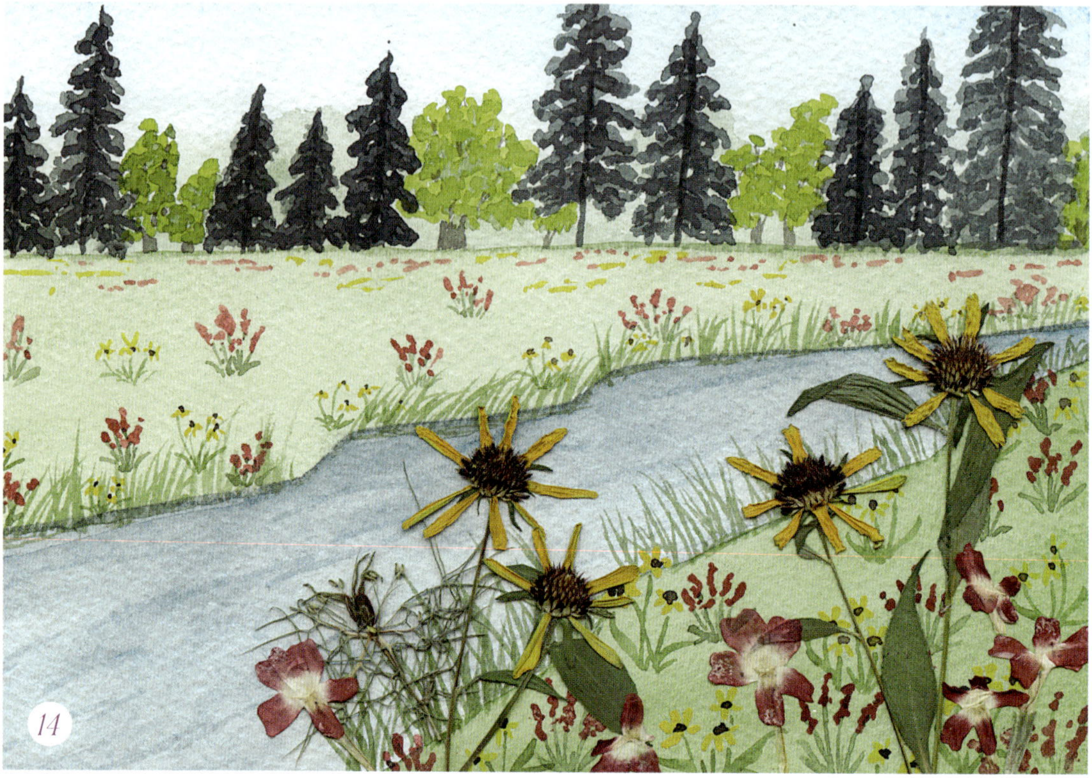

step 14

Choose your pressed flowers, and begin placing them on your paper. We are going to mount them only on the near bank of the river, on the bottom-right corner. Once you are happy with your layout, begin picking up the flowers one by one. Then, using your glue brush, carefully paint the backside of the flowers with a thin layer of glue and press them onto the paper. Once they are all mounted, set a piece of waxed paper on top of your piece and weigh it down with a few heavy books. Allow it to dry for at least 15 to 20 minutes before carefully peeling away the waxed paper. If you do this too quickly, you can peel your flowers off your page or break them. (See Mounting Flowers on page 22 for more details.) Your piece is now complete!

LOOKING UP

Lay down in the meadow with your face to the sky and be rewarded with a new perspective on wildflowers. We'll explore this unique point of view throughout this whimsical painting. I have chosen pinkish-purple cosmos, buttercups and pink sweet alyssum, as they correspond well with the colors and shapes in the painting. Since this is a "looking up" perspective, I chose a mix of flowers—some that I pressed head on and some that I pressed in profile.

size

8 x 10" (20 x 25 cm)

brushes

Wash brush
Size 10 round brush
Size 6 round brush
Size 8 filbert brush
Glue brush

flower palette

Cosmos
Buttercups
Pink sweet alyssum

materials

Tweezers (optional)
Scissors
Glue
Waxed paper
Heavy Books

color palette

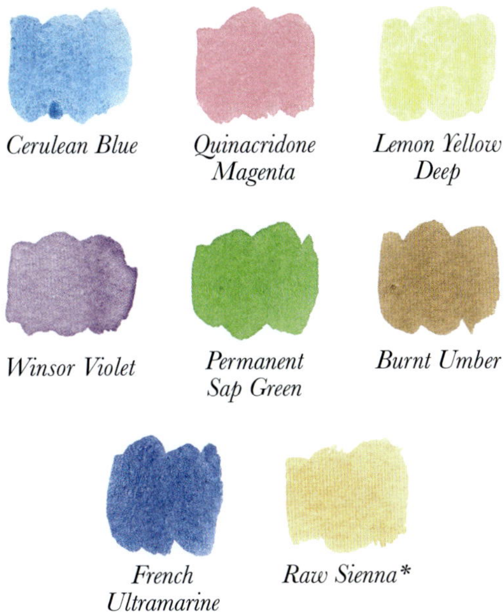

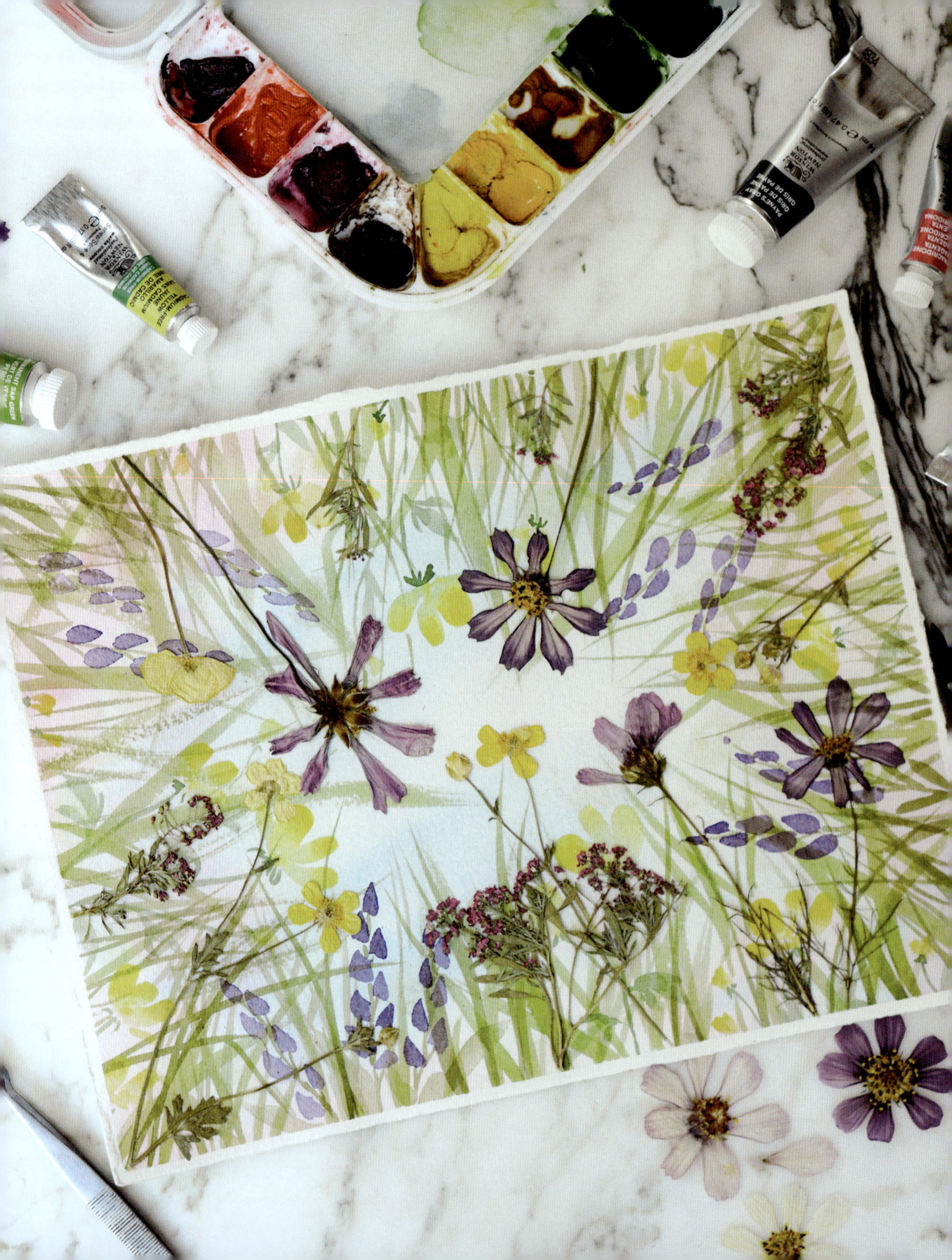

step 1

Dampen your entire paper with a large wash brush. Once the paper is damp, use your size 10 round brush to create a moderately pigmented wash of Cerulean Blue paint on your palette. Load your brush and create sweeping brushstrokes across the entire paper, allowing some portions to remain patchy and white. This is our base layer for the sky, and any white spots left will imply clouds. Clean your brush.

step 2

While the paper is still wet, create a moderately pigmented mixture of Quinacridone Magenta on your palette. (If the paper has dried, dampen it again with a wash of clean water.) Load your size 10 round brush with this color and make random blotches on the wet paper around the edges of the piece. We want only blue sky right in the center of the page. The wet paper will allow these marks to soften and bleed.

step 3

Make sure the paper is still wet, and create a moderately pigmented mixture of Lemon Yellow Deep on your palette. Load your size 10 round brush with this color and make small swirling motions with the tip of your brush to create yellow rounds (or roundish shapes). Spread these throughout the page, overlapping the pink in some areas and the blue in some others (but again, avoiding the very center of the paper). Allow the painting to dry.

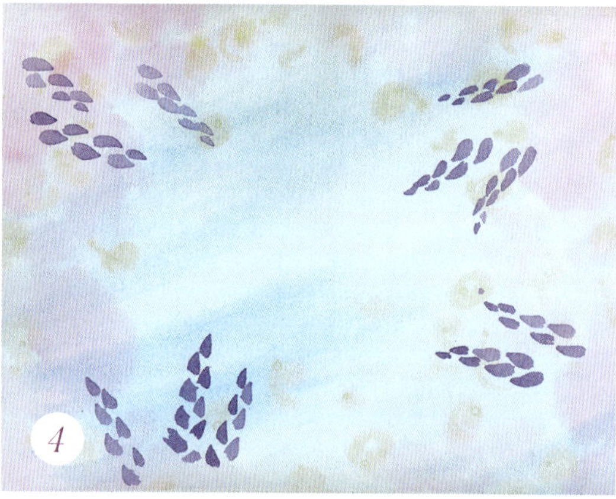

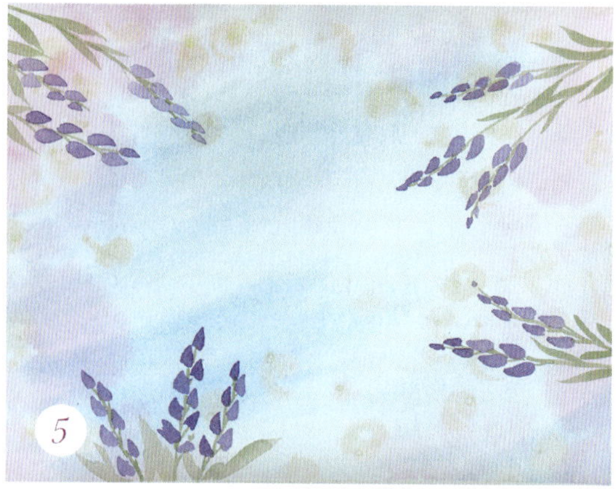

step 4

Create a pigmented mix of Winsor Violet on your palette. Then load your size 10 round brush with paint. Holding your brush like a pencil, press the point and then the belly of the brush to the paper before pulling the point down into the mark you just made and lifting the brush. This should create a sort of rounded triangular or teardrop shape. Make another of these marks right next to the first, starting the point of the brush just a little bit above the first and repeating this brushstroke. Make a third mark above the first. Then repeat, alternating side to side and shrinking the marks as you work upward, to make seven or eight marks in total. This is one flower. We will add the stems once the blooms are all painted.

Move to one side of your first flower and repeat the process, varying the direction of the line of blooms, creating a curve or varying the total number of marks per flower. I like to create clusters of flowers, grouping two or three together. Paint a few groups as if they are growing from multiple sides of your paper. Allow the painting to dry.

step 5

Create a pigmented mix of Permanent Sap Green and Burnt Umber on your palette. Then, load your size 6 round brush with this paint and, placing the tip of the brush at the end of the paper beneath one of your flowers, drag a line upward to the bottom of the flower. Continue the line up through to the top of the flower, either straight through (picking up your brush to avoid painting over the purple marks) or with branching stems to connect everything. Repeat, connecting each flower with a stem to the edge of the page.

Next, paint some leaves at the bottom of the stems. Making sure your size 6 brush is loaded with the same paint mixture as above; hold it so the tip is pointed downward and at an angle to the stem. Then, press first the point and then the belly of the brush to the paper to create a slender pointed leaf. (See Painting Leaves on page 36.) Repeat this process, alternating on either side of the stem and making smaller leaves as you move upward toward the flowers. Continue adding leaves to each of the stems you have painted.

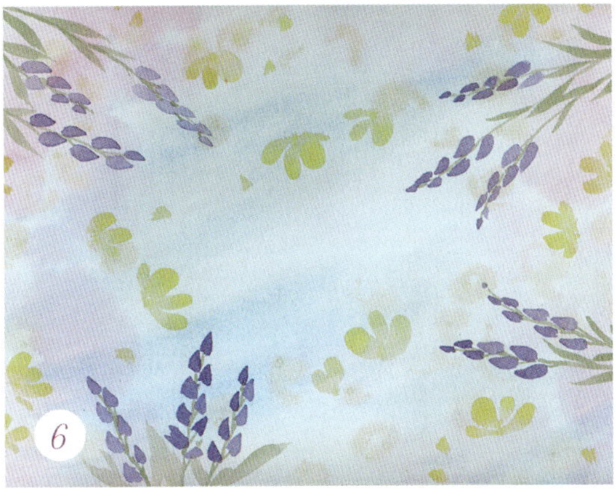

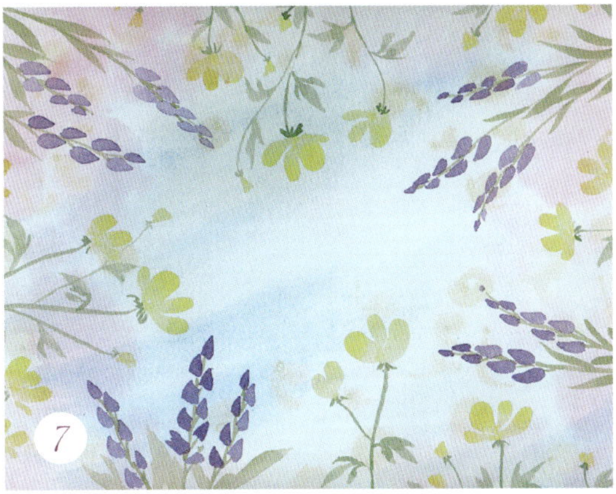

step 6

Activate some Lemon Yellow Deep with a little bit of water. Then, using a dampened size 8 filbert brush, pick up paint directly from the pan. Next, press the tip and belly of the brush (on the broad side) to the paper. Lift to create a rounded mark. This is one of our flower petals. Make another mark right next to it that connects at the bottom but has a space between them at their rounded tops. Make another mark or two, this time using the thinner edge of the filbert brush and still connecting them at the base of the flower. Your first yellow flower is finished.

Repeat this series of marks to create more flowers, moving around the paper. You can create a few small flower buds near the other flowers by using the broad side of the brush to create two small rounded strokes at opposing angles, so they connect in the center for a roundish heart shape.

step 7

Create a mix of Permanent Sap Green and a little French Ultramarine on your palette to create a cool-green color. Then, load your size 6 round brush with this mixture, and begin to lightly paint stems connecting your yellow flowers and buds to the edge of your paper. You can also use the point of the brush to make small marks right at the base of each flower and bud. These are called *sepals* and look like little collars beneath the flower heads.

Use your size 6 round brush to paint the leaves for these flowers. We will be making a variation on the leaf we did for the purple flowers in step 5. This time, we'll create a compound leaf with three leaflets using the same technique. Create one leaf near a stem. Then, create a smaller leaf at a slight angle to the first, connecting at the base of the first leaf. Finally, make a third leaf on the other side, connecting it again to the first two and dragging a line from the bottom of the leaf to connect it to the flower stem.

Repeat this process, adding leaves to other stems to fill the space. You can change the angle of the leaf in relation to each flower stem and make some with only two leaflets instead of three. Allow the painting to dry.

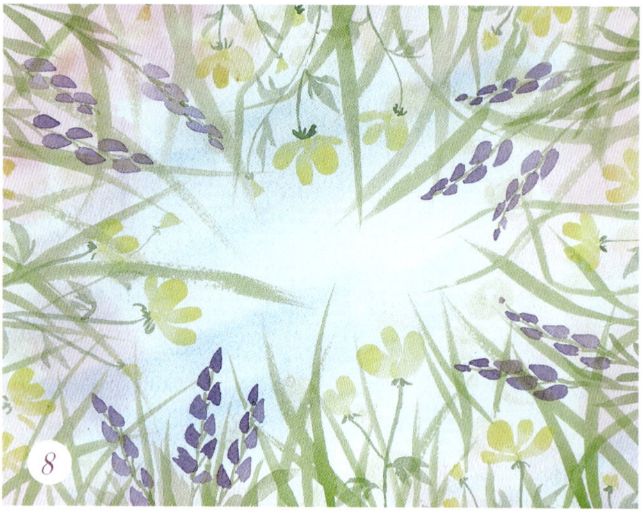

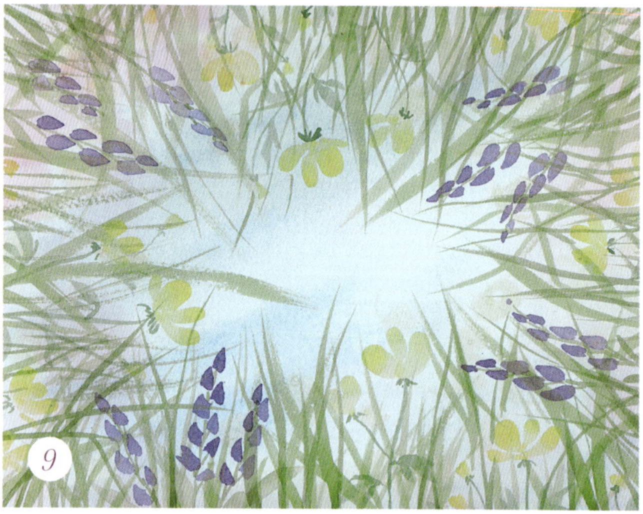

step 8

Create a pigmented mix of Permanent Sap Green with a little bit of Raw Sienna paint on your palette, and load your size 6 round brush with this green mixture. Begin loosely painting blades of grass, starting with the point of the brush at the edge of the page (pointed downward) and dragging it up into the painting, first giving pressure through the belly of the brush to broaden the stroke, then lifting the pressure until the brush leaves the paper to make a tapered end. This process should be loose and organic: Vary the angle of each blade of grass, add a bend here and there and make some longer and some shorter while working your way around all four edges of the paper. Don't forget to make some grass grow from the corners.

step 9

Create a pigmented mix of Permanent Sap Green and Burnt Umber on your palette for a darker, earthier green. Repeat the process in step 8 to add another layer of grasses, this time using less pressure on your brush to create some thinner grasses. Once you feel you have filled in the space to your liking, you can stop painting and clean your brushes. Allow the piece to dry. The painting portion is now complete!

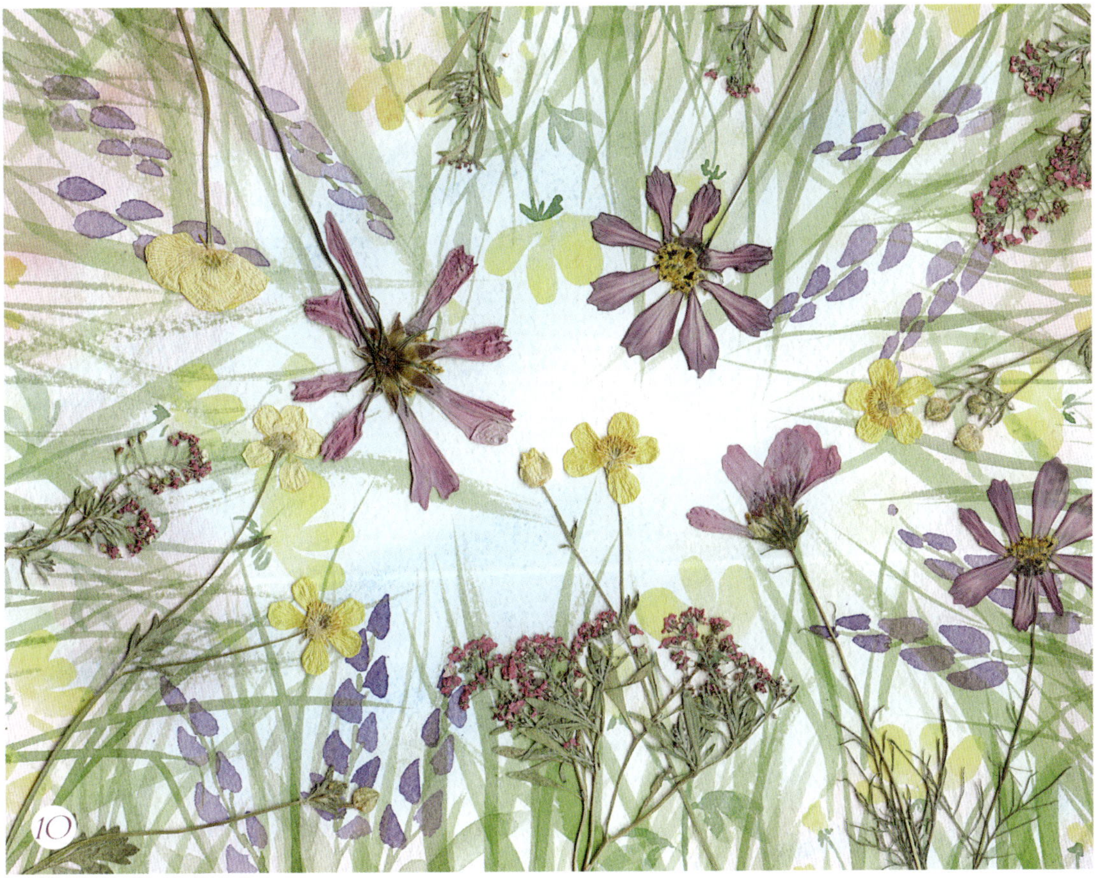

step 10

Choose your pressed flowers, and begin arranging them gently with your tweezers or fingers. This piece shows a different perspective than most of the other pieces in this book, so we will have flowers emerging from all four sides of the painting. Arrange them so the flowers are pointing roughly toward the center of the page. I also recommend varying the angle on some so the stems don't cross each other. (It's easier to mount them this way.) The stems should reach all the way to the edge of the painting. Once you are happy with the layout, you can begin mounting the flowers one by one.

Using your glue brush, coat the back of each flower and stem with a thin layer of glue before mounting it to the artwork. Press down with your fingers or tweezers to ensure it sticks. Once they are all mounted, set a piece of waxed paper on top of your piece and weigh it down with a few heavy books. Allow it to dry for at least 15 to 20 minutes before carefully peeling away the waxed paper. (See Mounting Flowers on page 22 for more details.) Your piece is now complete!

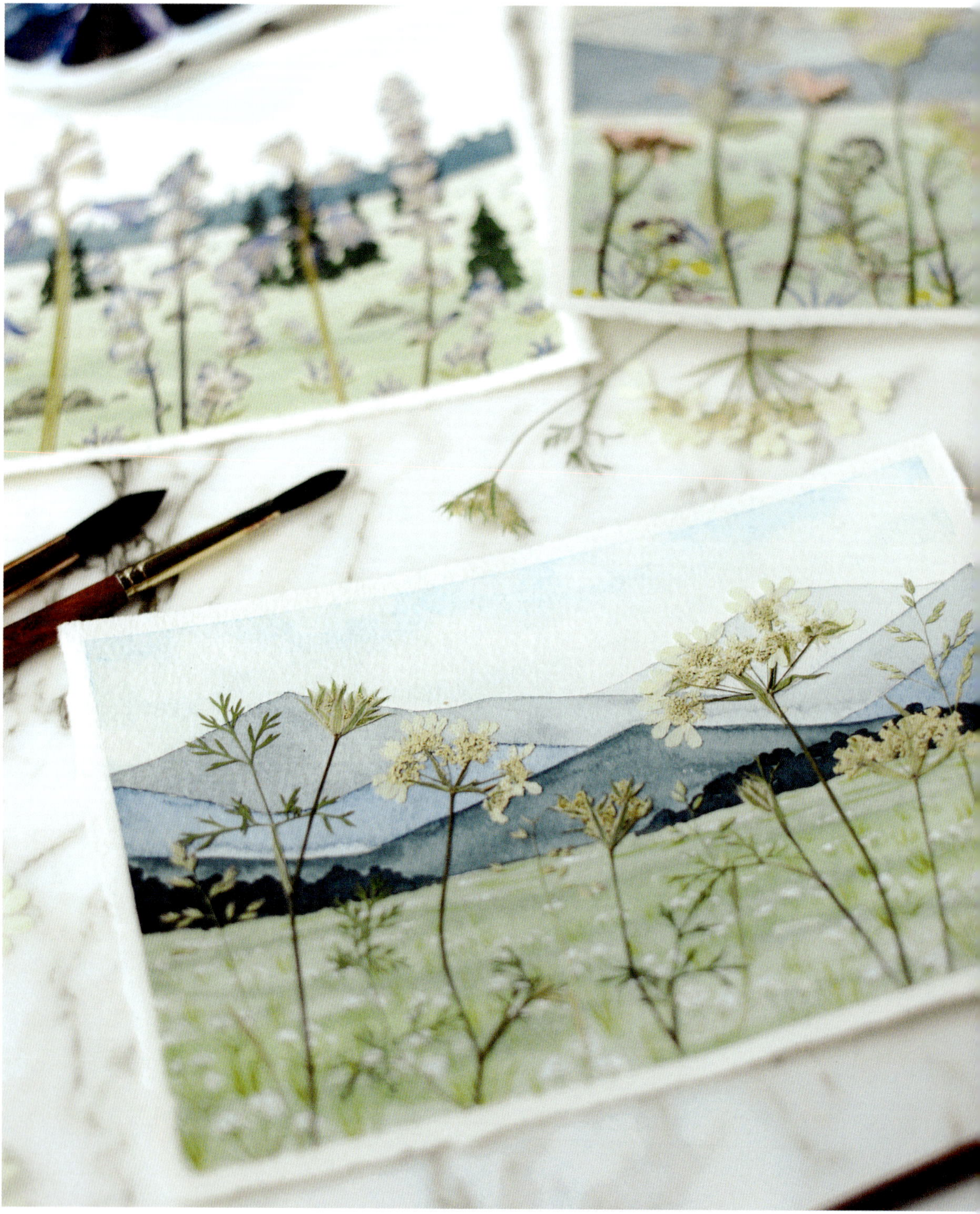

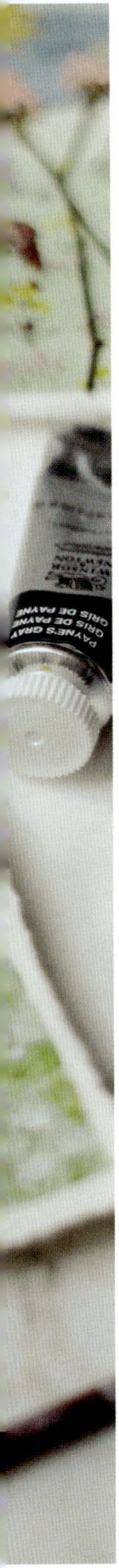

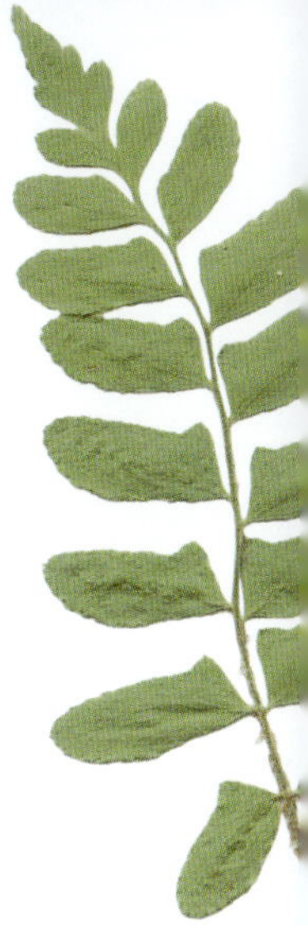

mountain MEADOWS

Mountains can form a beautiful and fun-to-paint backdrop to many different wildflower ecosystems. In this chapter, we will paint gentle mountains in Blue Ridge Wildflowers (page 111), dramatic snow-capped peaks in Rocky Mountain Meadow (page 125), an autumn mountaintop vista in Autumn Overlook (page 117) and a whimsical sunset scene in Cotton Candy Skies (page 131).

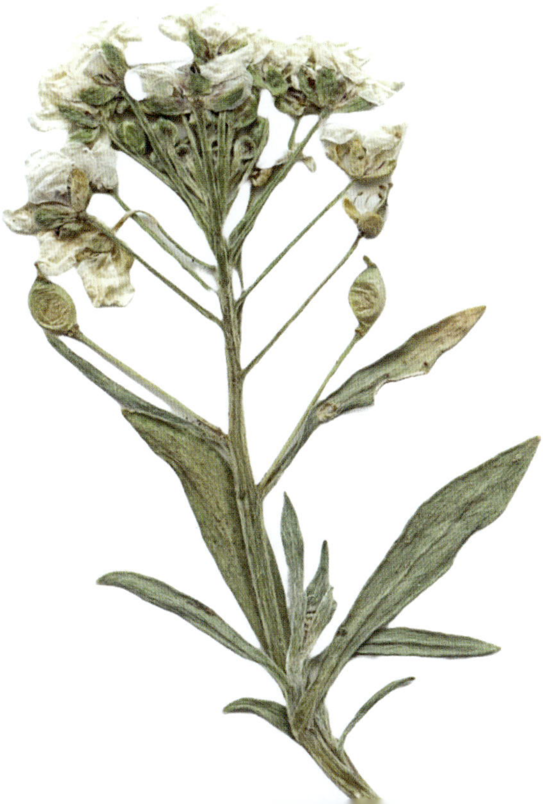

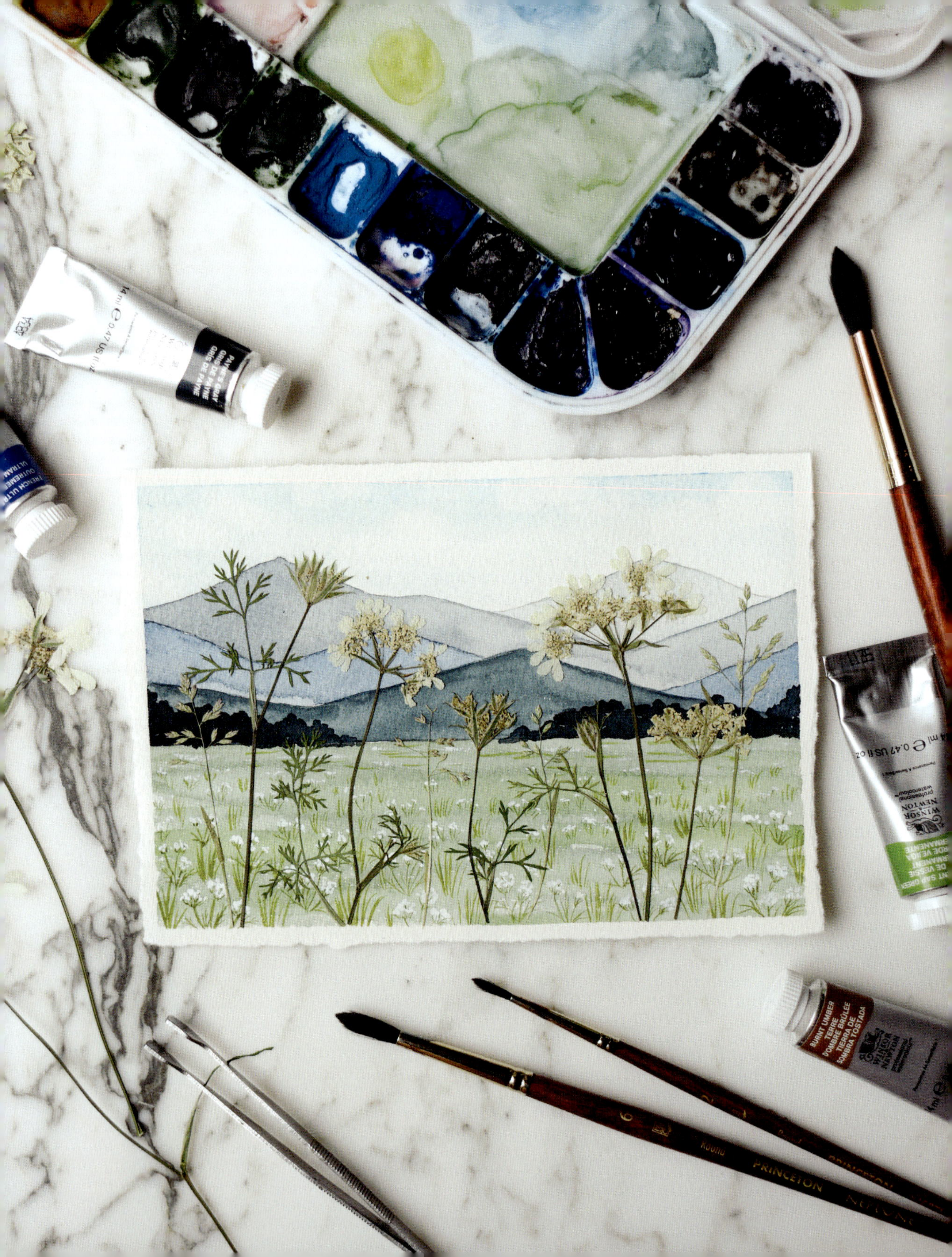
PRINCETON

BLUE RIDGE WILDFLOWERS

Fields of swaying green grasses and masses of white wildflowers lay before the beautiful Blue Ridge Mountains, all beneath a calm blue sky. This simple, serene scene employs a modest color palette and will transport you to a warm afternoon in the countryside. In this piece, I am using orlaya flowers, which are related to Queen Anne's Lace. I also like to use pressed grasses and other wispy elements in a meadow like this one.

size

5 x 7" (12.5 x 18 cm)

brushes

Size 10 round brush
Size 6 round brush
Size 2 round brush
Glue brush

flower palette

Queen Anne's lace or orlaya
Grasses

materials

Tweezers (optional)
Scissors
Glue
Waxed paper
Heavy Books

color palette

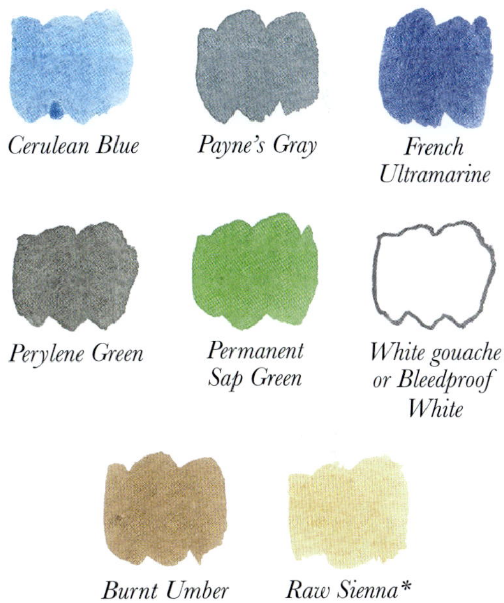

1

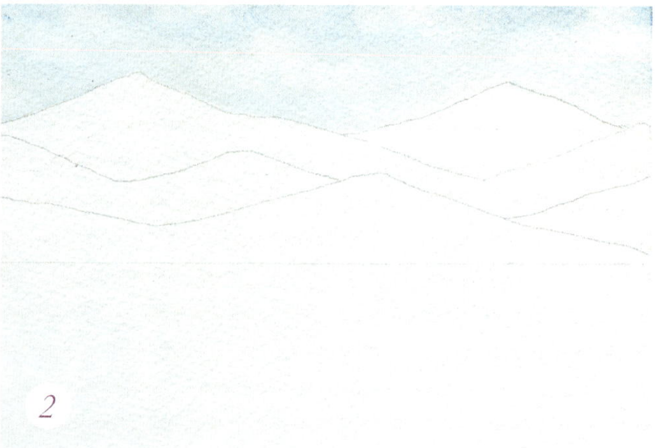

2

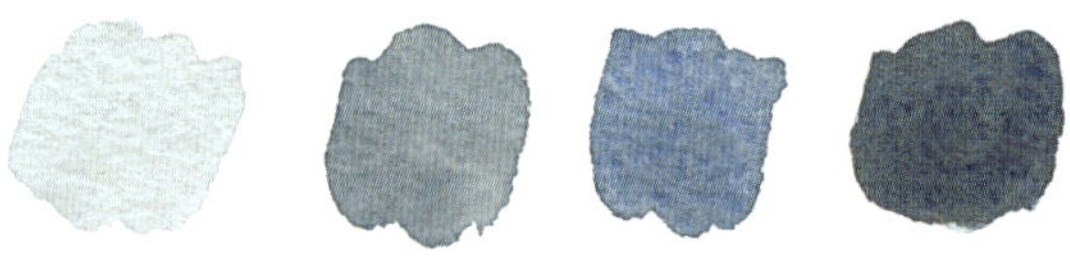

3a

step 1

Using a pencil, lightly draw in some lines for the layers of mountains we will be painting. I like to create multiple mountain planes using a series of asymmetrical *M* shapes and inverted *V* shapes.

step 2

Create a watery mix of Cerulean Blue on your palette. Load your size 10 round brush with this mixture, and paint in the top portion of the page above the pencil lines (the sky), carefully dragging the brush along the pencil marks. While the paint is still wet, take a crumpled-up paper towel and blot at a few places within the sky to create clouds. Allow the painting to dry.

step 3

To paint the different mountain layers, we will need to create several mixes of paint in varying concentrations of Payne's Gray and French Ultramarine. On your palette, make these four mixes: Mix 1 is a very watery Payne's Gray; Mix 2 is a slightly more pigmented Payne's Gray (but not full concentration); Mix 3 is a mix of Payne's Gray with a little bit of French Ultramarine; Mix 4 is a pigmented mix of French Ultramarine with a little bit of Perylene Green. Mix 4 should be the boldest color.

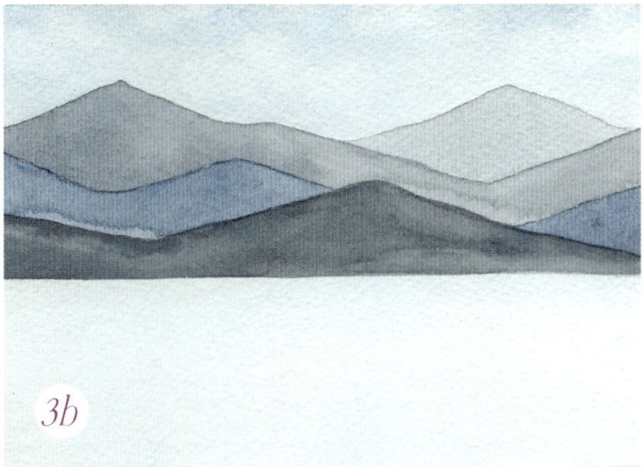

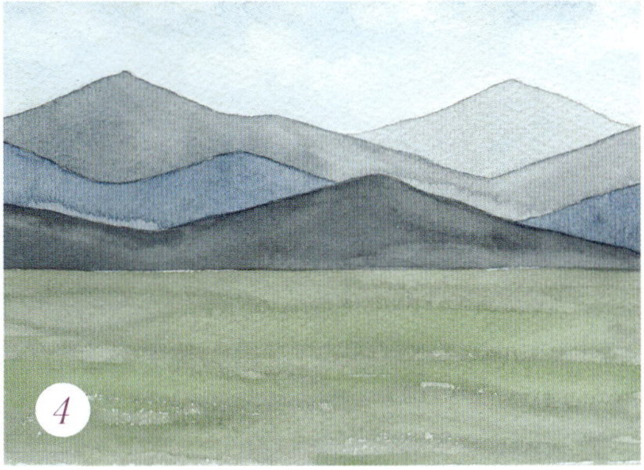

We're going to work our way down the page, starting with the highest mountain peaks down to the lowest. Pick up some of Mix 1 on your size 10 round brush and paint in the very top mountain segment. Allow the painting to dry. Next, fill in the second mountain segment with Mix 2 and allow it to dry. Then, use Mix 3 to paint in the third mountain segment. Allow the painting to dry. Finally, pick up some of Mix 4, and paint in the very bottom mountain segment. Allow the painting to dry.

step 4

Mix up some moderately pigmented Permanent Sap Green and Perylene Green on your palette for a cool-green color. Then, using your size 10 round brush, make sweeping brushstrokes to fill in the meadow below the horizon line. Next, while the paper is still damp, clean your brush and create a watery mixture of Permanent Sap Green on your palette. Finally, use some of that mixture to lightly paint a few more horizontal strokes within the meadow here and there. Allow the painting to dry.

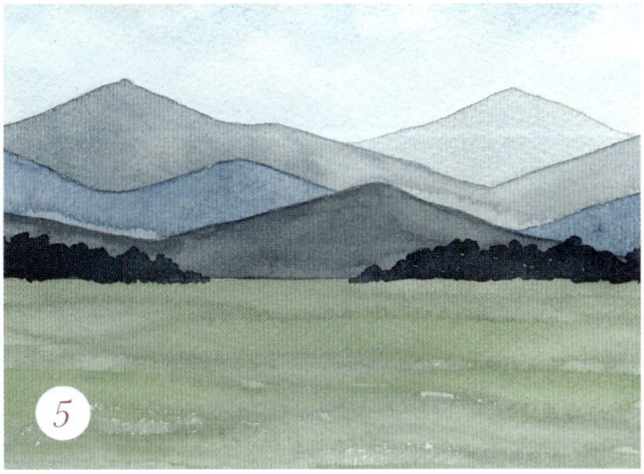

step 5

Mix up some Perylene Green and Payne's Gray for a pigmented deep green color. On your size 10 or 6 round brush, pick up some of this paint and, starting on the left side of the page, tap the brush repeatedly to make connected clusters of marks, stopping about a quarter to a third of the way from the edge of the page. This will be a distant line of trees. Make sure that the bottom edge of this tree line is in line with the horizon. I like to drag the point of the brush along this line to clean it up. Repeat this process, starting at the opposite edge of the paper. There should be a gap between the two lines of trees.

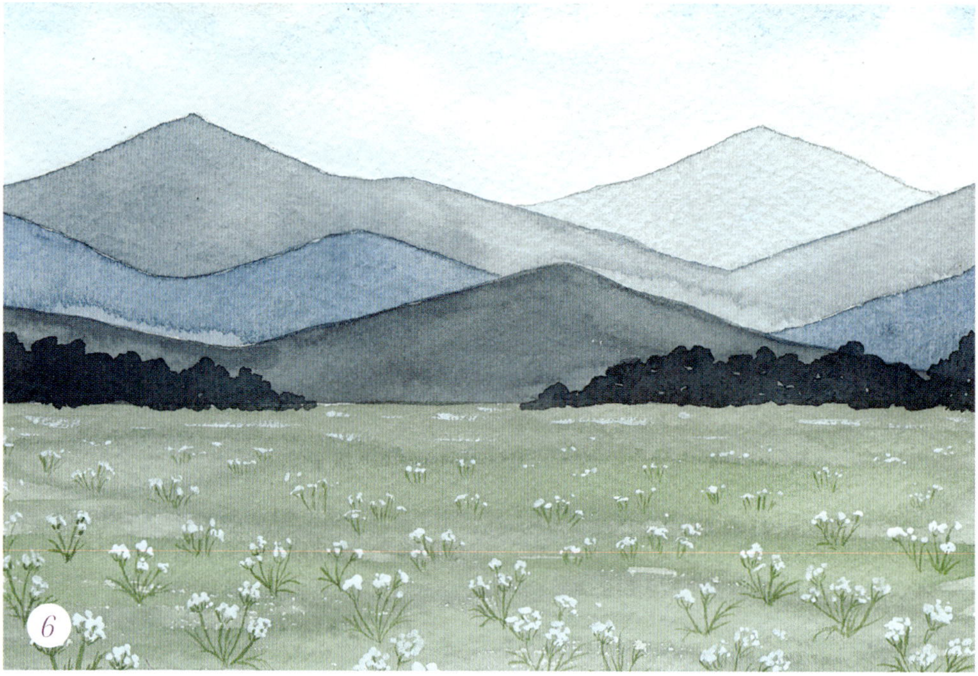

step 6

Now it's time to add flowers and grasses to the meadow. We will be using white paint for the wispy white wildflowers of summer. (I'm using Dr. Ph. Martin's Bleedproof White, but you can use another opaque white watercolor or gouache if you prefer.) Pick up some of your chosen white paint on your size 2 round brush and, in the bottom half to two-thirds of the meadow, use the brush point to tap small clusters of dots in rough round or half-moon shapes to resemble umbel flowers. (For more details, see the instructions for painting tiny flowers on page 37.) The flowers should be slightly larger toward the bottom of the page and smaller as they move up toward the horizon. You can loosely paint some blobs or strips of white closer to the horizon for distant, less-defined flowers.

Once you have added white flowers throughout the space, allow them to dry, and clean your brush. Then create a mixture of Permanent Sap Green and Burnt Umber, load your size 2 round brush with this mixture and use it to paint the stem structure for the white flowers. Since I imagine these to be Queen Anne's lace flowers, I like to lightly paint a few tiny, thin lines in a sort of fan shape under one white cluster. This can be a loose, imprecise process; don't worry too much about making perfect fan shapes.

Paint a slightly thicker line for a stem connecting the base of the fan to a spot on the ground, and then repeat this process with other nearby white clusters to create a plant with multiple blooms. Add a few wispy leaves by sweeping the brush lightly upward from the base of the plant or along the stems. As you move up the page, you can be even looser (or smaller) with your marks, adding less detail to the plants farther into the background.

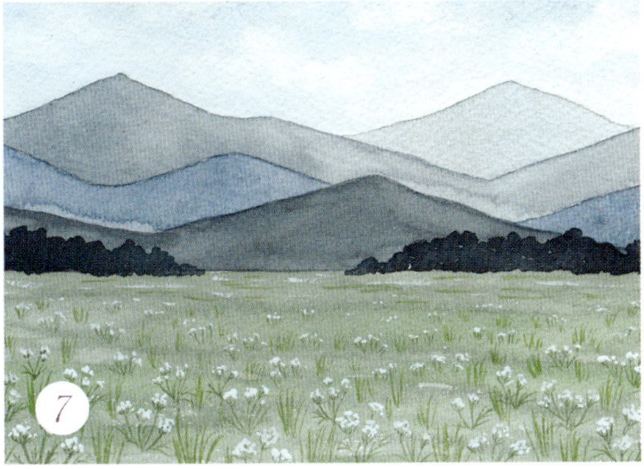

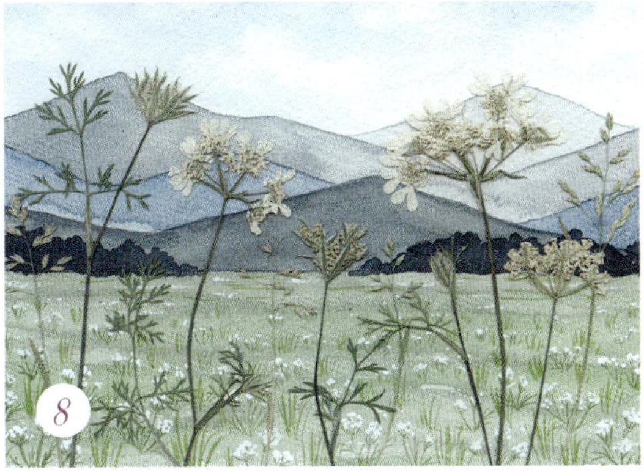

step 7

Create a pigmented mix of Permanent Sap Green and Raw Sienna on your palette. Making sure not to introduce too much additional moisture from your brush, load your size 2 round with this pigment. Then, holding the brush perpendicular to the page, add clusters of grasses in between the flowers. To do this, place the point of the brush lightly to the paper and swipe upward, lifting the brush as you go to create a tapered end to the brushstroke. Place the point of the brush right next to or on top of the same spot. Then make another brushstroke, this time varying the angle slightly, and repeat to make a clump of grass (see Painting Grasses on page 36 for more details). Make your grasses smaller and slightly closer together as you move toward the tree line. You can loosely and lightly paint horizontal strokes close to the tree line for very distant grasses. Set the watercolor to dry—the painting portion is now complete!

step 8

We will now add our pressed flowers to finish this piece. Take your selected pressed materials and, using your tweezers or hands, gently arrange them on top of your watercolor painting. I like to have them growing out of the bottom of the page. Play with the heights of your materials, and don't worry about the length of the stems if they're too long, because you can always shorten them. Once you have an arrangement you like, trim any stems that are too long.

Mount your flowers to your artwork by carefully picking them up one by one with your tweezers or fingers. Flip your flower over onto some scrap paper and, with your glue brush, pick up a little bit of glue and carefully paint the back of the flower with it. Then, pick the flower back up and press it to your artwork in its correct spot, glue side down, and press on it carefully with your tweezers or fingers. Repeat with the remaining flowers.

Once they are all mounted, set a piece of waxed paper on top of your piece and weigh it down with a few heavy books. Allow it to dry for at least 15 to 20 minutes before carefully peeling away the waxed paper. If you do this too quickly, you can peel your flowers off your page or break them. (See Mounting Flowers on page 22 for more details.) Your piece is now complete!

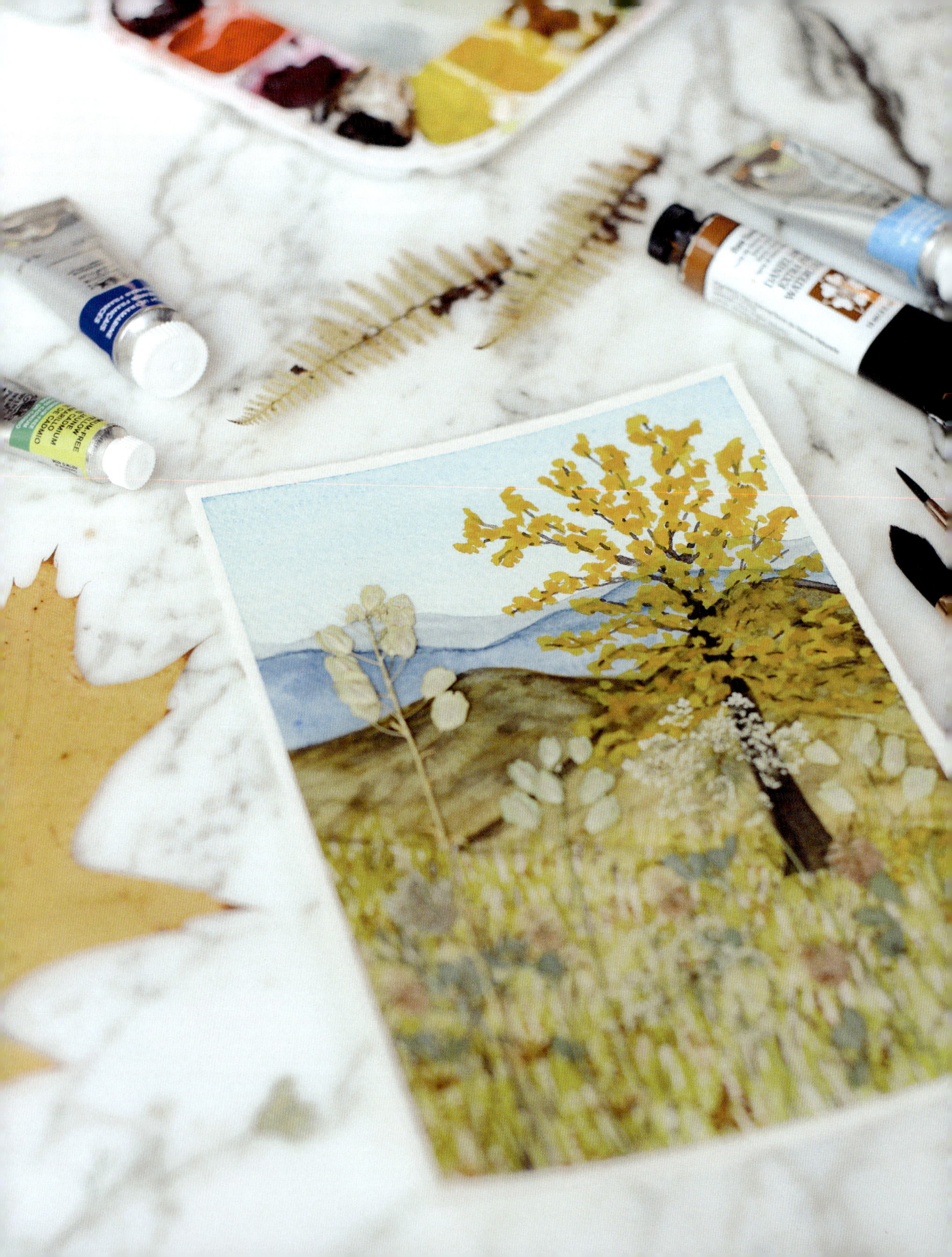

AUTUMN OVERLOOK

In this project, we paint mountains from a slightly different point of view. Well into the autumn season, we stand atop a ridge and look down into the valley and to the hills beyond. A meadow of pressed late-season wildflowers and seed pods fills the foreground. I am using pennycress, Queen Anne's lace, black medic and a few other small flowers.

size

5 x 7" (12.5 x 18 cm)

brushes

Size 10 round brush
Size 6 round brush
Size 2 round brush
Glue brush

flower palette

Pennycress
Queen Anne's Lace
Black medic
Other small wildflowers in yellows and browns

materials

Tweezers (optional)
Scissors
Glue
Waxed paper
Heavy Books

color palette

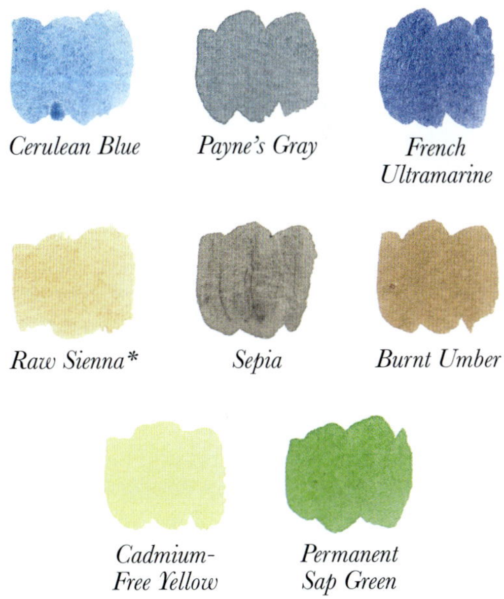

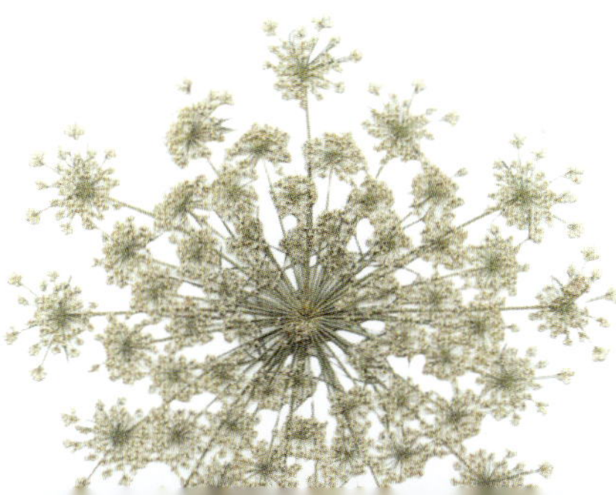

1

2

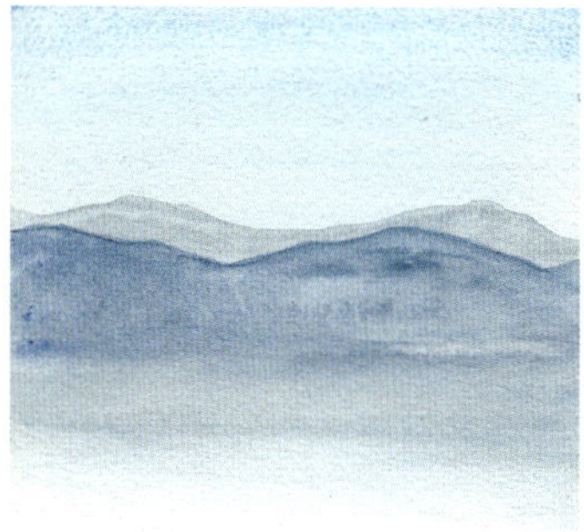

3

step 1

Pick up some Cerulean Blue paint and create a watery mix of it on your palette. Load your size 10 round brush and, starting at the top of your paper, paint sweeping horizontal strokes to fill in the sky. As you move down the page—slightly above the halfway point—dip your brush in clean water. Then drag it lightly along the edge of your water container to remove some excess water, and continue making the same sweeping brushstrokes at the bottom of the blue portion to blend it. The goal is to avoid a harsh line. You can stop about halfway down the page. Allow the painting to dry.

step 2

Create a very watery, pale mix of Payne's Gray on your palette. Pick up some of this paint with your size 6 round brush and, using the brush point, drag a wavy and jagged line horizontally across the page about a quarter of the way from the top. This is your most distant mountain. Fill in below this line with the same paint, and blend it out using the same water technique as the previous step so there are no harsh lines. Allow the painting to dry.

step 3

Next, create a watery mix of Payne's Gray and French Ultramarine on your palette. Pick this paint up with your size 6 round brush, and create a second wavy line just below the first (a slightly closer mountain). Again, fill in below it and blend it out to avoid any harsh lines. Allow the painting to dry.

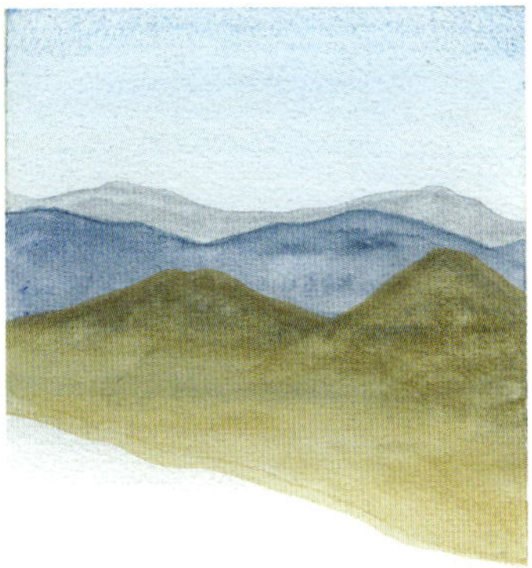

4

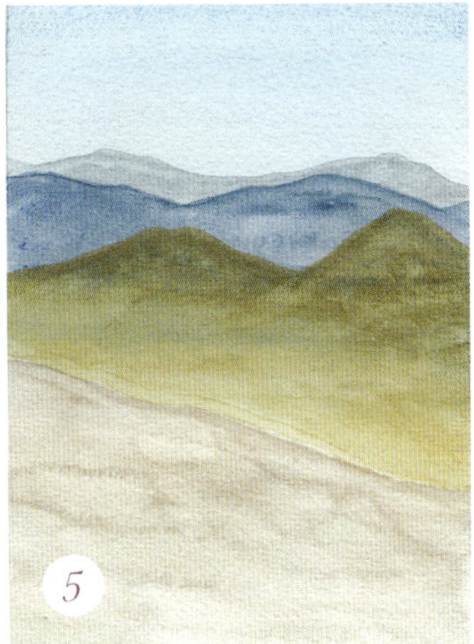

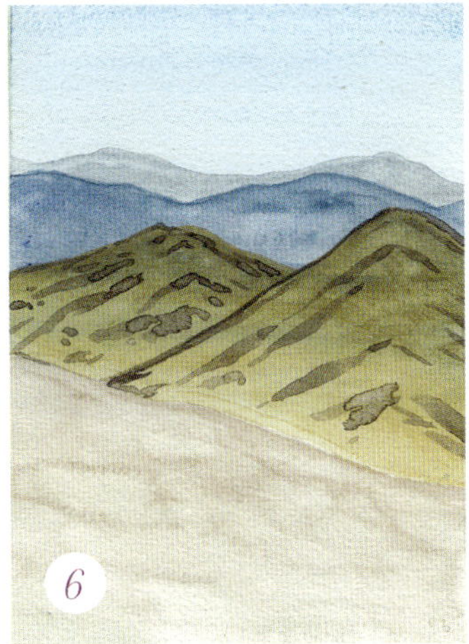

step 4

Pick up some Raw Sienna paint on your size 6 round brush, and use it to paint a third jagged mountain line. For reference, this one should be about a third of the way from the top of the paper. I like to create two main peaks. Fill in these mountains with your Raw Sienna paint, leaving a diagonal line moving downward from left to right on your page with white space below. Allow the painting to dry.

step 5

Create a moderately pigmented mixture of Sepia and Burnt Umber on your palette. Load your size 6 round brush with this pigment, and carefully paint along the diagonal line from step 4. Fill in the paper below. Allow the painting to dry.

step 6

Create a moderately pigmented mixture of Sepia on your palette. Load your size 6 round brush with this pigment, and use the brush point to paint blobs and rough patches on the yellow mountainside. I decided that the right peak will sit just in front of the left, so I used similar markings to paint a line down where the mountains meet the ground. This adds more dimension to the painting.

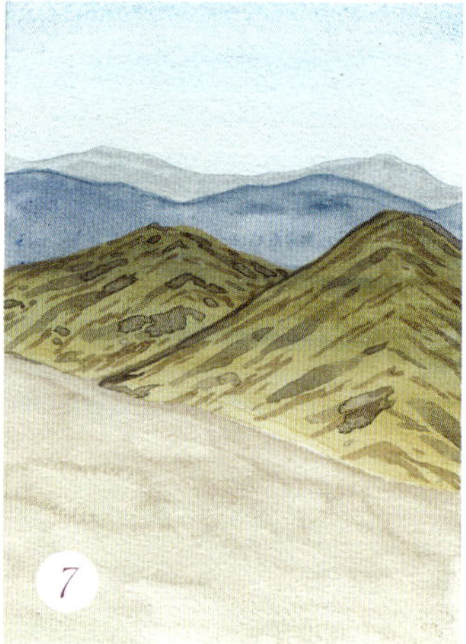

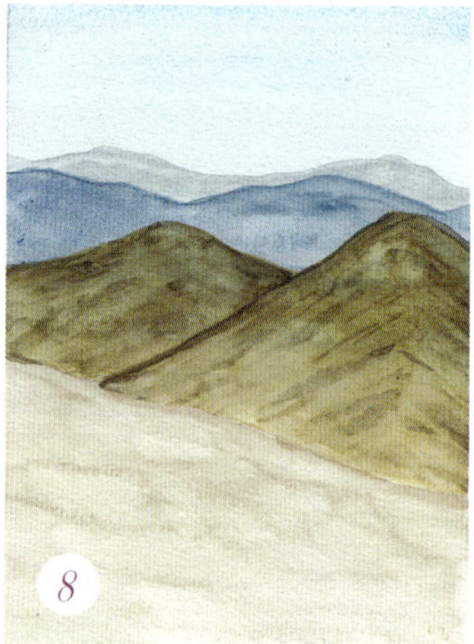

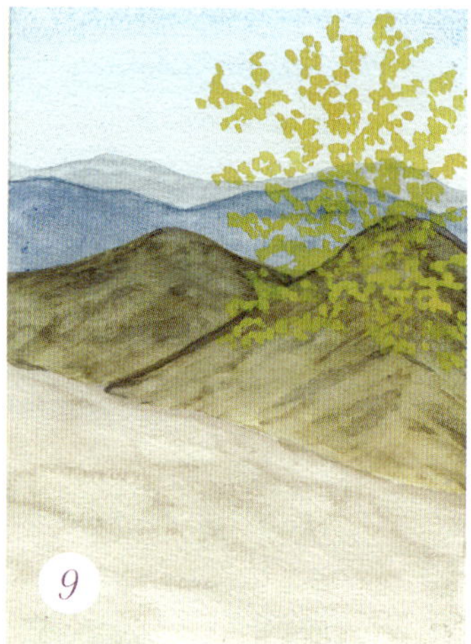

step 7

Mix up some Burnt Umber and Raw Sienna paint on your palette, and use it to add more blobs and rough patches—just like we did with the Sepia paint in the previous step. We want to add some contrast to this mountainside, but don't cover up all of the base layer.

step 8

If you like the way your mountains look right now, feel free to skip this step. Otherwise, we are going to do something that usually we wouldn't want to do: We are going to muddy our painting a bit. Clean your brush and pick up some clean water. Then, paint over the yellowish-brown mountainside. Use the brush to blend out some of the lines and allow the colors to bleed together, but keep your brushstrokes roughly moving in the direction of the slopes you want to convey. Allow the painting to dry.

step 9

On your size 6 round brush, pick up some Cadmium-Free Yellow (either a highly pigmented mix on your palette or straight from the pan). Use the point of the brush to paint dots and blobs in the upper-right quadrant of your page. These will be golden leaves on a tree. Paint blobs in rough lines reaching into the sky—some reaching to the side, and some at different angles. Keep in mind that the branches are mostly originating from a central trunk, which we will add next.

step 10

Create a pigmented mix of French Ultramarine and Burnt Umber on your palette for a grayish-brown color. Remove any excess moisture from your size 6 round brush by blotting it on a paper towel. Then, load it with this pigment and begin painting a trunk and branches for your tree. To start, paint a broad vertical line starting beneath the lowest portion of your yellow leaves, somewhere within the foreground (the Sepia and Burnt Umber area from step 5). Bring it up to the place where the leaves start, and begin painting thinner branching lines—using lighter pressure on the brush for thinner lines—roughly along the shapes of the leaves. Paint small segments of branches rather than sweeping lines to give the impression that you can see only glimpses of branches and limbs through the leaves. Use your imagination to predict/depict where the branches will be visible.

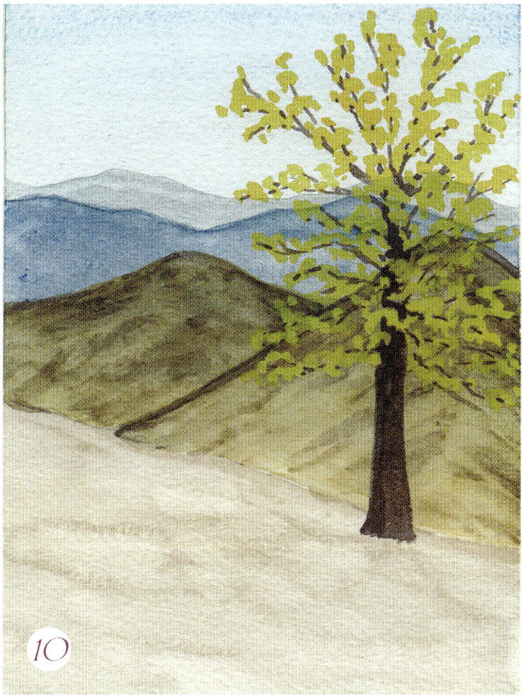

step 11

Mix some Cadmium-Free Yellow with Raw Sienna for a darker yellow. Then, with your size 6 round brush, make some overlapping leaves to add dimension and shadow. Make sure you don't cover up all of the lighter yellow color.

Create a moderately pigmented mix of Permanent Sap Green and Raw Sienna on your palette. Again, using your size 6 round brush (or a smaller round brush, if you prefer), load it with paint and begin painting loose grass in the foreground. To do this, place the point of the brush on the page and sweep it quickly upward, lifting it from the page as you go to form a tapered end on each brushstroke. Using these same brushstrokes, fill the entire foreground area, all the way up to the diagonal line (hillside), varying the angle and length of the grasses to allow them to overlap and create a natural field. Allow the painting to dry.

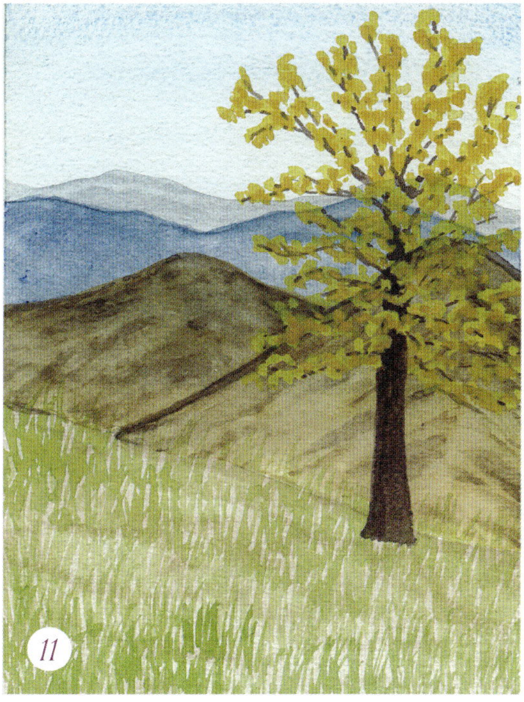

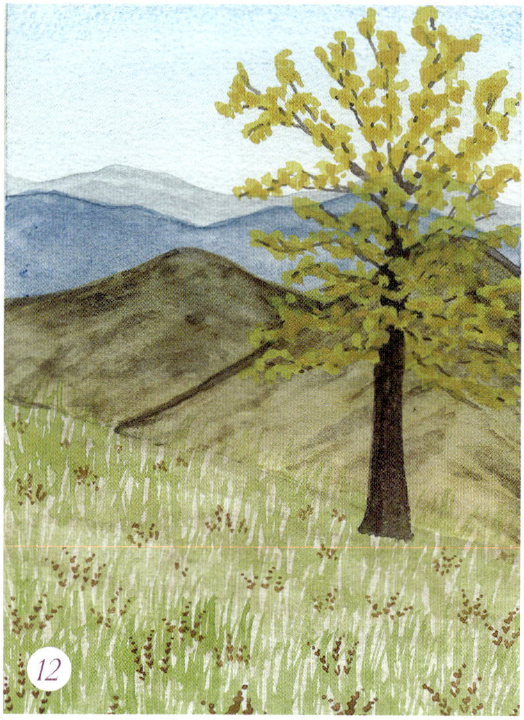

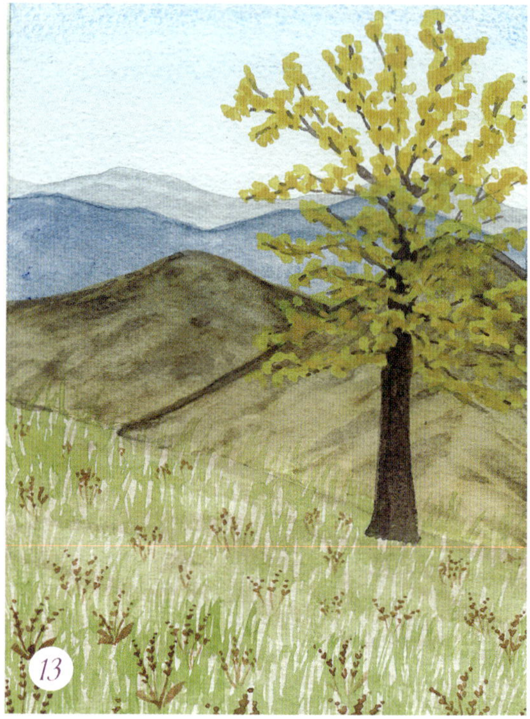

step 12

Make a pigmented mixture of Burnt Umber paint on your palette, and pick up some of it with your size 2 round brush. Using the brush point, begin to paint tiny *V* shapes within the meadow grasses. Paint one, then another just above it, and another just above that to create little stacks of three to six *V* shapes. These will be seed pods of spent autumn plants. At the top of each stack, you can make a few more simple marks (dots or blobs). Make two to four more stacks like this one nearby, at slightly varying angles, and then move around the page, creating more clusters of these stacks. They can become smaller and less defined as you move up toward the top of the hillside meadow.

step 13

Once you have finished painting these little *V*-shaped marks, you can use the same brush and paint to lightly paint short, thin vertical lines for stems through each stack of seed pods and beneath. These plants are growing within taller grasses so the stems can—but don't *need* to—visibly connect with the ground, which is hidden from our view. You can add a few leaves as well by painting slightly thicker lines (using more pressure through the brush) upward and at an angle from some of the stems.

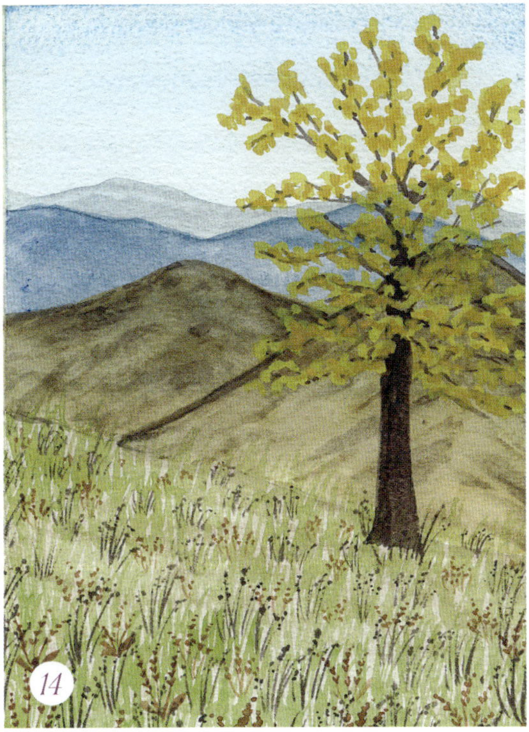

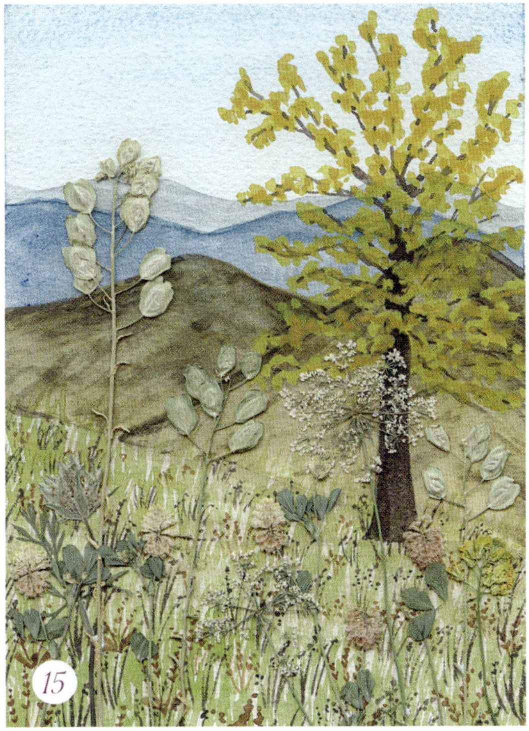

step 14

Make a pigmented mixture of Sepia paint on your palette, and pick up some of it with your size 2 round brush. With light pressure and the point of your brush, create thin wild grasses (see "Painting Grasses" on page 36 for more details). Space these out, and place them in clusters all across the meadow. Work quickly and loosely so these grasses lend wildness and texture to the painting.

Once you have finished adding grasses, pick up some more Sepia paint. Then, again using a light hand and the point of the brush, tap the paper to make tiny dots roughly around the tops of the grasses to add even more texture. This can be a very loose, organic process; autumn meadows tend to be full of movement and interest with all of their plants gone to seed. The painting portion is now finished! Allow the painting to dry.

step 15

Choose your pressed plants, and begin placing them on your piece. We want to fill up the bottom edge of the painting to create a full foreground of plant material. Once you are happy with your layout, begin picking up the flowers one by one. Using your glue brush, carefully paint the backside of the flowers with a thin layer of glue and press them onto the paper. Once they are all mounted, set a piece of waxed paper on top of your piece and weigh it down with a few heavy books. Allow it to dry for at least 15 to 20 minutes before carefully peeling away the waxed paper. If you do this too quickly, you can peel your flowers off your page or break them. (See Mounting Flowers on page 22 for more details.) Your piece is now complete!

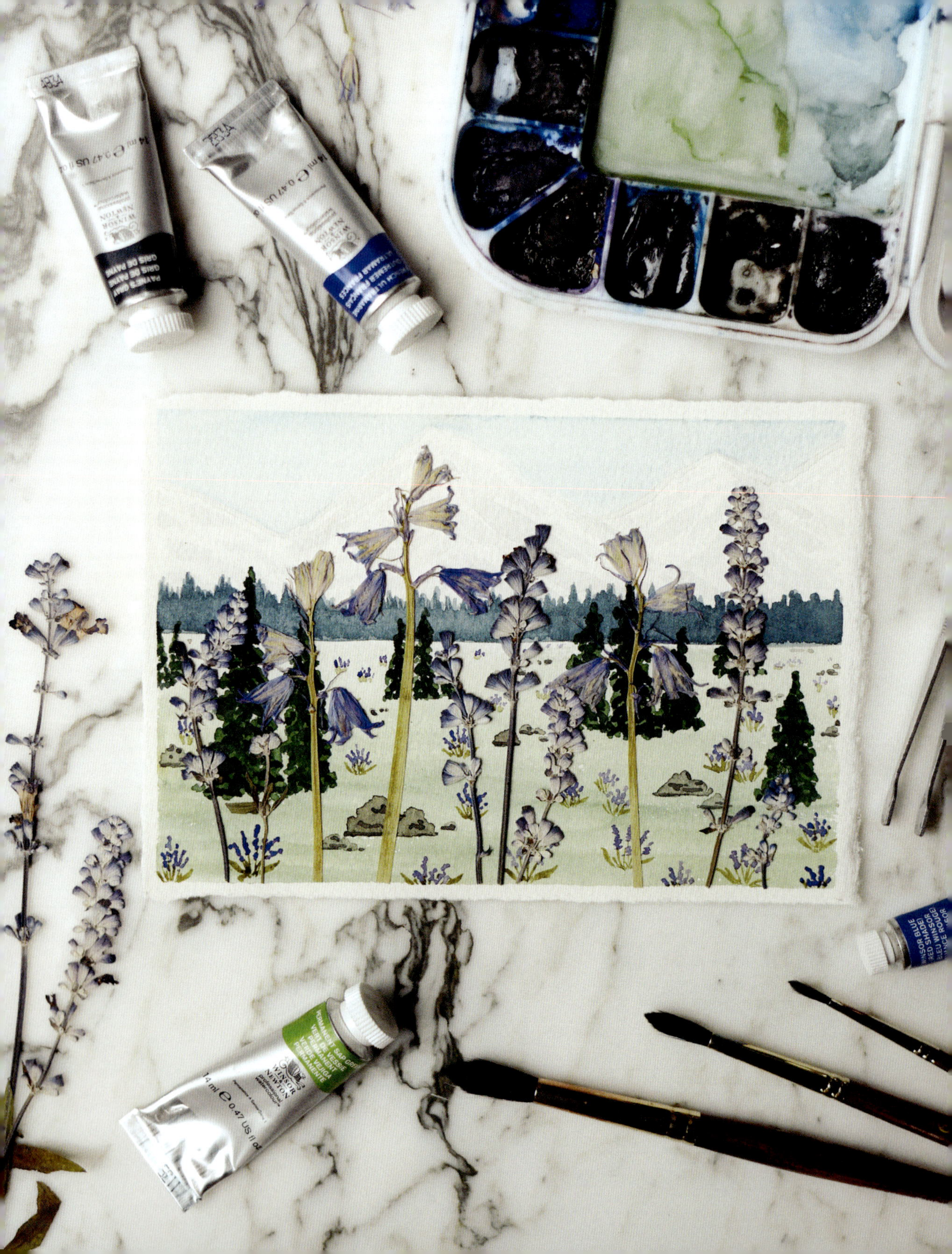
WINSOR BLUE
PERMANENT SAP GREEN

ROCKY MOUNTAIN MEADOW

The mountain meadows of the western United States possess a unique kind of beauty. Snow-capped mountains form the backdrop to groves of tall evergreen trees and swaths of vibrant wildflowers. In this painting, we create a cool landscape of blues, greens and purples and finish it with some bright pressed flowers in the same color palette. For this project, I chose some linear flowers to mirror the ones in the painting (blue salvia) and some Spanish bluebells to add another unique shape.

size

5 x 7" (12.5 x 18 cm)

brushes

Size 6 round brush
¼" (6-mm) square brush
Size 10 round brush
Size 2 round brush
Glue brush

flower palette

Blue salvia
Spanish bluebells

materials

Tweezers (optional)
Scissors
Glue
Waxed paper
Heavy Books

color palette

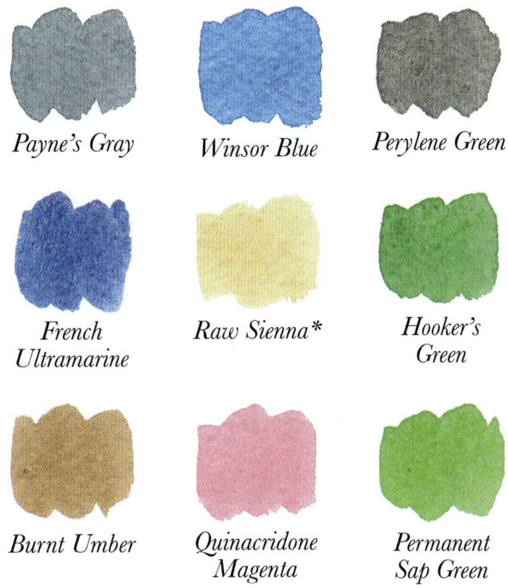

1

2

3

step 1

Create a very watery, diluted mixture of Payne's Gray on your palette. Load your size 6 round brush with this pigment and, with the brush perpendicular to the paper, use very light pressure to drag the point of your brush to paint mountains with distinct peaks and steeper sides. Paint these toward the top of your page, with the tallest peak nearly touching the top. I like to create slightly jagged, irregular lines by wiggling the paint brush very slightly.

step 2

Dry your brush slightly before dipping it back into the same mixture. Using varying pressure on the point and through the belly of the brush, paint irregular lines beneath the mountain peaks. It is okay if some of the paper texture shows through—or not! Angle these marks roughly perpendicular to the angle of the peak, giving the impression of melting snow amid the rocky mountainside. Be sure to leave white space to depict remaining snow. The mountains should fill about a quarter to a third of the page.

step 3

Create a watery mixture of Winsor Blue on your palette. Then, using the same brush, carefully fill in the sky above the mountains. Use the broadest strokes you can manage without painting over the mountains.

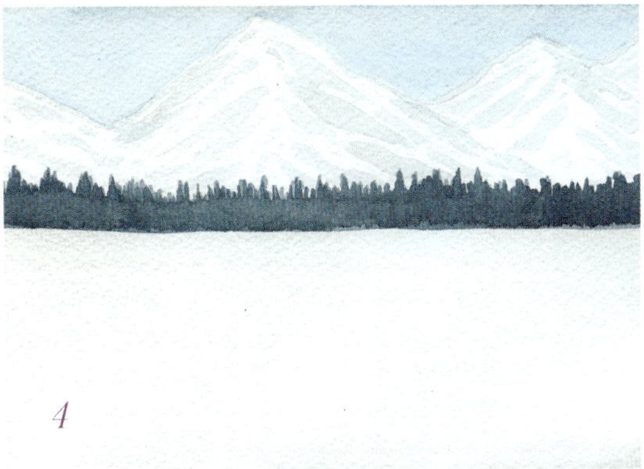

4

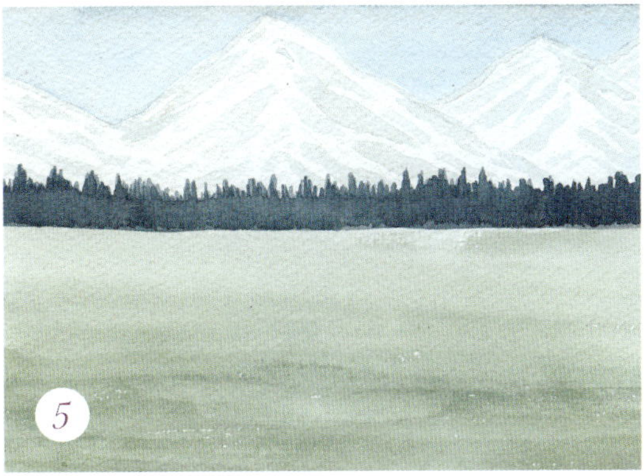

5

step 4

Create a moderately pigmented mixture of Perylene Green with a little bit of French Ultramarine on your palette. Using a ¼-inch (6-mm) square brush, pick up some of this paint. At the bottom of the mountain portion, place the flat side of the brush at the edge of the paper and parallel with the edge. Then, start dragging the brush up and down in short strokes as you pull it slowly away from the edge. Keep the brush in contact with the paper as much as possible as you move, except to reload with paint as necessary. We are basically creating a tight zigzag line, with variations in height and spacing of the marks, to create a distant line of evergreen trees. Continue all the way to the opposite edge of the paper.

Reload your brush with paint and, starting back at the beginning, use a similar brush-stroke to fill in beneath the first zigzag line. This time, finish it at the bottom edge with a relatively straight edge. We can achieve this simply with our square brush, but be sure to blend it in with the existing brushstrokes by working back and forth and adding paint as needed. Allow the painting to dry.

step 5

Pick up some Winsor Blue and Raw Sienna to create a moderately pigmented green mixture on your palette. Using a size 10 round brush, load up with paint and begin painting broad, sweeping horizontal brushstrokes at the bottom of the page. Cover the area, working upward toward the distant tree line. Dip your brush in water as needed, moving up the page and allowing the green to become lighter toward the horizon. Allow the painting to dry.

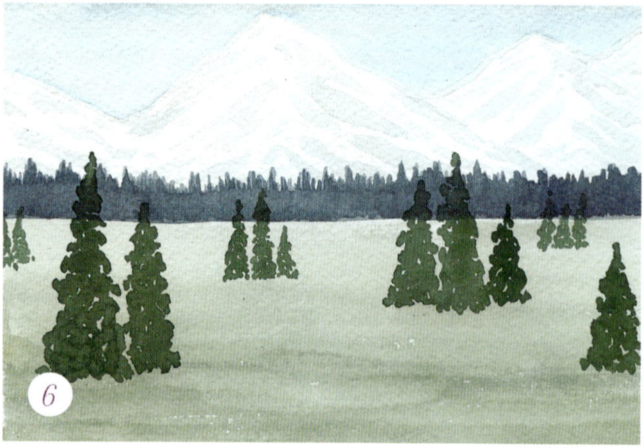

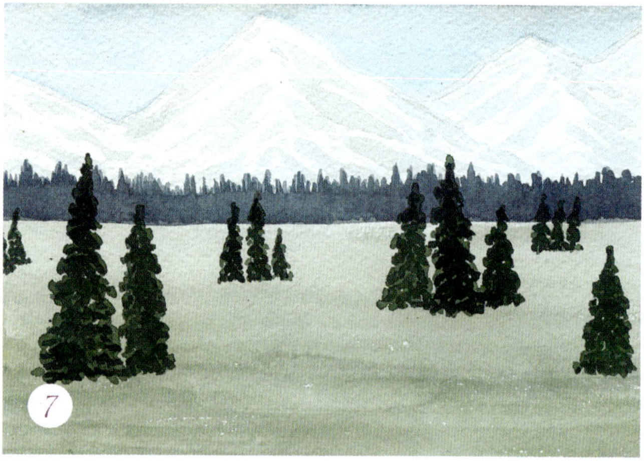

step 6

Mix up some Perylene Green and Hooker's Green on your palette for a pigmented dark-green mixture. Load your size 10 round brush with this paint, and begin painting clusters of evergreen trees within the meadow. (For details on painting evergreen trees, see page 42.)

Once you have finished one tree, add a second tree of a different height next to it, and then a third if you'd like. We are painting clusters or groupings of two to four trees here within the meadow. Remember, trees that appear farther down the page should be larger and taller, while trees closer to the mountains and distant tree line should be shorter and thinner. Allow the painting to dry.

step 7

Add some Payne's Gray to the mixture used for the trees to darken it slightly. Then, using the same brush and mark-making technique as in step 6, add shadows and dimension to the trees. To do this, tap the brush toward the center of the tree and in downward diagonal marks to imply the undersides of limbs. Take care not to cover up all of the initial marks, as the contrast between the two shades is what gives it dimension. Allow the painting to dry.

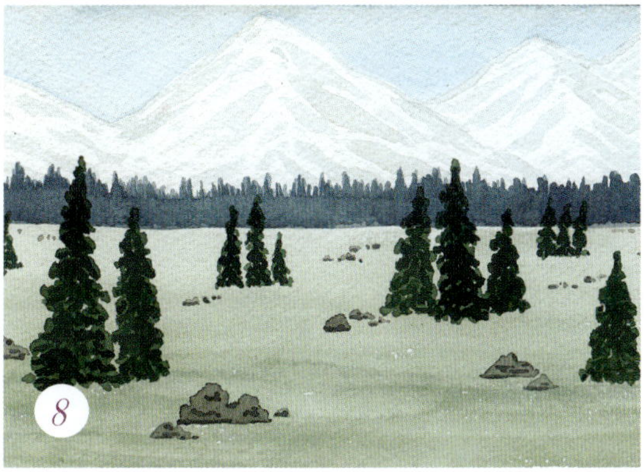

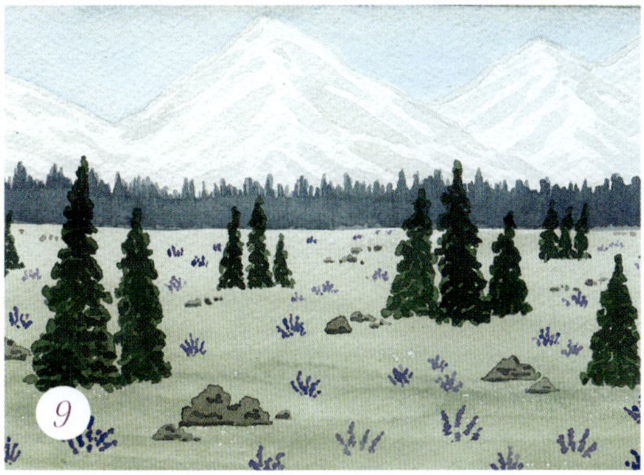

step 8

Mix up some Payne's Gray and Burnt Umber on your palette, moderately pigmented. Using your size 6 round brush, paint a small irregular blob with a flat bottom near the bottom of your page. This will be a boulder within the meadow. Add a few more boulders sparingly across the meadow, some in groups of two or three, varying them in size and shape, and making them smaller toward the distant tree line. Allow the painting to dry.

Add a bit more Payne's Gray to the mixture to darken it, and then—sparingly—add a few shadows on the rocks with this pigment. A shadow along the flat bottom, plus a few irregular marks here and there on the rock, will give this impression. Allow the painting to dry.

step 9

Mix up some French Ultramarine and Quinacridone Magenta on your palette with a little bit of water for a pigmented mix. Then, using a size 2 round brush, paint groupings of three to five purple linear flowers. To do this, tap the brush point to the paper lightly within the meadow somewhere near the bottom of the page. Then, tap it a few more times beneath the initial mark in a rough linear shape. This will be one flower. (See Painting Tiny Flowers on page 37 for more details.) Move to a different spot within the meadow and do this again, keeping your marks and flowers organic and imperfect. Space your flower clusters out around the rocks painted in step 8. These flowers and clusters should become smaller and closer together as you move up toward the distant tree line and mountains, and they can become light horizontal brushstrokes in the far distance. Allow the painting to dry.

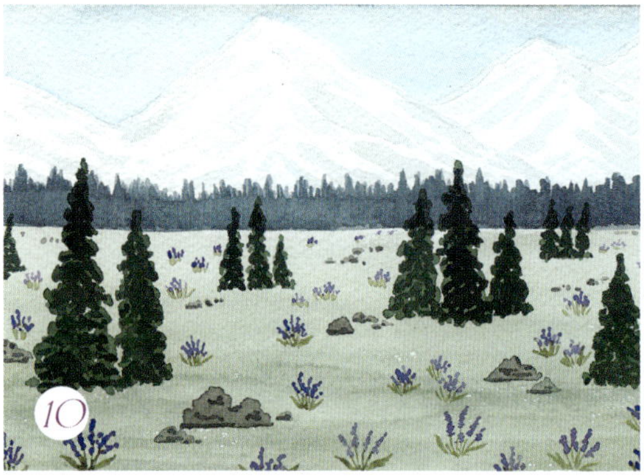

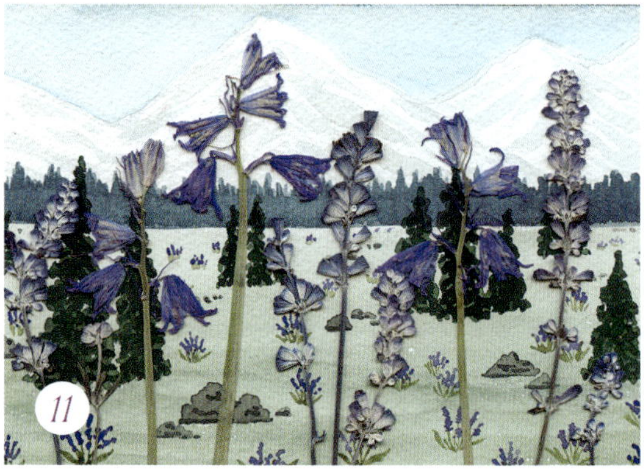

step 10

Create a pigmented mixture of Permanent Sap Green and Burnt Umber on your palette. Pick up some of this paint with your size 2 brush and use it to paint stems for the purple flowers. Using the brush point and holding the brush perpendicular to the paper, lightly drag the brush from the bottom of one of the flowers to a point just below within the meadow. Repeat with the rest of the flowers in the cluster, varying their angles as needed to make organic-looking plants. Make a few more brushstrokes within the same cluster but not connected to any purple flowers, and apply a little bit more pressure through the belly of the brush to create a thicker mark. These will be leaves. Add a few leaves at the base of each plant cluster or along the stems before moving on to complete the remaining plants in the same way. Once you have added stems and leaves to all the purple flowers, the painting portion is complete! Allow the painting to dry.

step 11

Choose your pressed flowers, and begin placing them on your paper. Once you are happy with your layout, trim the stems to length and begin picking up the flowers one by one. Using your glue brush, carefully paint the back of each flower with a thin layer of glue, and press them onto the paper using your fingers or tweezers.

Once they are all mounted, set a piece of waxed paper on top of your piece and weigh it down with a few heavy books. Allow it to dry for at least 15 to 20 minutes before carefully peeling away the waxed paper. If you do this too quickly, you can peel your flowers off your page or break them. (See Mounting Flowers on page 22 for more details.) Your piece is now complete!

COTTON CANDY SKIES

A colorful sunset is a treat at the end of any day, especially in summer. This whimsical scene incorporates a smooth sky gradient dotted with cotton candy clouds, a few distant mountains and a meadow filled with wildflowers. For this scene, I selected quite a few different pressed plants. They appear to grow from the bottom of the page and fill the foreground. Included are stems of sea lavender, catmint, fleabane, sweet alyssum and hawkweed.

size

8 x 10" (20 x 25 cm)

brushes

Size 10 round brush
Size 6 round brush
Size 2 round brush
Glue brush

flower palette

Sea lavender
Catmint
Fleabane
Sweet alyssum
Hawkweed

materials

Tweezers (optional)
Scissors
Glue
Waxed paper
Heavy Books

color palette

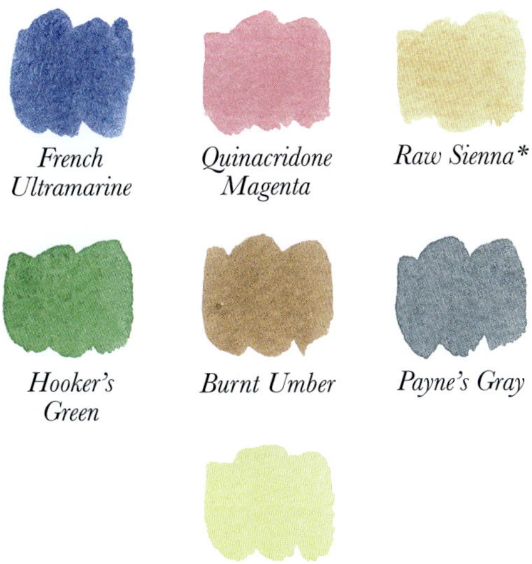

French Ultramarine, *Quinacridone Magenta*, *Raw Sienna**

Hooker's Green, *Burnt Umber*, *Payne's Gray*

Cadmium-Free Yellow

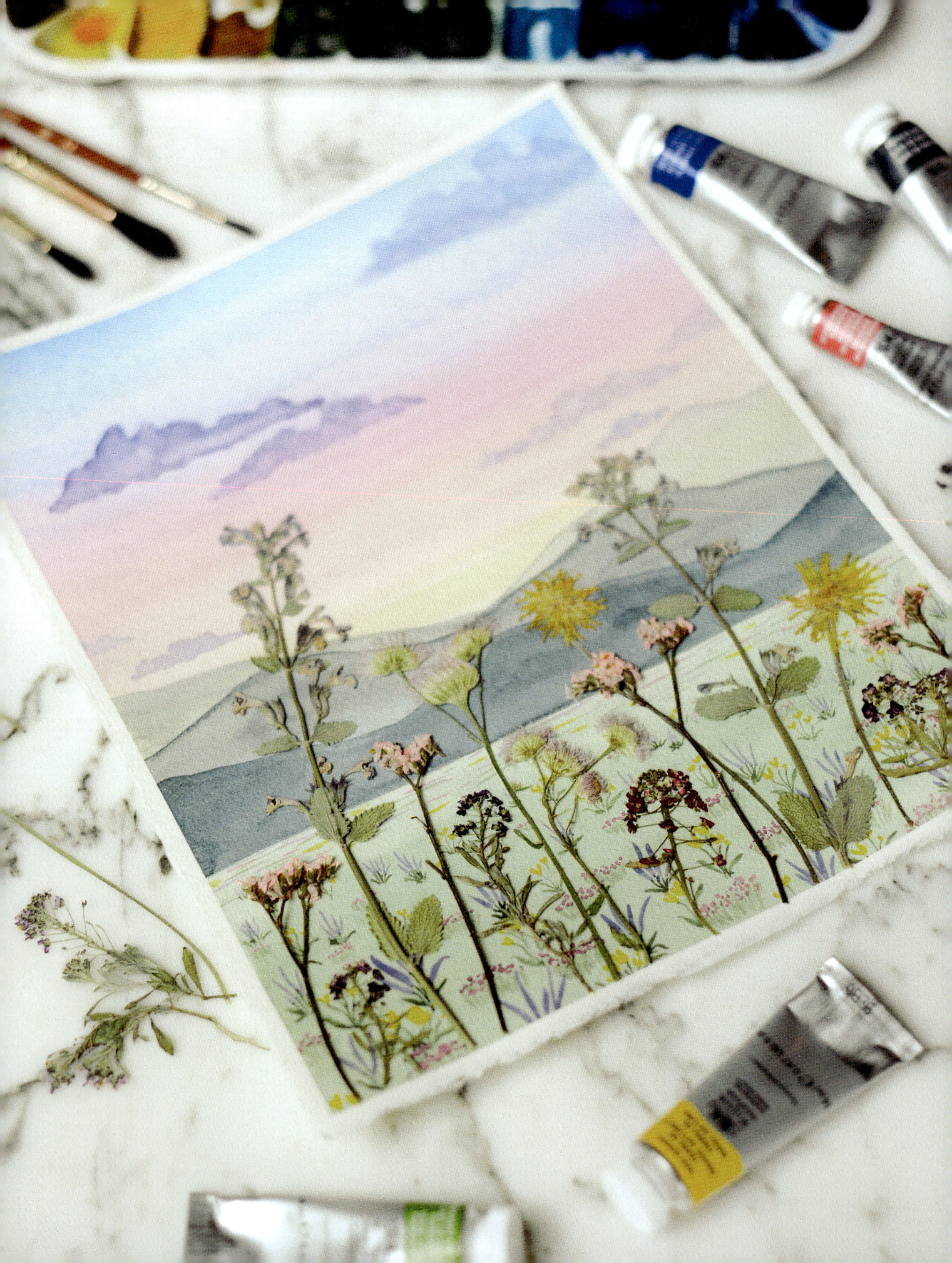

step 1

On your palette, make these four mixes: Mix 1 is a moderately pigmented French Ultramarine; Mix 2 is a moderately pigmented mix of French Ultramarine and Quinacridone Magenta; Mix 3 is a moderately pigmented Quinacridone Magenta; Mix 4 is water and Raw Sienna.

Working quickly, start at the top of the page and use your size 10 round brush loaded with Mix 1 to make broad, sweeping horizontal brushstrokes to cover the top of the page. Then, dip the brush into Mix 2 and make more strokes at the bottom of the blue section, overlapping it slightly and blending them together. Dip the brush into Mix 3 and repeat at the bottom of the purplish section, again blending into a smooth color gradient.

Clean your brush, then pick up some of Mix 4 from your palette and paint a band of this color beneath the pinkish edge (don't overlap it just yet). Then, working upward from this yellowish stripe, blend the colors with horizontal brushstrokes. This will be a warm band of sunlight peeking from behind our mountains. Make sure your colors are well blended with no hard lines or obvious stripes, but be careful not to overwork this portion or it can become patchy. This gradient should cover a little more than the top half of the paper. Allow the painting to dry.

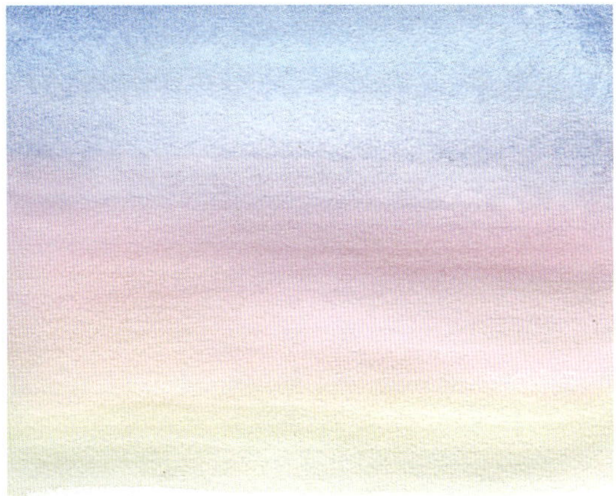

1

step 2

Create a mixture of Hooker's Green, Burnt Umber and a little bit of French Ultramarine on your palette for an earthy cool-green color. Load your size 10 round brush with it and, using similar horizontal brushstrokes as in step 1, paint in a grassy area within the bottom third of the page. Leave some space between this and the sky portion. Allow the painting to dry.

2

step 3

In this step, we will paint several layers of mountains, using three different concentrations of Payne's Gray and starting with the farthest mountain peaks. To ensure crisp lines, we will allow each layer to dry before moving on to the next one.

To begin, create a watery mixture of Payne's Gray on your palette. Using your size 6 round brush, pick up some of this paint and, using the point of the brush, carefully paint an uneven wavy line, starting about halfway from the top on the left-hand side of the page (or the right-hand side, if that's more comfortable for you). Using this same paint, fill in beneath the line all the way down to the top of the grass portion. Allow the painting to dry.

Next, add a little bit more Payne's Gray pigment to your mixture to make it darker, and then paint in your second mountain just beneath the first, adding peaks at different spots. Again, paint all the way down to the top of the grass portion with this paint. Allow the painting to dry.

Finally, add just a bit more Payne's Gray pigment to the mixture for an even darker color, and repeat the same process beneath the second mountains to paint a third and final mountain, this one with more subtle peaks. Each layer should be darker than the last and allow the ones behind it to show.

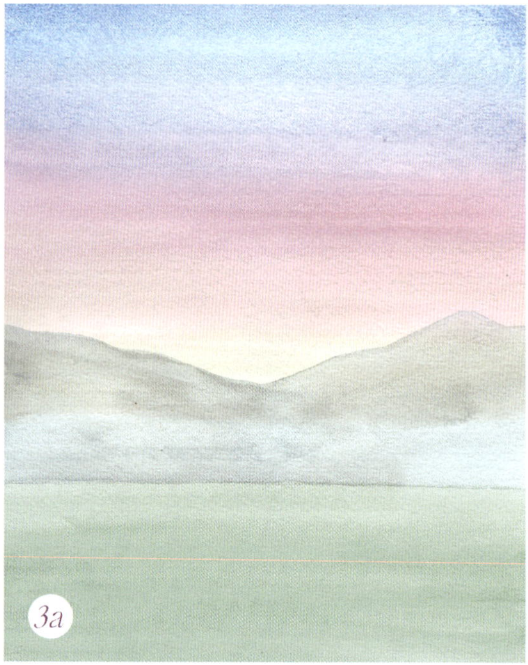

3a

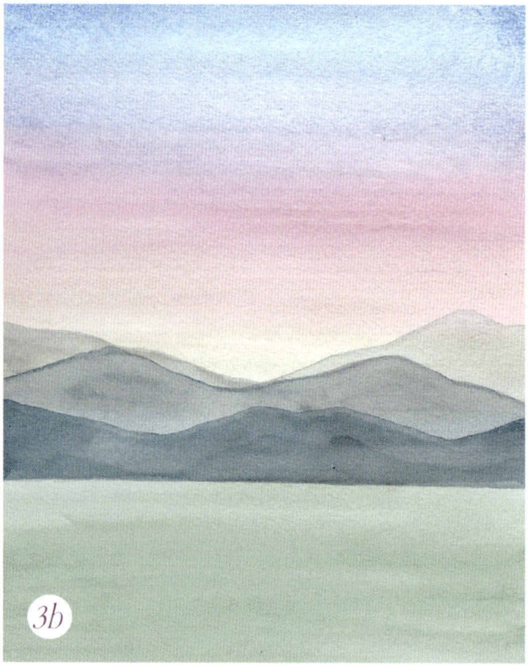

3b

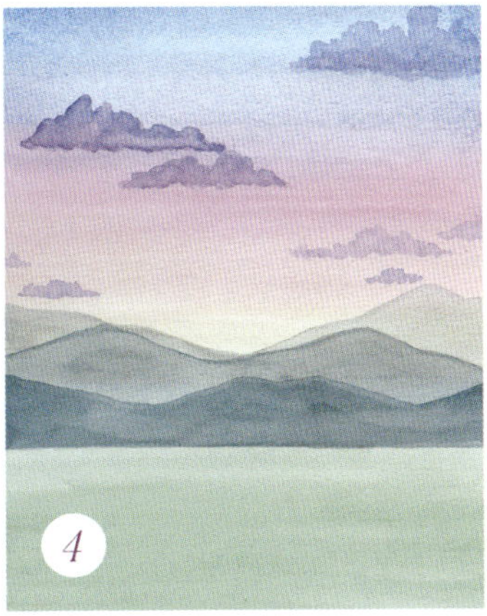

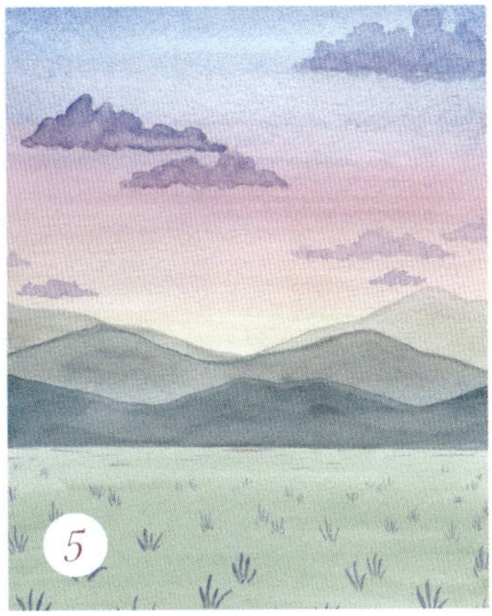

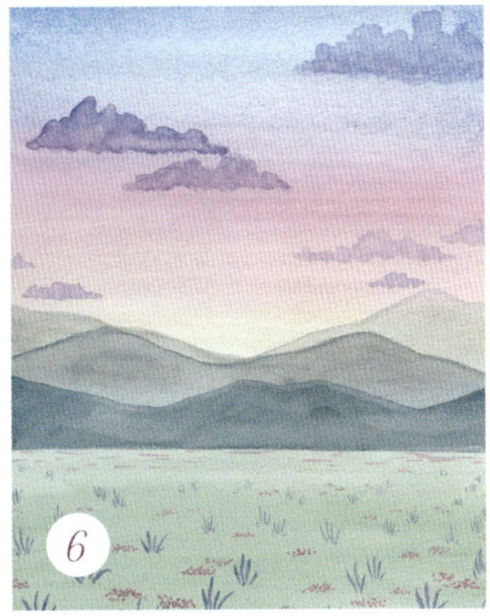

step 4

Return to Mix 2 (from step 1) on your palette. If it is not still a watery mixture of French Ultramarine and Quinacridone Magenta, then add a little more pigment and water to achieve a watery mixture. Next, pick up some of this paint with your size 6 round brush and begin painting clouds in the sky above the mountains. To do this, swirl the brush point around loosely to create organic blobs, and fill in a bit along the bottom of each cloud so it has a roughly flat (straight) underside. Add clouds across the sky, making them smaller closer to the horizon and larger toward the top of the page. You can experiment with groupings and small single clouds, but be sure not to cover up your beautiful gradient too much.

step 5

Add a bit more French Ultramarine and Quinacridone Magenta to Mix 2 to make it more pigmented. Then, pick up some of this paint with your size 2 round brush and use the brush point to lightly paint short vertical lines at varying heights and angles in clusters throughout the green meadow. Make smaller (shorter) clusters farther up the page toward the mountain, and lightly paint sweeping horizontal strips of purple just below the mountains for very distant flowers.

step 6

Return to Mix 3 (from step 1) on your palette, adding a bit more paint from the pan if necessary to make it more pigmented. Dab most of the moisture off your size 2 round brush with a paper towel and pick up some of this paint. Then, lightly tap little dots in the meadow using the brush point. Cluster these dots together in horizontal groupings, spaced across the meadow between the purple flower clusters. Again, your marks should be smaller as you move up toward the mountain, and you can add sweeping horizontal strips of color just below the mountains for distant flowers. Clean your brush.

step 7

Add some Cadmium-Free Yellow to your palette with a little bit of water for a pigmented mixture. Then, load your size 2 round brush and lightly paint little *V* marks and dots within the meadow, both in groupings and on their own.

step 8

Create a moderately pigmented mixture of French Ultramarine with some Cadmium-Free Yellow on your palette for a cool, earthy-green color. Pick up some of this paint with your size 2 round brush, and use it to paint stems on the flowers that connect to a single point on the ground. Start with the purple linear flowers, making the stems short and fairly straight. Be sure to make them even shorter (in proportion with the smaller flowers) as you move up the page toward the mountains.

Moving on to the yellow flowers, paint even lighter, thinner lines with very light pressure through the point of the brush. These can be a bit longer, bendy and airy. You can add a few leaves to either side of the cluster, originating from the same point as the stems, by pressing through the belly of the brush as you drag it away from the plant, lifting at the end of the brushstroke to give a slightly tapered end to the leaf.

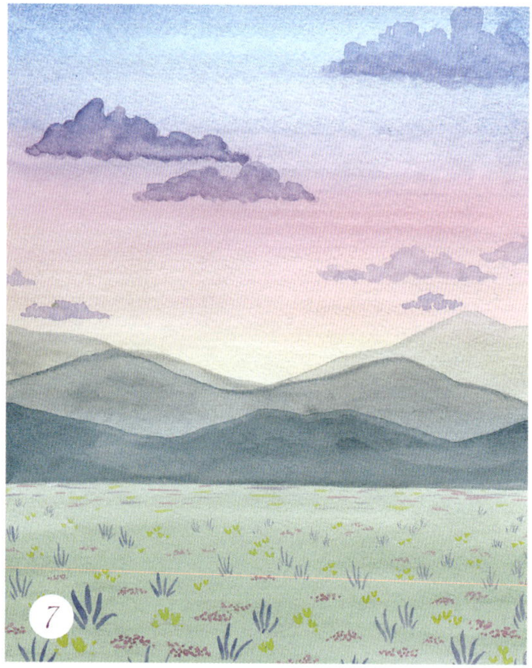

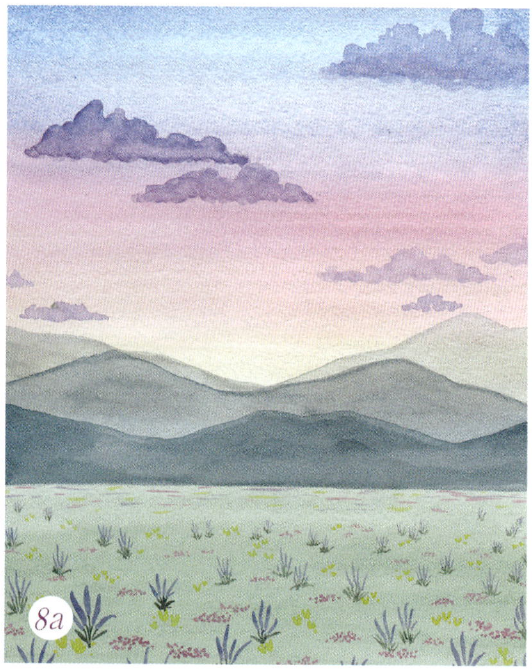

Finally, add tiny short stems to the pinkish flower clusters. Instead of focusing on individual stems, use the point of the brush to lightly paint several short vertical lines close together beneath each cluster of pinkish dots. By varying both the color and shape of the flowers and the styles of the stems, we've created a wild landscape full of different types of plants.

Using the same paint and brush, you can add a few light, sweeping horizontal brushstrokes to the background near the mountain along with the other strips of purple, pink and yellow to add more dimension. Allow the painting to dry. The painting portion is complete!

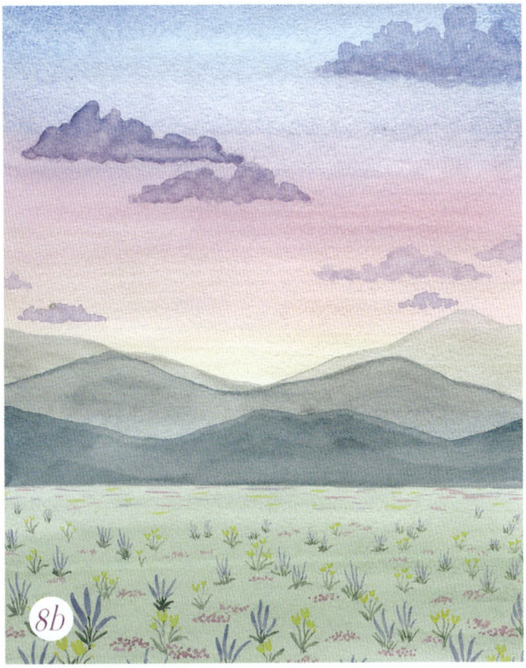

step 9

Choose your pressed flowers, and begin placing them on your paper. Once you are happy with your layout, trim the stems to length and begin picking up the flowers one by one. Using your glue brush, carefully paint the back of each flower with a thin layer of glue, and press them onto the paper. Repeat for each flower.

Once they are all mounted, set a piece of waxed paper on top of your piece and weigh it down with a few heavy books. Allow it to dry for at least 15 to 20 minutes before carefully peeling away the waxed paper. If you do this too quickly, you can peel your flowers off your page or break them. (See Mounting Flowers on page 22 for more details.) Your piece is now complete!

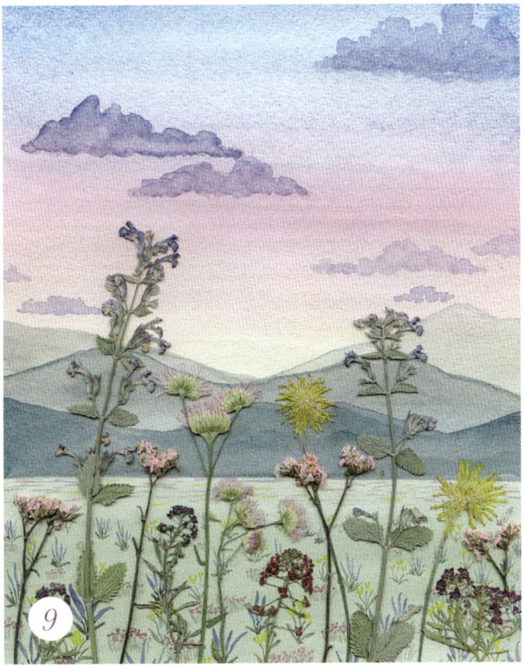

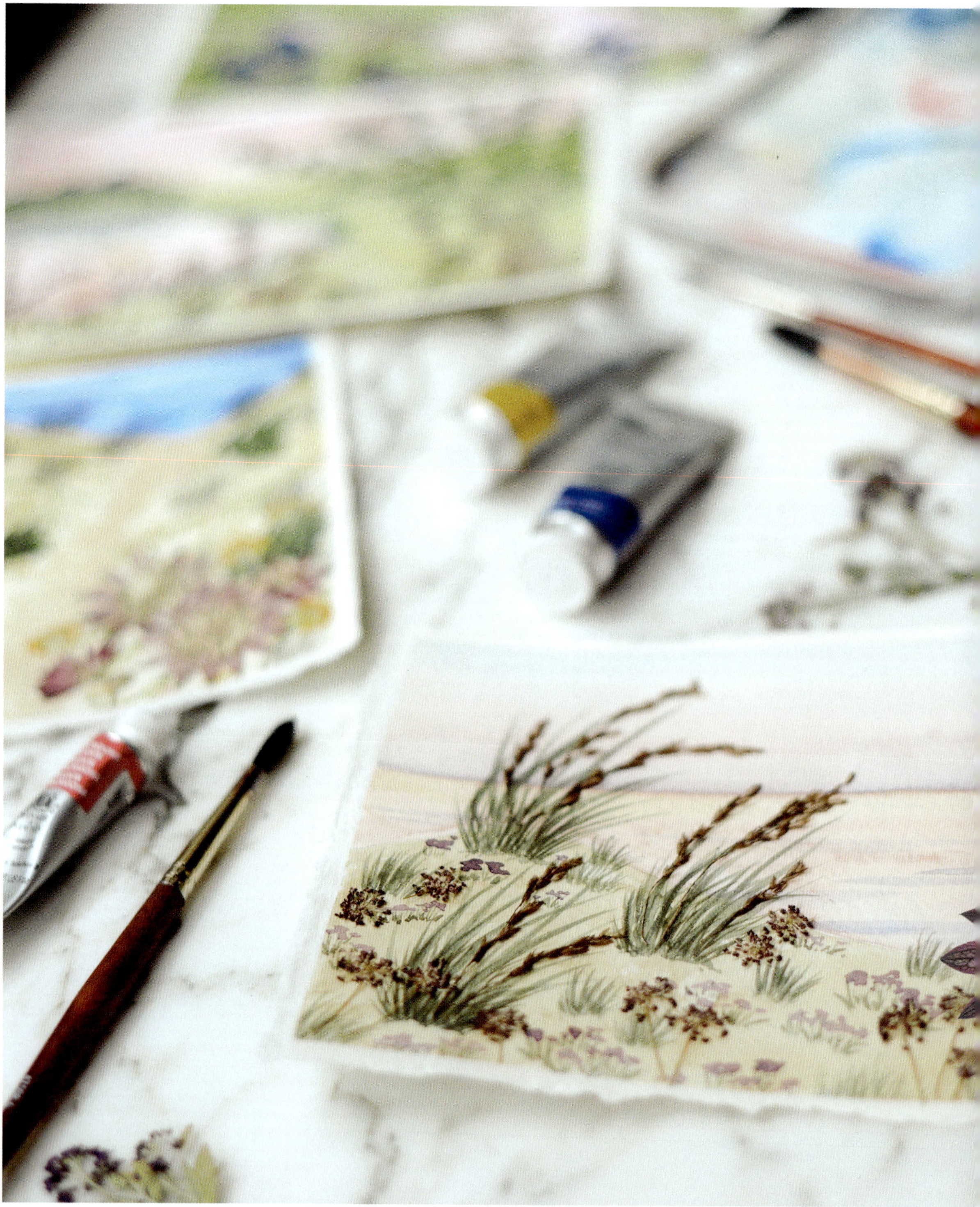

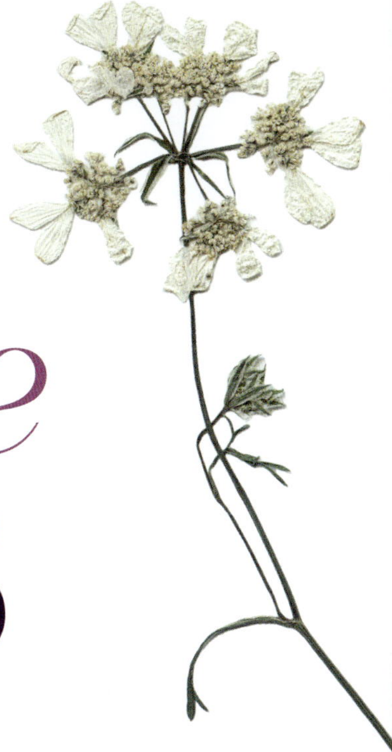

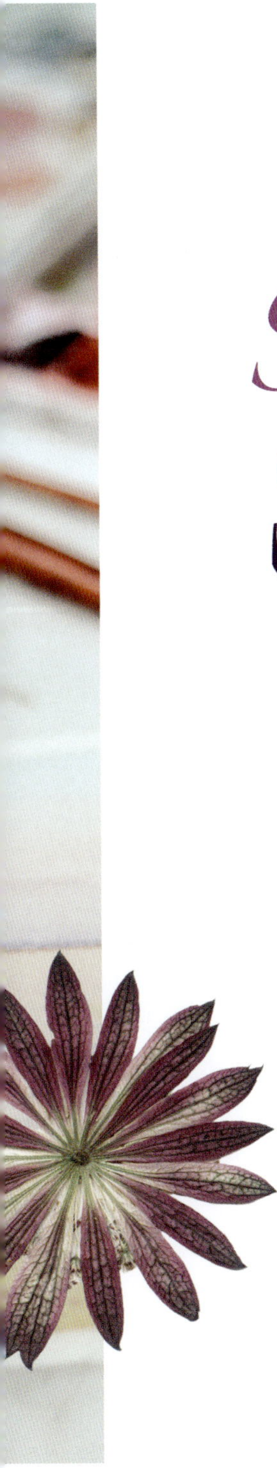

shoreline SCENES

Unique and beautiful landscapes are born where shorelines and plants meet. An ocean landscape accented by beach grasses and sandy plants (page 149), a tranquil saltwater marsh full of reeds, rushes and wildflowers (page 155) or a glassy pond surrounded by a meadow of blooms (page 141)—we will explore all of these compelling subjects in this chapter.

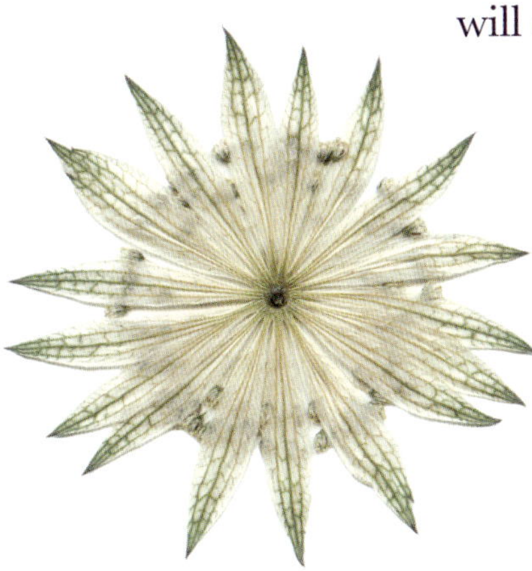

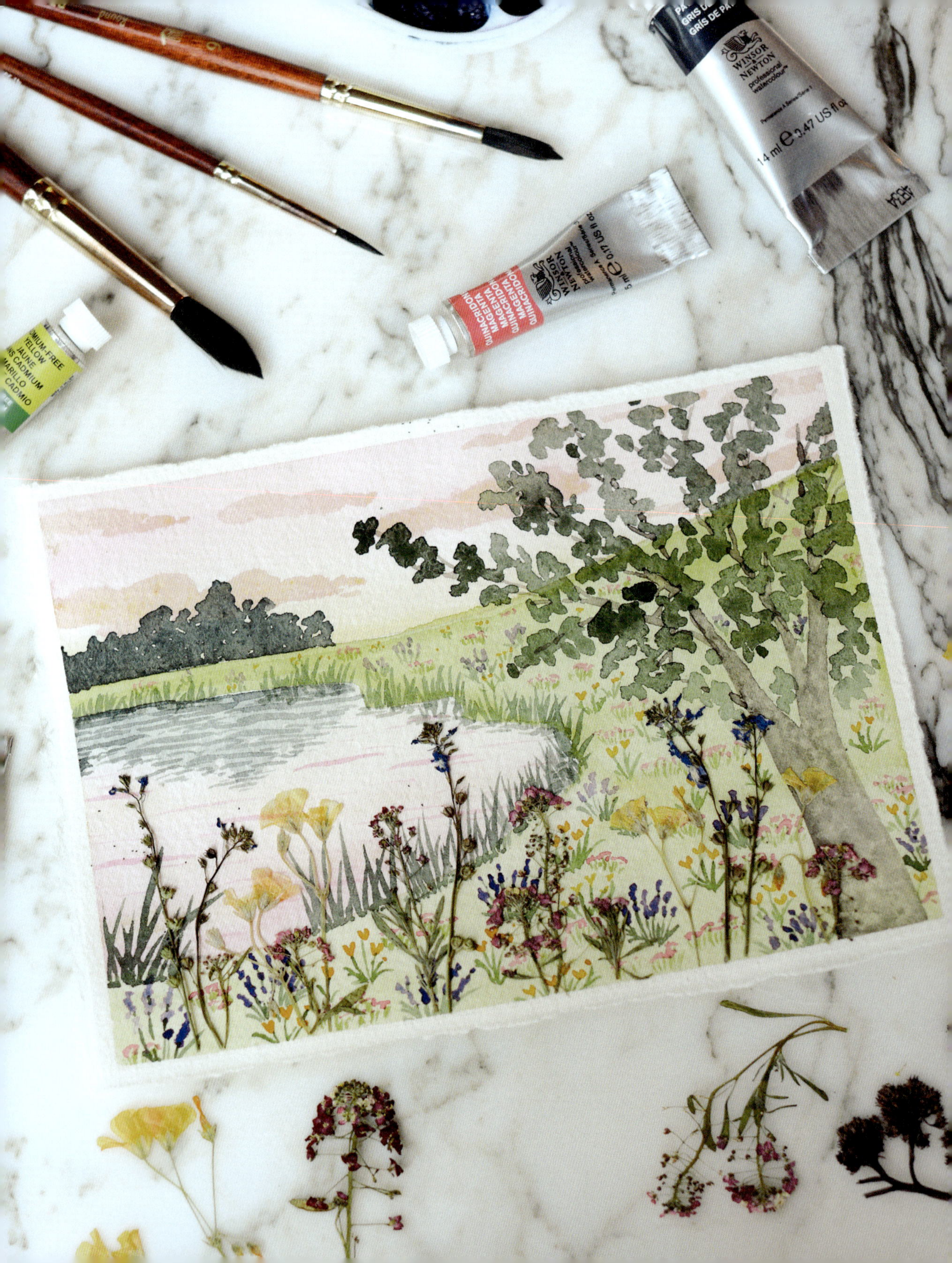
WINSOR NEWTON
professional watercolour
14 ml e 0.47 US fl oz
MAGENTA
YELLOW
JAUNE

SHERBET REFLECTIONS

One of my favorite views is the reflection of a beautiful sky within the glassy surface of a pond. This scene showcases a sherbet-colored sunset, doubled by a small pond and surrounded by a meadow of colorful flowers. A magnificent tree opposite the pond balances the composition. I chose a mixture of pressed flowers to mimic the ones in the painting: toadflax (linear purple flowers), pink sweet alyssum (cluster flowers) and yellow oxalis flowers (cup-shaped flowers).

size

5 x 7" (12.5 x 18 cm)

brushes

Size 10 round brush
Size 6 round brush
Size 2 round brush
Glue brush

flower palette

Toadflax
Sweet alyssum
Oxalis flowers

materials

Tweezers (optional)
Scissors
Glue
Waxed paper
Heavy Books

color palette

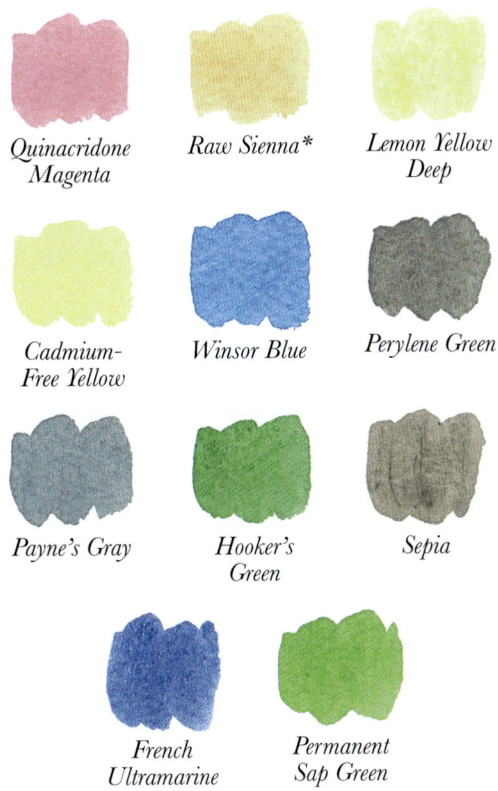

1a

1b

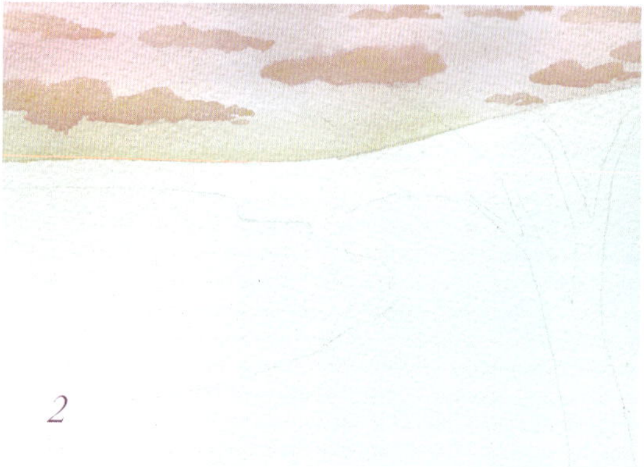

2

step 1

With a pencil, lightly draw an oval shape on the left-hand side of your paper, with part of the oval running off the side of the paper and with a few wavy bits on the right-hand side. This will be our pond. Then, lightly draw a sloping line above the oval, which will be our hilly horizon. Be sure to leave a little gap between the far edge of the pond and the horizon line. Then, lightly pencil in the trunk of a large tree in the bottom-right corner, reaching up into the paper and branching out.

Using your size 10 round brush and clean water, dampen the area above the hilly horizon line (the sky). Then, mix up a watery wash of Quinacridone Magenta on your palette. Load your brush with this pigment, and begin painting broad horizontal strokes across the sky, starting at the top of the page and stopping about half to two-thirds of the way down to the horizon.

Create a watery mix of Raw Sienna on your palette. Then, pick up some of this paint with your size 10 brush, and carefully drag it along the horizon line. Next, blend upward to meet the pinkish portion of the sky.

step 2

While the sky is still a bit damp (but not wet), create a mixture of Lemon Yellow Deep and Quinacridone Magenta on your palette for a pink-orange color. Pick up some of this pigment on your size 6 round brush, and drag the point of the brush in short wavy strokes across the sky.

step 3

Use clean water on your size 10 round brush to carefully paint in the penciled-in pond shape to the left of your page. Then, pick up a bit of the Quinacridone Magenta wash from your palette, and paint along the bottom edge of the pond, working up toward the top edge of the pond without picking up more pigment. We are trying to create a gradient that is darker at the bottom. Next, while the paper is still a little damp, pick up some of the pinky-orange color from step 2 on your size 6 brush, and make brushstrokes to mimic the clouds you painted in the sky above. They should be roughly the same in terms of distance from the horizon and position left-to-right (as a reflection). Allow the painting to dry.

3

step 4

Create a moderately pigmented mixture of Cadmium-Free Yellow with a little bit of Winsor Blue on your palette for a greenish color. Then, load your size 10 round brush with this color, and carefully trace between the pond and the horizon. Continue painting in the hillside area, and fill the entire white space with this greenish paint. Allow the painting to dry.

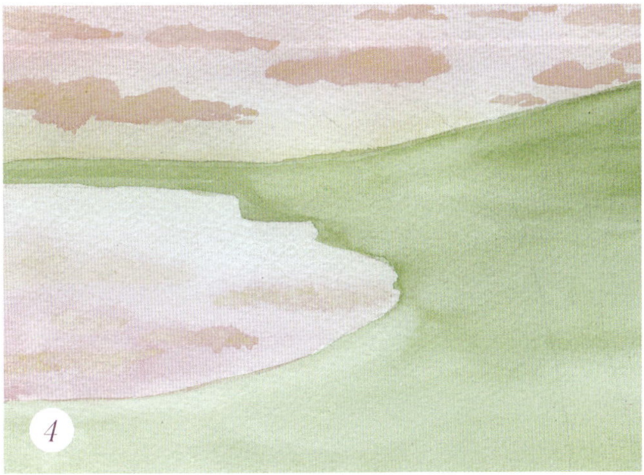

4

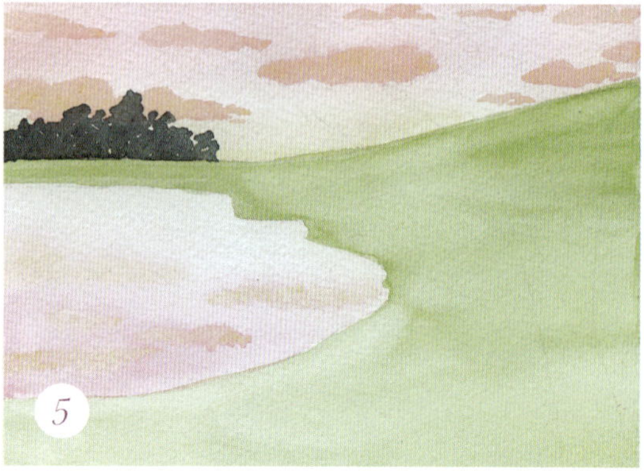

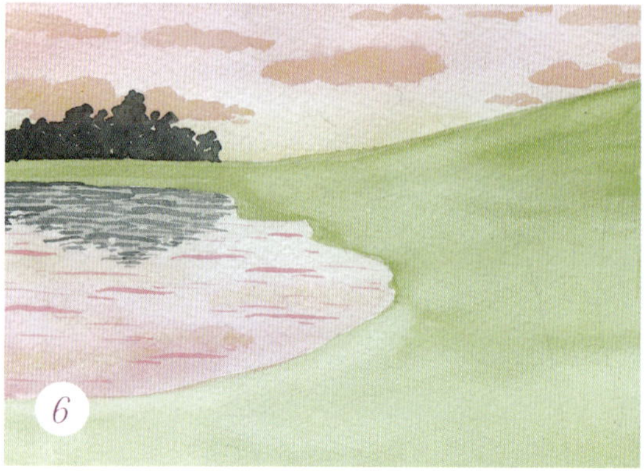

step 5

Create a pigmented mixture of Perylene Green and Payne's Gray together on your palette. Then, pick up some of this pigment on your size 6 round brush and begin tapping the point of the brush at the horizon to make a lot of loose, connected marks. This will be a distant line of trees. Make lots of these marks, leaving a few spaces here and there for the sky to peek through. The top of this tree line should be an irregular shape, with some areas taller and others shorter.

step 6

Dampen the pond area with clean water on your brush, and then use a paper towel to blot away most of the water from the paper. Next, turn the paper sideways and, using the same green-gray paint mixture with a little bit of extra water mixed in, paint a mirror image of your tree line inside the pond for the reflection. We don't want the paper to be too wet or this mirror image will be too blurry and get lost, but it can be just a little bit softer than the real tree line above the horizon. Allow the painting to dry.

Make a slightly darker mixture of Perylene Green and Payne's Gray, like the one we used to paint the trees and reflection. Using your size 2 brush, pick up some of this paint and loosely paint horizontal lines in the pond, within the reflection of the trees. Some of these lines should be thin, a few should be a bit thicker (from more pressure on the brush), and they can all vary in length. These will be ripples in the surface of the water. You can drag some out a bit beyond the existing tree reflections, but don't stray too far outside this area.

Next, create a slightly darker mixture of Quinacridone Magenta and, using the same technique, create just a few horizontal strokes within the pink area of the pond. Try using the lightest possible hand to loosely paint horizontal lines—so light that the point of the brush barely grazes the paper. Be careful not to overdo it.

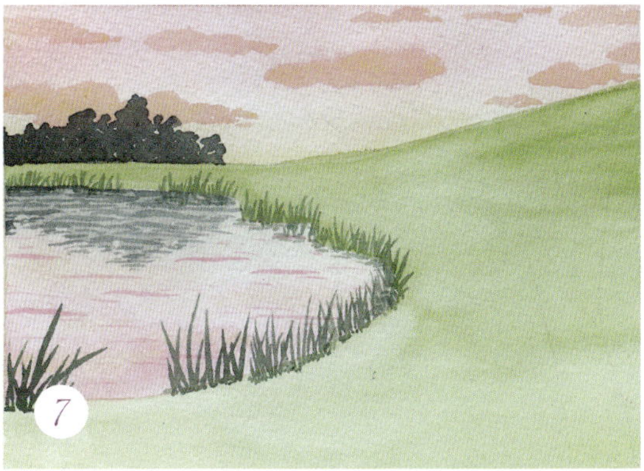

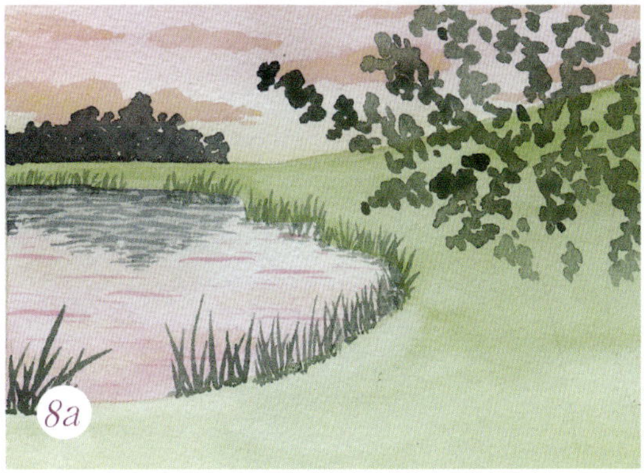

step 7

Create a pigmented mixture of Hooker's Green and Perylene Green on your palette. We will use this to paint reeds around the edge of the pond. Using your size 6 or size 2 round brush, pick up some of this pigment. Then, holding the handle of the brush perpendicular to the paper, place the point of your brush at the near edge of the pond. Sweep it upward in a quick motion, lifting it to create a pointed end on the mark. Continue painting these reeds or grasses in clumps at the pond's edge, working your way around and painting the marks smaller (shorter) as you move toward the far edge of the pond. You can leave some gaps here and there so it looks a bit more natural. (See "Painting Grasses" on page 36 for more details.)

Using the same paint mixture and brush, add some small horizontal strokes at the base of the grasses where they meet the water. You can also add some loose dots where the reeds meet the bank.

step 8

Mix up a pigmented combination of Perylene Green, Sepia and a bit of Hooker's Green for a dark-green color. Load your size 6 round brush with this paint, and locate the pencil marks made in step 1 for the tree in the foreground. We are going to first add the leaves to the tree by tapping the paper with the point of the brush, using enough pressure to make larger blobs. Make these marks roughly along the upper branches, leaving space for the sky and hill beyond to show through. Allow the painting to dry.

(continued)

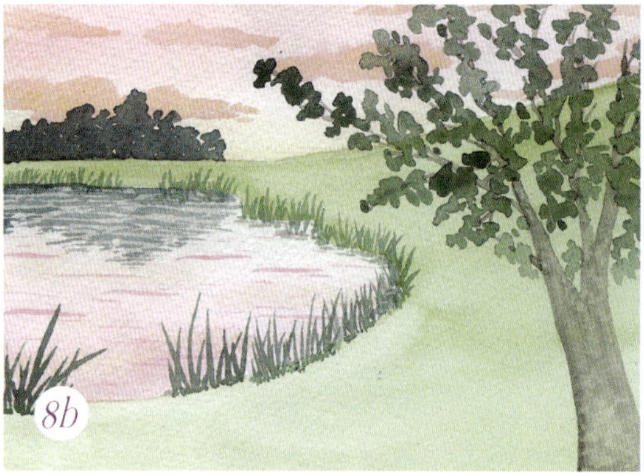

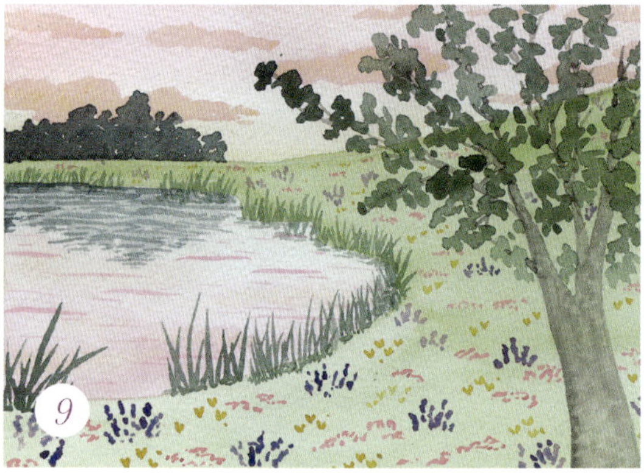

Next, create a pigmented mixture of Sepia and Payne's Gray for a dark-brown color on your palette. Load your size 6 round brush with this pigment, and begin painting in the trunk and branches based on the pencil lines drawn in step 1. Once you have painted the main trunk and lower branches, you can take a crumpled paper towel and blot at it to create a mottled look.

Continue adding branches all the way up the tree, bridging gaps between leaves. You can switch to a smaller brush for this part, if necessary, to make thinner lines higher in the tree.

step 9

Create a pigmented mixture of French Ultramarine and Quinacridone Magenta together on your palette for a nice purple color. Pick up some of this paint with your size 2 round brush. Using a light touch and the point of the brush, paint tiny dots in a vertical line somewhere near the bottom of the page in the green area. Then, paint a few more of these lines of dots on either side. Each of these groupings will be a cluster of purple linear flowers. Continue painting similar groupings here and there across the meadow, making them smaller as you move up the hill. Clean your brush.

Next, return to your Quinacridone Magenta wash on your palette (or make a little bit more), and pick some up with your brush. We will make similar marks with this pinkish paint, but this time instead of vertical lines, we will make horizontal ones in clusters. Add these pink clusters in the gaps between the purple clusters.

Finally, mix up some Cadmium-Free Yellow and Raw Sienna on your palette. With your size 2 round brush, pick up this paint and make little *V* marks throughout the page. The marks can be simple little dots farther back on the hill.

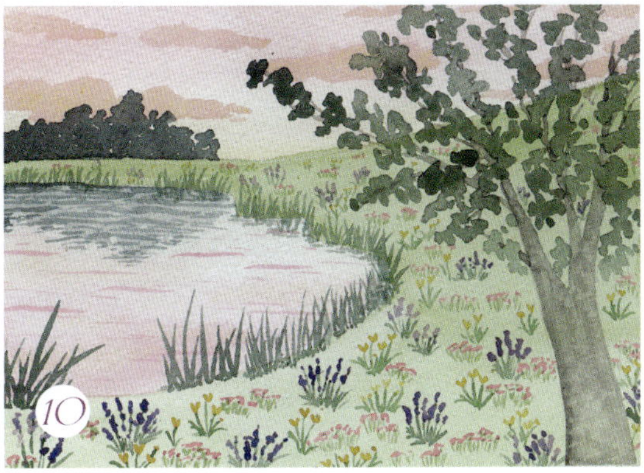

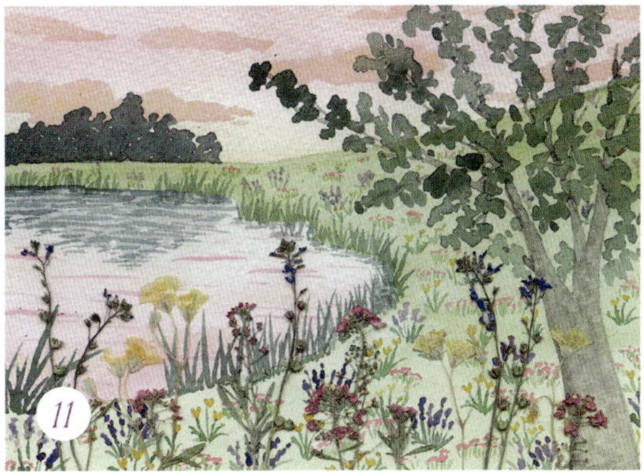

step 10

Create a moderately pigmented mixture of Hooker's Green and Perylene Green on your palette. Use your size 2 round brush and this paint to begin painting stems. Starting with the purple linear flowers, lightly paint long, graceful stems beneath them, connecting the stems at their bases and adding a few additional brushstrokes on either side for leaves.

Add a little bit of Permanent Sap Green to the mixture you were using to change it slightly. Then, pick up this paint and continue painting stems on the little yellow flowers.

Finally, add a little bit of Sepia paint to the mixture to change it again. Pick up some of this paint, and lightly paint lots of tiny vertical dashes beneath the pink clusters of flowers. Allow the painting to dry. The painting portion is now complete!

step 11

Choose your pressed flowers, and begin placing them across the bottom edge of your piece. Once you are happy with your layout, trim the stems to length and begin picking up the flowers one by one. Using your glue brush, carefully paint the back of each flower with a thin layer of glue and press them onto the paper.

Once they are all mounted, set a piece of waxed paper on top of your piece and weigh it down with a few heavy books. Allow it to dry for at least 15 to 20 minutes before carefully peeling away the waxed paper. If you do this too quickly, you can peel your flowers off your page or break them. (See Mounting Flowers on page 22 for more details.) Your piece is now complete!

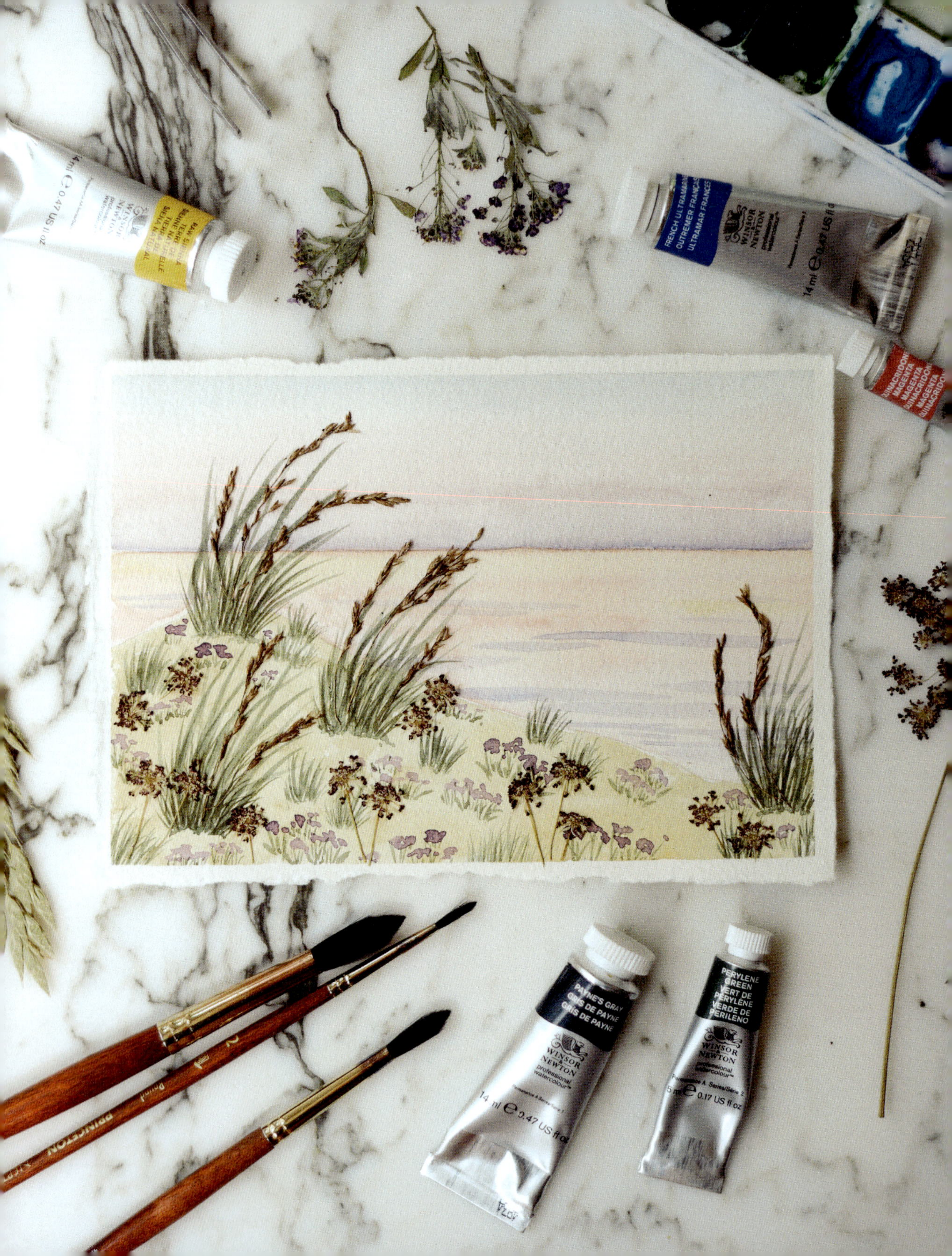
PAYNE'S GRAY
GRIS DE PAYNE
GRIS DE PAYNE
WINSOR & NEWTON
14 ml 0.47 US fl oz
PERYLENE GREEN
VERT DE PÉRYLÈNE
VERDE DE PERILENO
WINSOR & NEWTON
5 ml 0.17 US fl oz
PRINCETON
FRENCH ULTRAMARINE
ULTRAMAR FRANCÉS
14 ml 0.47 US fl oz

COASTAL DAWN

For this coastal scene, a gentle sky gradient meets a tranquil sea, and gently swaying grasses stand out in silhouette. A few flowers are sprinkled along the sand in between, but the unique placement of pressed grasses is the main visual focus of this piece. A relatively simple composition, this one can be scaled up or down depending on the scale of the pressed plants you have. I have chosen some grass seed heads, collected and pressed in late spring and early summer, along with some small purple (chocolate) Queen Anne's lace florets, which correspond with the purple flowers we will paint in this piece.

size

5 x 7" (12.5 x 18 cm)

brushes

Size 10 round brush
Size 6 round brush
Size 2 round brush
Glue brush

flower palette

Chocolate Queen Anne's lace
Grasses with seed heads

materials

Tweezers (optional)
Scissors
Glue
Waxed paper
Heavy Books

color palette

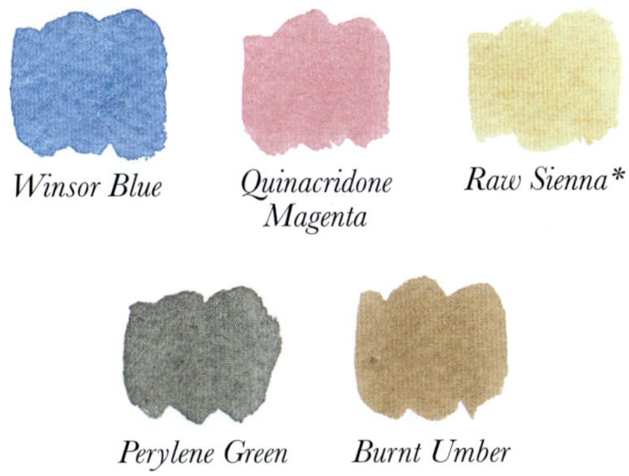

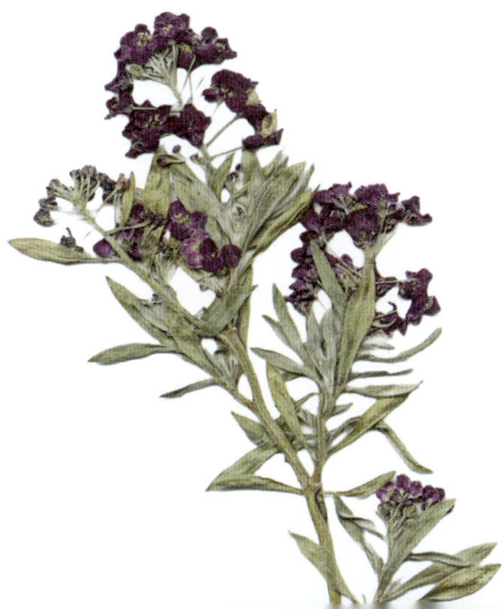

1a

1b

step 1

Sketch a straight line for the horizon about a quarter to a third of the way from the top of the page, as well as the sloping dunes about a quarter to a third of the way up from the bottom of the paper. A nice, straight horizon line where the ocean meets the sky is important, so I recommend using a ruler or other straight edge if you can.

We'll start with painting the sky. Make separate watery washes of both Winsor Blue and a mixture of Quinacridone Magenta with Raw Sienna on your palette. Load up your size 10 brush first with the watery Winsor Blue. Using sweeping horizontal brushstrokes, paint a band across the top of the sky portion. Clean your brush and paint a band with just clear water at the bottom of your blue. Then, clean the brush again and load it with the dusty-pink wash. Starting at the horizon line, use the same brushstrokes to paint a band of this color across the bottom of the sky portion. The two bands of color should meet at the band of wet paper we established with the clean water. You can use your brush to push the paint around a little bit on the wet paper to encourage a smooth gradient, but be careful not to add too much water or overwork it. Allow the painting to dry.

2

step 2

Picking up the same dusty-pink paint that we used for the sky, use your size 10 round brush to paint in the ocean all the way down to the sloping pencil line for the sand dune. Then, pick up a moderately pigmented mixture of Raw Sienna and paint a horizontal band of color right beneath the horizon line, so it's in the ocean. Then, place another horizontal brushstroke or two beneath the first one to add in a little more of this golden color in the top half of the ocean portion. Allow the painting to dry.

step 3

Create a watery mixture of Winsor Blue and Quinacridone Magenta on your palette. Using the same size 10 round brush and some of this mixture, paint a straight horizontal band of color right above the horizon line, so it's in the sky. If there is a hard edge at all, use clean water to carefully soften it with another brushstroke at the top edge of the first. You should have a smooth, soft gradient of pre-sunrise color.

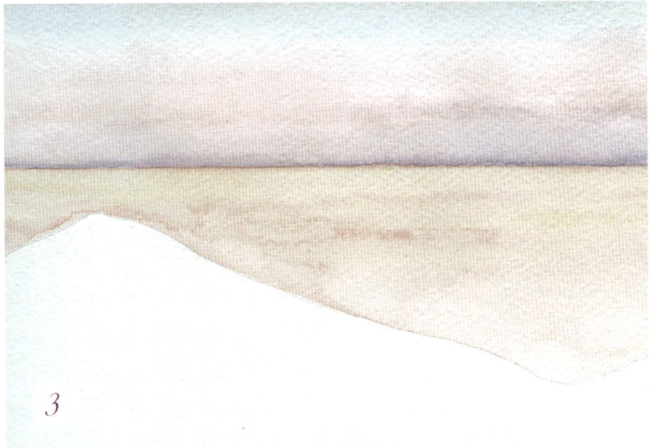

3

step 4

Pick up some more of the purplish mixture from step 3 with your size 6 round brush. Then, paint a few horizontal lines in the lower two-thirds of the ocean segment, followed by thinner and fewer lines mid-ocean and thicker and closer lines together in the lower segment near the dunes.

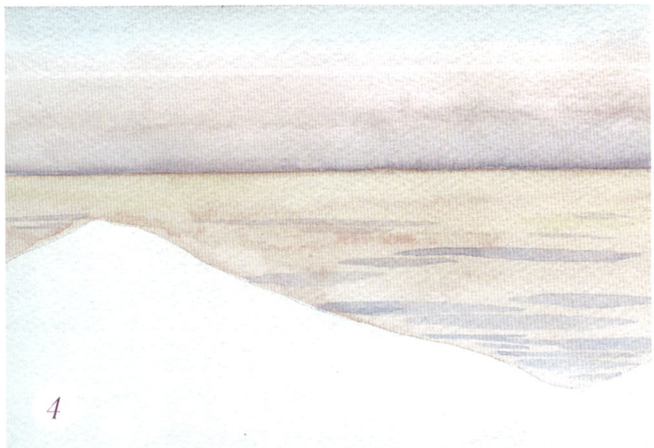

4

step 5

Create a moderately pigmented mixture of Raw Sienna with just a little bit of the purplish mixture from the previous two steps to create an earthy, sandy color. Then, use your size 10 round brush and swirling brushstrokes to fill in the sand dune area below the pencil line in the bottom portion of the page. Allow the painting to dry.

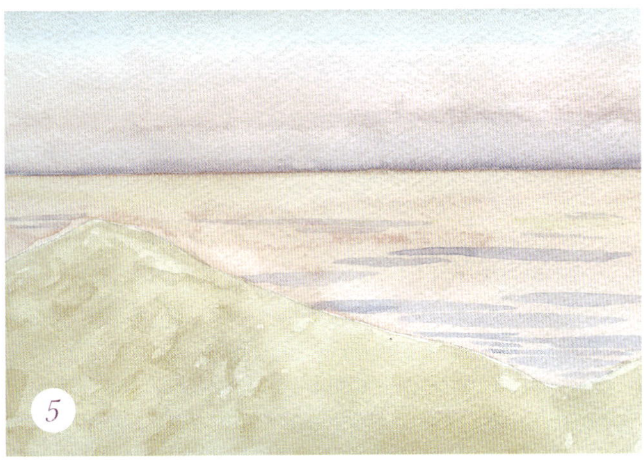

5

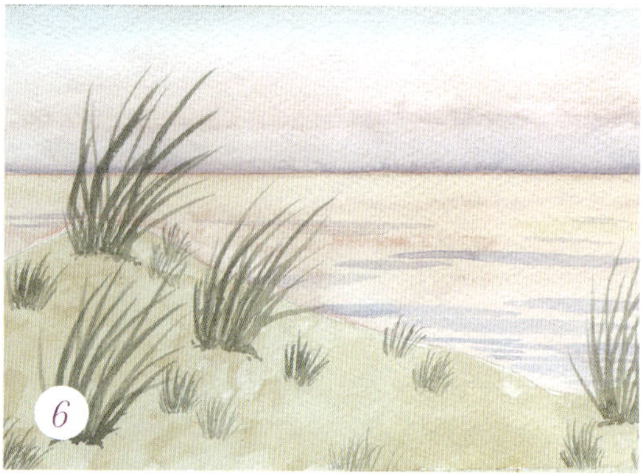

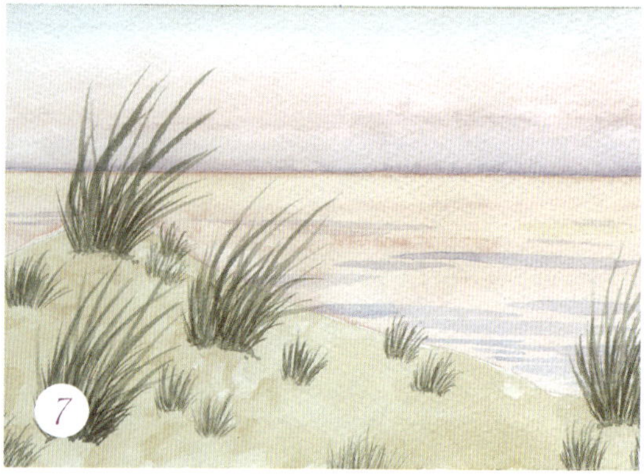

step 6

Next, we will add beach grasses to the dunes. Create a pigmented mix of Perylene Green and Burnt Umber. Using your size 2 brush and holding it with the tip pointing toward the bottom of the paper, lightly touch the brush to the paper and quickly flick it upward, lifting it as you go to create a tapered blade of grass. Repeat this process, starting right next to the base of the previous mark, making a cluster of grass blades to create a clump of grass. Vary the direction that you flick the brush upward each time to keep it loose and organic and give the impression of a light breeze. Once you are satisfied with your clump of grass, move to a different spot on the dune and create another, varying the size and spacing of these grasses. I made a handful of large clumps with longer grasses and added smaller, shorter grasses in clumps around them. Allow the painting to dry.

step 7

Add more Burnt Umber to your original mixture to darken the shade, and then revisit your grass clusters. Add more blades of grass to each clump, this time making them even thinner and shorter, using a lighter hand but the same swishing brushstroke. If the base of any of your grass clumps looks uneven, you can tap in a few marks with your paint to fill it in so it appears to be growing more naturally from the sand.

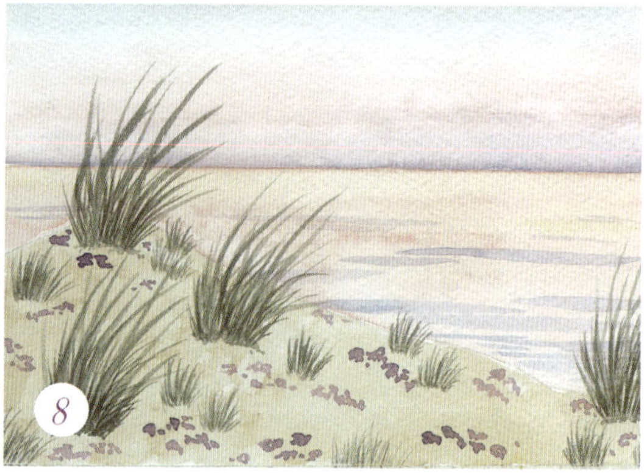

step 8

Create another mixture of Quinacridone Magenta and a little bit of Winsor Blue, this time making it more pinkish-purple. Then, add some Burnt Umber to dull it to a more earthy-purple tone. Pick up some of this paint with your size 2 round brush, and use the brush point to tap little clusters of dots across the sand dune here and there, in between the grasses. Allow the painting to dry.

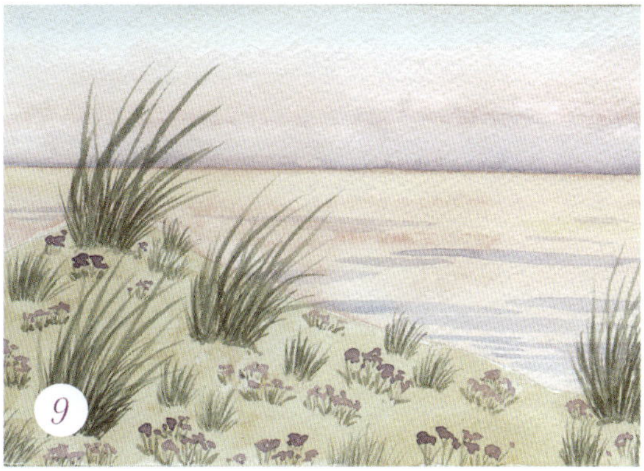

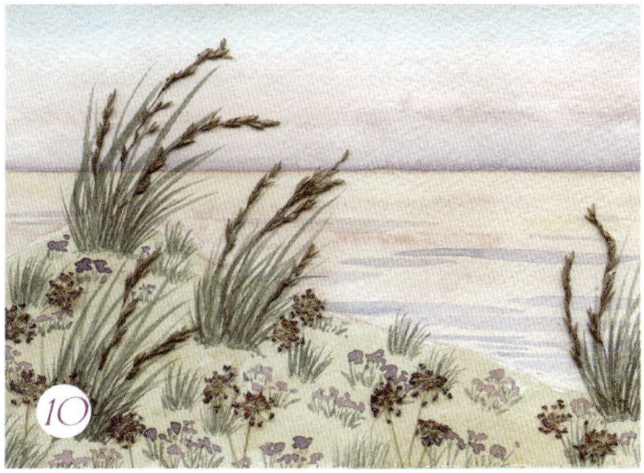

step 9

Make up a moderately pigmented mix of Perylene Green and a little bit of Burnt Umber. Take your size 2 round brush, load it with paint and use a light hand to paint loose, tiny clusters of stems beneath each grouping of flowers. These can simply be a series of vertical or diagonal dashes. You can connect them at the bottom with small dots or blobs as leaves. Allow the painting to dry. The painting portion is now complete!

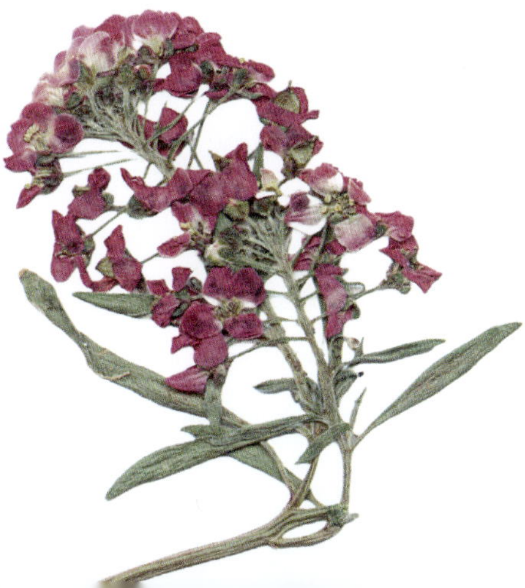

step 10

Select your pressed plant material for this scene. The grass I used had many miniature "flower stalks" branching off the main stem, so I removed each of those and used them as individual grasses in this piece, gluing them right on top of the large grass clusters so they appear to be growing there.

Pick each stem or flower up with your tweezers or hands, and gently use your glue brush to paint the backside of each with a thin layer of glue. Press them onto your painting and repeat until everything is stuck down.

Once they are all mounted, set a piece of waxed paper on top of your piece and weigh it down with a few heavy books. Allow it to dry for at least 15 to 20 minutes before carefully peeling away the waxed paper. If you do this too quickly, you can peel your flowers off your page or break them. (See Mounting Flowers on page 22 for more details.) Your piece is now complete!

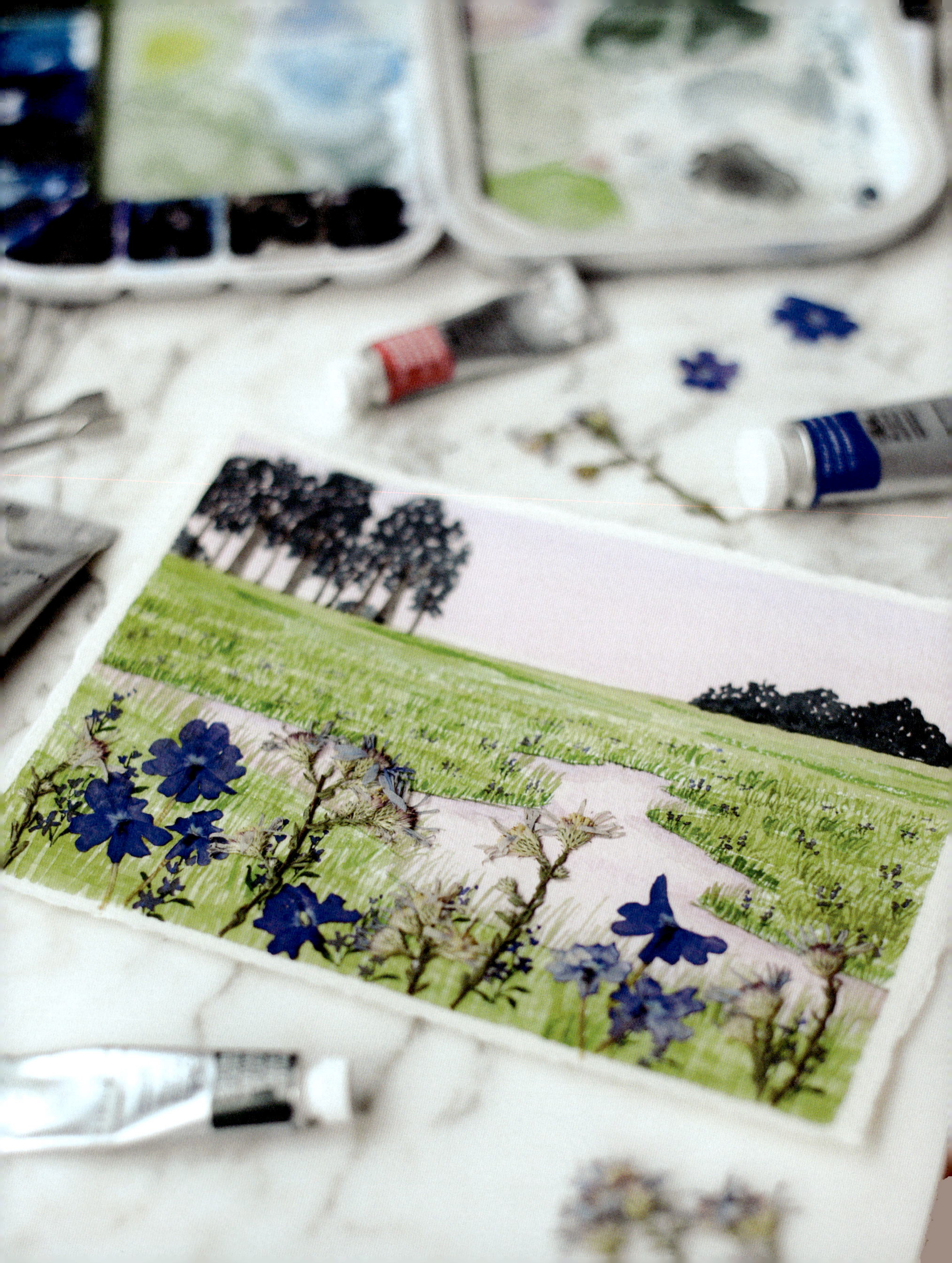

TRANQUIL MARSH

Another landscape where flowers meet water is the marsh. While marshes are typically dominated by herbaceous plants like grasses, rushes and reeds, you can also find flowers here and there. In this imagined landscape, a pink sky is reflected in the still water, and the grasses are punctuated by purple flowers. To match the painted purple flowers within the marsh, I chose some vibrant-purple verbena blossoms and wildflower asters on their stems.

size

5 x 7" (12.5 x 18 cm)

brushes

Size 10 round brush
Size 6 round brush
Size 2 round brush
Glue brush

flower palette

Purple verbena blossoms
Small wild asters

materials

Tweezers (optional)
Scissors
Glue
Waxed paper
Heavy Books

color palette

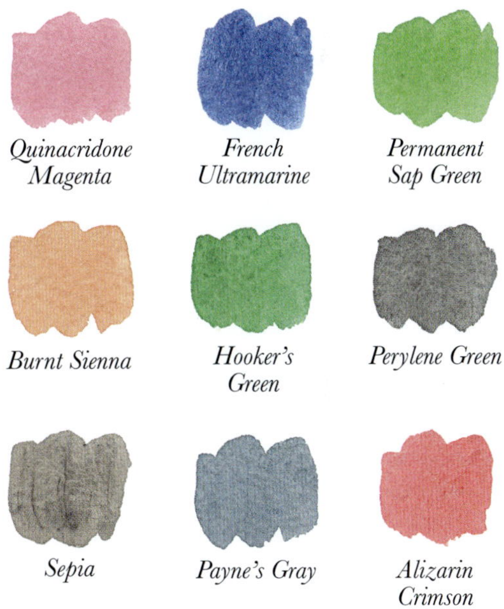

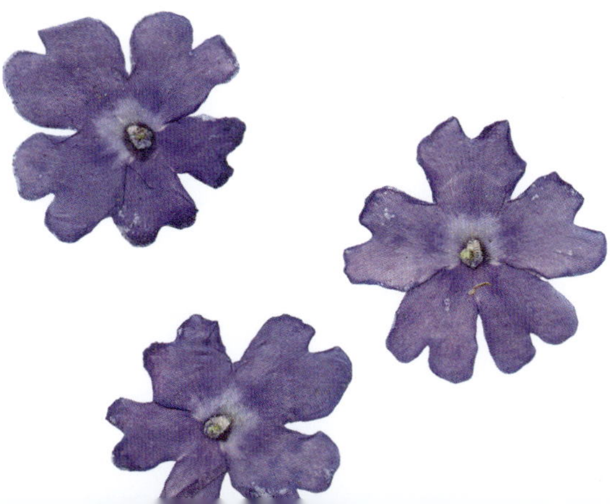

1

2

step 1

With a pencil, lightly sketch in some of the major shapes for the painting: First, draw a straight horizon line about a third of the way down the page. Then, draw a marsh made up of a few curved lines that snake back and forth about two-thirds of the way down the page, and a curved line about a quarter of the way up from the bottom.

step 2

Mix up a moderately pigmented wash of Quinacridone Magenta (this will be pinkish in hue). Then, mix a wash of Quinacridone Magenta with a little bit of French Ultramarine added in (this will be purplish in hue). Load your size 10 round brush with the French Ultramarine mixture, and paint a band of color across the top of the page, using a broad, sweeping horizontal stroke. Then, pick up the Quinacridone Magenta mixture and continue painting horizontal strokes under the first one to fill in the space down to the horizon, making sure you overlap your strokes enough to blend it into a smooth sky gradient. The gradient should be subtle, appearing slightly more purple up top and pinkish at the horizon.

Next, flip your paper upside down so the sky is at the bottom, and repeat the color sequence, starting with what is the bottom of the marsh (now at the top) beneath the curved line. Starting with the purplish paint, carefully drag your brush along this line, and then continue filling in the space with the pinkish pigment. Once you have finished, turn your paper right side up again. This is the still water in the marsh.

step 3

Create a mixture of Permanent Sap Green and Burnt Sienna, moderately pigmented, on your palette. Pick up some of this paint with your size 6 round brush. Using quick, light horizontal strokes, begin making marks beneath the horizon (sky), allowing some white space and paper texture to show through. When your brush runs out of paint, dip it into some water and continue painting, allowing for a lighter, more transparent color to show on the paper. Fill in the area between the sky and the water, and then move down to the area below the water and do the same. Allow the painting to dry.

Add a little bit of Hooker's Green to this mixture, and add a few more similar brushstrokes to fill in some of the bare patches and add variation.

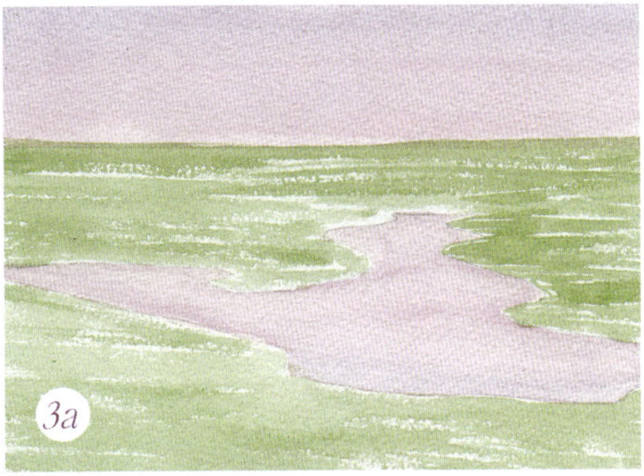

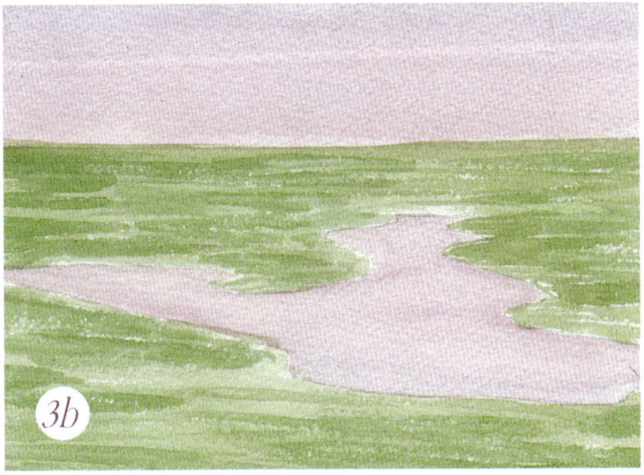

step 4

Create another slightly more pigmented mixture of Permanent Sap Green and Burnt Sienna on your palette, and fill your size 2 round brush with it. We will be painting the marsh grasses with lots and lots of little vertical lines. With the brush held perpendicular to the paper, lightly paint vertical brushstrokes, swiping upward and pulling the brush away from the paper to create a tapered end. (See Painting Grasses on page 36 for more details.) The grasses in the foreground (at the bottom of the page) can be longer, while the ones farther up the page should be shorter. They should all be vertical but can vary in their angles. Overlap the grasses and fill in the area just to give texture, but not so much that your individual brushstrokes are lost.

Leave the area just beneath the horizon alone. The horizontal brushstrokes from the last step convey distance and depth to the painting.

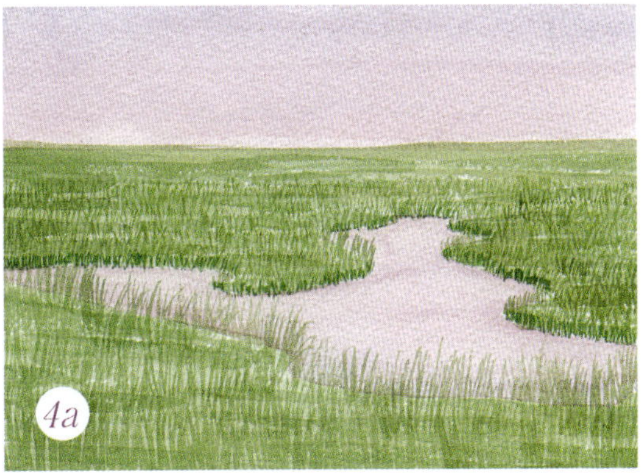

(continued)

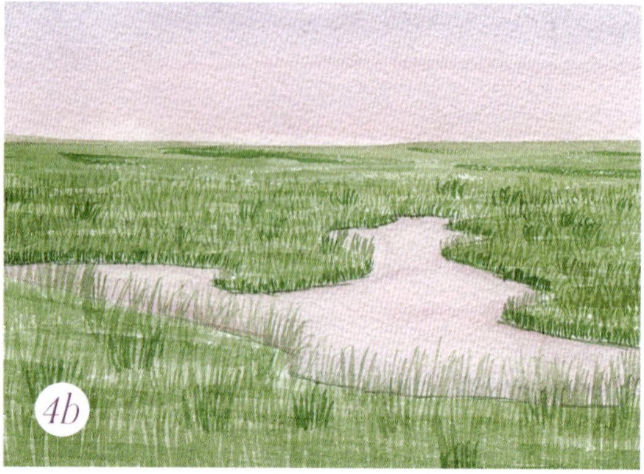

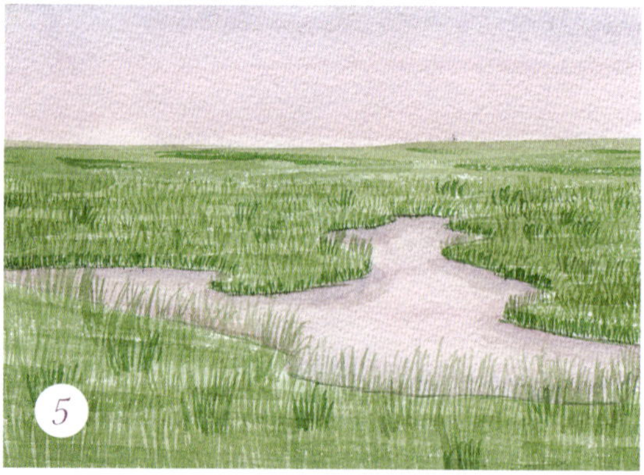

Mix some Hooker's Green into this mixture, and add grasses of this new color to your marshy meadow along the water's edge and in random spots, using the same technique as before. Lightly add in some choppy horizontal brushstrokes right at the water line, at the base of the grasses. Then, make a few broad horizontal brushstrokes just below the horizon to add this new color to the distant, undefined grasses. Allow the painting to dry.

step 5

Create a watery mixture of French Ultramarine and Quinacridone Magenta on your palette. With your size 6 round brush, paint a band of this purplish color just below the water line where the grasses meet the water, following just along the bottoms of the grasses (but not to the side of the grasses; don't trace the entire curve, just the horizontal portions). Clean off your brush and then, with just clear water and no paint, blend the purplish marks slightly so there are no hard edges. These are the reflections and shadows from the grasses on the surface of the unmoving water.

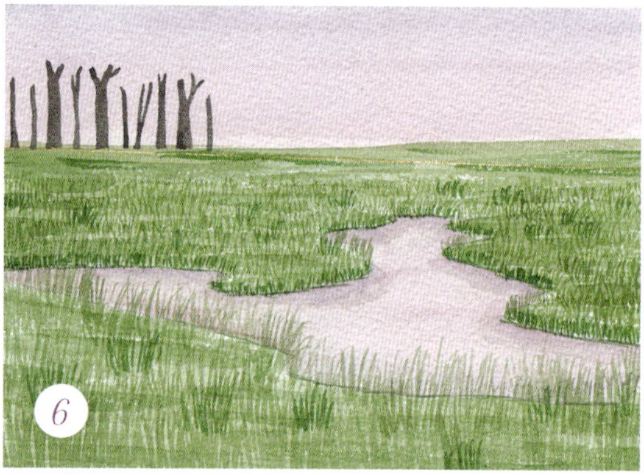

step 6

Combine Perylene Green and Sepia on your palette in a moderately pigmented mixture. Pick up some of this paint using your size 6 round brush (size 2 if it makes you feel more comfortable) and paint a series of thin vertical lines upward from the horizon on the left side of the page. These will be tree trunks for some distant pine trees, and you can vary their width, spacing and height. You can also add branches—or not. Allow the painting to dry.

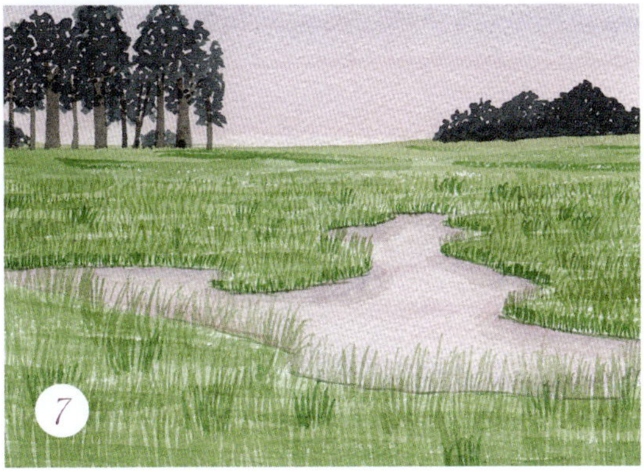

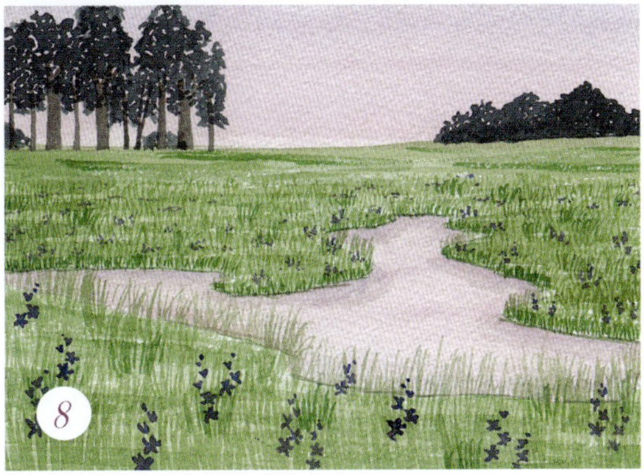

step 7

Combine Perylene Green with a little bit of Payne's Gray on your palette in a moderately pigmented mixture of deep, cool green. Load your size 6 round brush with this paint, and use the brush point to tap dot marks in clusters just above the horizon at the right-hand side of the page. Continue adding dots in clusters until there is a dense mass of color (some sky showing through is okay), with an uneven silhouette at the top and a roughly straight line at the bottom, resting on the horizon.

Move over to the tree trunks on the left-hand side of the page, and begin adding more dots in clusters around the tops of each trunk. Keep them irregular and allow them to reach up into the sky at different heights, to depict the evergreen leaves of pine trees. You can add some marks at the base of some of the trees as lower-growing trees or shrubs.

step 8

Create a pigmented mixture of Alizarin Crimson and French Ultramarine on your palette. Pick up some of this paint with your size 2 round brush. Then, with light pressure through the brush point, begin painting little star-shaped flowers within the lower portion of the marsh meadow. (See Painting Tiny Flowers on page 37 for more details.) Paint two or three of these in a little grouping, with a few little marks (dots or *V* shapes) nearby or above. We will connect them with stems soon.

Add more groupings across the marsh meadow, making the marks smaller and less defined as you move into the background and up the page.

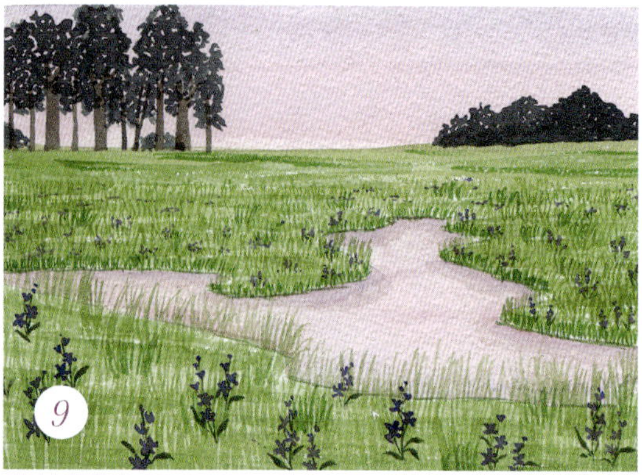

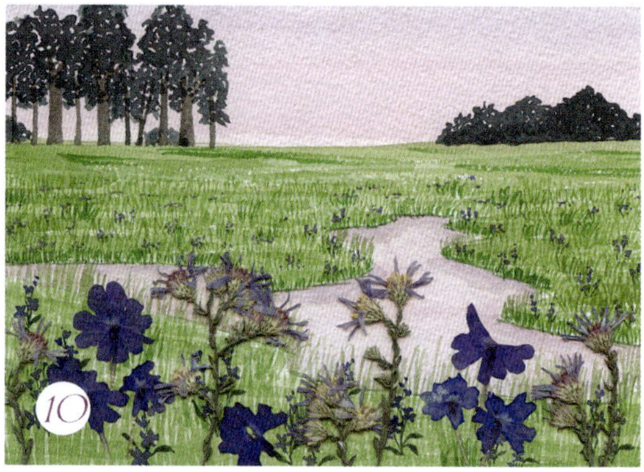

step 9

Once these flowers have dried, make a cool-green mixture on your palette with some Perylene Green and Permanent Sap Green. Pick up some of this mixture with your size 2 round brush, and lightly paint stems to connect the flowers. With the brush perpendicular to the paper, lightly paint a line downward from each flower, and add a leaf here and there by placing the brush point on top of the stem, pressing down through the belly of the brush as you drag it away from the stem and lift to create a tapered end to the leaf.

These stems and leaves don't need to connect to the ground, since they are growing out of dense grasses. They should simply imply growth upward through the grasses and give the flowers something to connect them to the landscape.

Once you have added stems to the nearest flowers (there's no real need to do the distant ones, unless you want to), allow the painting to dry. The painting portion is complete!

step 10

Select your pressed flowers, and begin laying them across the bottom edge of your piece. Once you have a layout you are happy with, trim the stems to length and begin picking up the flowers one by one. Using your glue brush, carefully paint the back of each flower with a thin layer of glue and press them onto the paper.

Once they are all mounted, set a piece of waxed paper on top of your piece and weigh it down with a few heavy books. Allow it to dry for at least 15 to 20 minutes before carefully peeling away the waxed paper. If you do this too quickly, you can peel your flowers off your page or break them. (See Mounting Flowers on page 22 for more details.) Your piece is now complete!

DUNE PATH

The sandy dunes on the coast are often home to large clumps of grasses, anchoring the dunes with their roots and swaying in the ocean breeze. Other plants populate these ecosystems as well, including flowering vines and shrubs. In this project, we imagine some colorful flora among the grasses and include some pressed specimens in the foreground. Pink astrantia and golden alyssum work well with the colors and atmosphere of this piece.

size

5 x 7" (12.5 x 18 cm)

brushes

Size 6 round brush
Size 2 round brush
Glue brush

flower palette

Pink astrantia
Golden alyssum

materials

Tweezers (optional)
Scissors
Glue
Waxed paper
Heavy Books

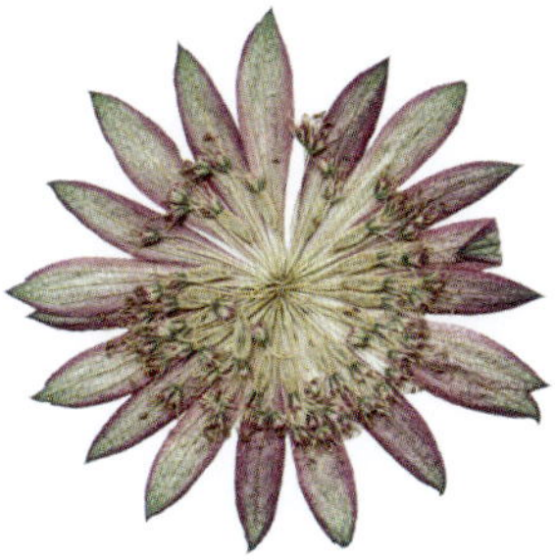

color palette

*Raw Sienna**

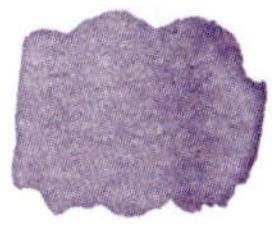

Winsor Violet

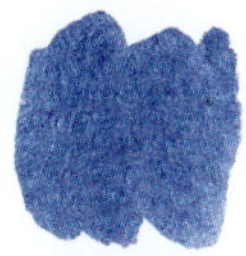

French Ultramarine

Perylene Green

Cadmium-Free Yellow

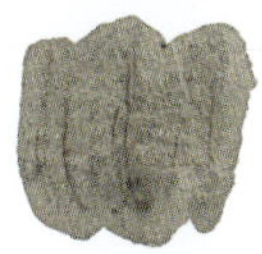

Sepia

Quinacridone Magenta

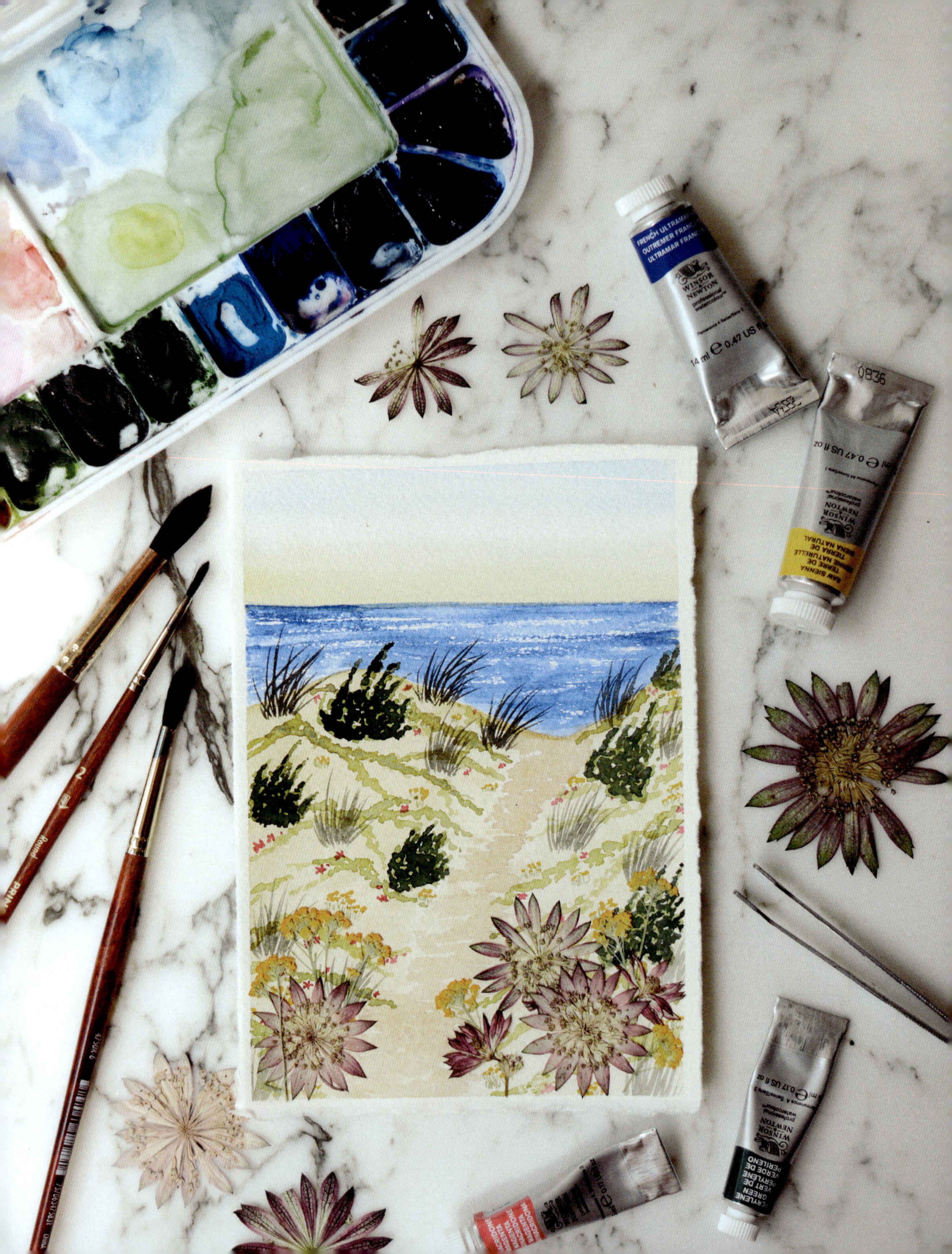
FRENCH ULTRAMARINE
OUTREMER FRANÇAIS
ULTRAMAR FRANCÉS
WINSOR & NEWTON
14 ml ℮ 0.47 US fl oz
RAW SIENNA
TERRE DE SIENNE NATURELLE
TIERRA DE SIENA NATURAL
PERYLENE GREEN
VERT DE PERYLENE
VERDE DE PERILENO

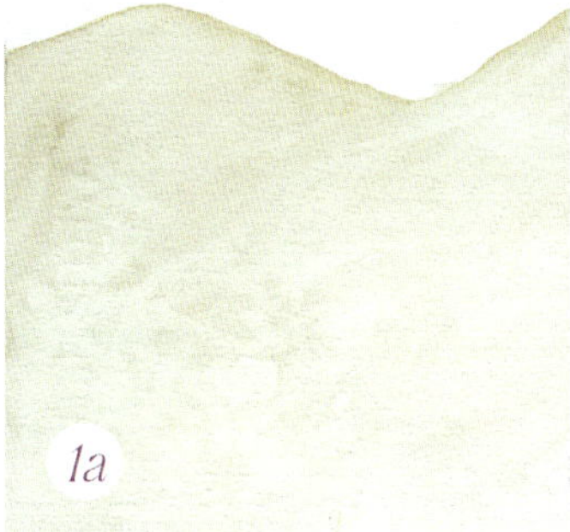

1a

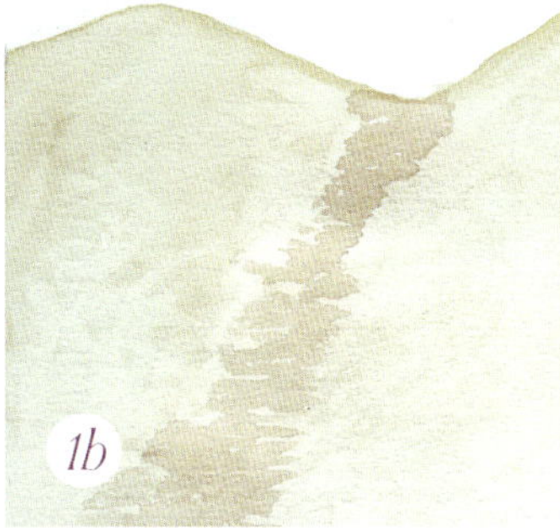

1b

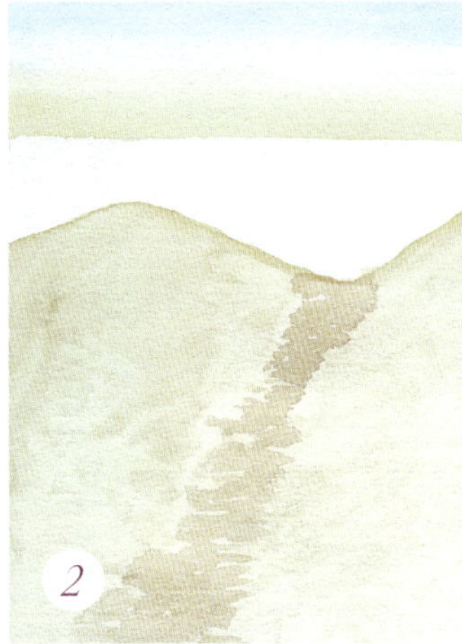

2

step 1

Create a very watery mixture of Raw Sienna and just a touch of Winsor Violet to create a sandy light-brown color. Using your size 6 round brush, pick up some of this mixture and paint an uneven, wide *V* shape from the left edge of your paper to the right, about a third of the way from the top. This will be a sand dune, so the line should be wavy and organic.

Using quick, random brushstrokes, fill in the entire space below the line you just painted. It is okay if the texture of the paper shows through in some spots. Once the paper has almost dried, add a little bit more Winsor Violet to the mixture on your palette to darken it. Starting at the lowest point of the *V*, make small horizontal brushstrokes with this darker paint, leading in an uneven line down toward the bottom of the page, getting slightly larger as you go. These are shadows in the sand, like a path of footprints to lead the way to the ocean.

step 2

On your palette, mix a watery puddle of French Ultramarine and another watery puddle of Raw Sienna. Pick up some of the blue with your size 6 round brush. Then, using a smooth horizontal brushstroke, paint a thin band of blue across the top of the page. Dip your brush in clean water, and paint another band at the bottom of the first, overlapping slightly. Then, clean your brush and pick up some of the Raw Sienna, and paint another band of color beneath that, again overlapping slightly. This should fill in approximately the top fifth of the page. You shouldn't have any hard lines here in the sky; it should be a smooth gradient. Set to dry.

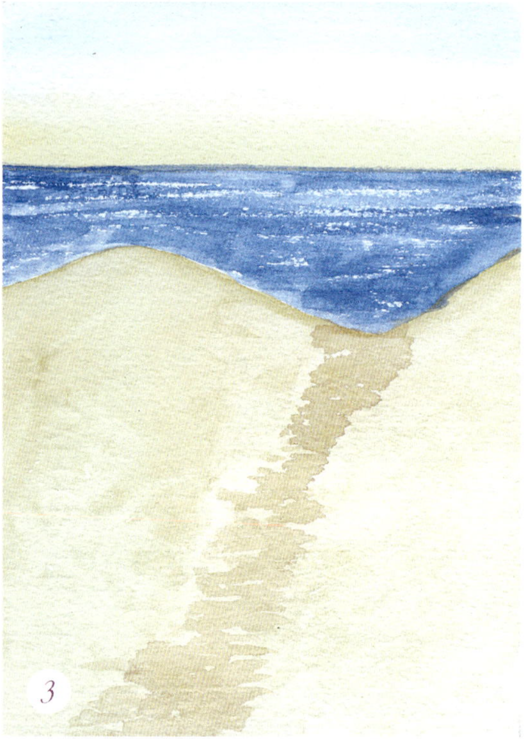

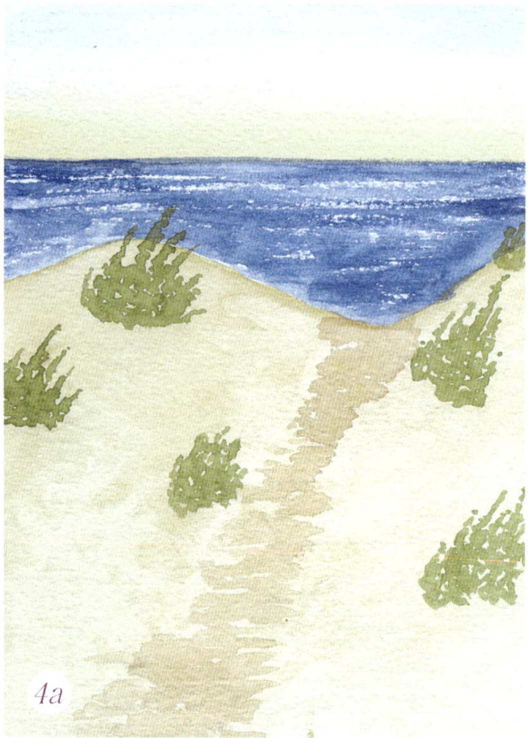

step 3

Create a more pigmented mixture of French Ultramarine on your palette. Blot some of the moisture off your size 6 round brush with a paper towel before picking up some of this paint. Using a smooth horizontal brushstroke and light touch, drag the side of your brush across the paper in a straight line at the bottom of the sky portion. Take care with this step: You want the horizon to be very straight and level. By using light pressure and a brush that is not saturated with water, you should get plenty of paper texture showing through, which is good! Continue with these light horizontal brushstrokes to fill in the area between the sky and sand dunes, picking up more paint as needed. Carefully paint around the contours of the sand.

step 4

Mix some Perylene Green and Cadmium-Free Yellow on your palette for a concentrated earthy, yellowy-green color. Load your size 6 round brush with this pigment and, using the brush point, begin to loosely paint dots and marks just below the top of the sand dune on the left-hand side. Continue making dots, close enough together that most of them touch and bleed together, but with some gaps and spaces in between, to create a windswept shrub. Using this dotting motion, paint "fingers" reaching up from the plant and leaning to one side (mine lean to the right) at slightly varying angles and heights. Once you are happy with your shrub, create a few more in different spots across the dune, varying their sizes and shapes so they look loose, organic and natural.

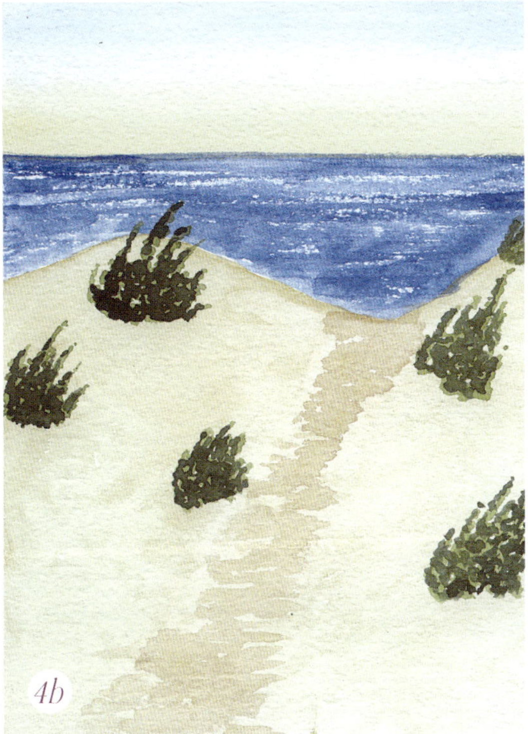

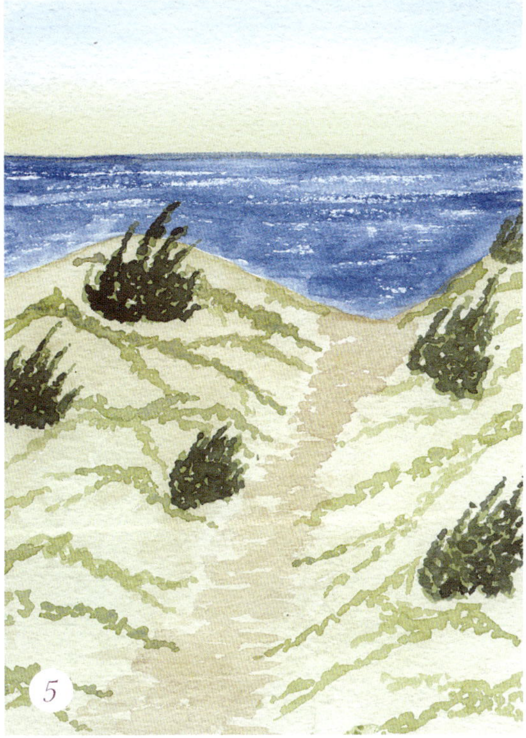

Allow the shrubs to dry, and then create a moderately pigmented mixture of Perylene Green on your palette. Pick up some of this paint with the same size 6 round brush, and add more marks to the shrubs using the same method as before. These will be shadows within the shrubs. Don't cover up all of the lighter-green color in this step; simply add dimension along the existing lines.

step 5

Mix some French Ultramarine with a little bit of Cadmium-Free Yellow for a pigmented mixture of a different earthy-green color. Pick up some of this paint with your size 2 round brush. We are going to be painting some vines across the dunes—and again, it's going to be a natural, loose process. Dab at the paper with the point and belly of the brush to create marks of different shapes. Envision that each mark is a leaf or clump of leaves, and form these leaves in organic lines the way a vine might grow across the sand. Since two sand dunes meet with a path in between, the vines can appear to grow down at an angle toward the center path, branching and clumping at different points. Paint these vines across the sand dunes and between the shrubs.

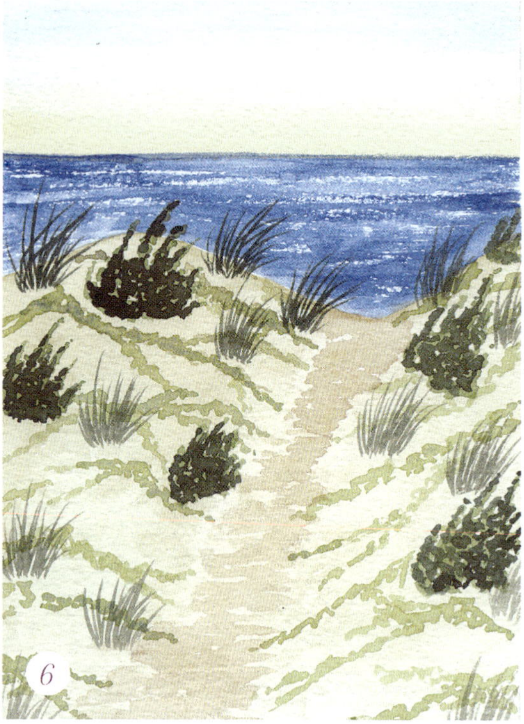

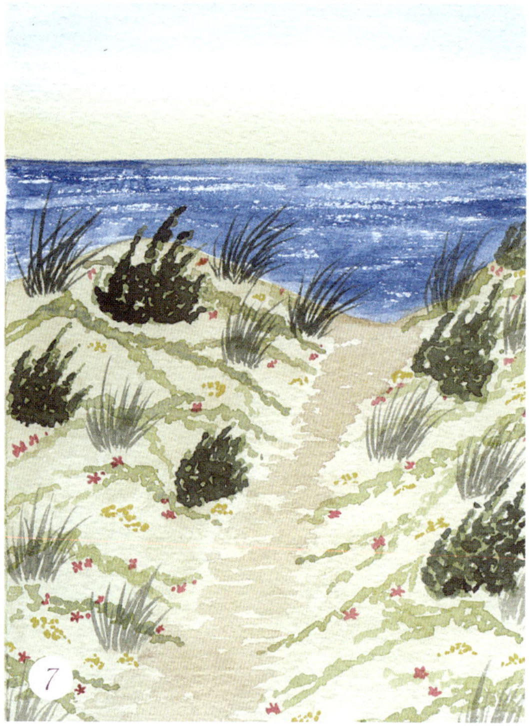

step 6

Combine some Perylene Green and Sepia to form a pigmented mixture, and then load your size 2 brush with it. Paint clumps of grasses throughout the dune. First, lightly sweep the point of the brush vertically along the paper to create a long, thin brushstroke. Then, place the brush point at the base of this first brushstroke and repeat, varying the height and/or angle of the second line. Continue adding lines to this first clump; the total number of individual grasses can vary, from eight to more than twenty. (See Painting Grasses on page 36 for more details.) Once you feel that this clump of grass looks good, move on to a different spot and create another, repeating the process across the dunes.

step 7

Pick up some Cadmium-Free Yellow paint from the pan with your size 2 round brush. Using a quick, light dotting motion, dab the brush point to the paper within the sand dunes (between the vines and shrubs) to make small clusters of yellow dots. Sprinkle these clusters throughout the dune in random places.

Create a watery mixture of Quinacridone Magenta on your palette, and pick some up with your size 2 round brush. Create short, thin lines in little star or flower shapes—five or six little lines radiating outward from a central point—by using very light pressure through the brush. (See Painting Tiny Flowers on page 37 for more details.) Sprinkle these individually or in small groups throughout the sand dune, as we did with the yellow clusters. Farther up the dune toward the ocean, the pink marks can be little blobs rather than defined flowers.

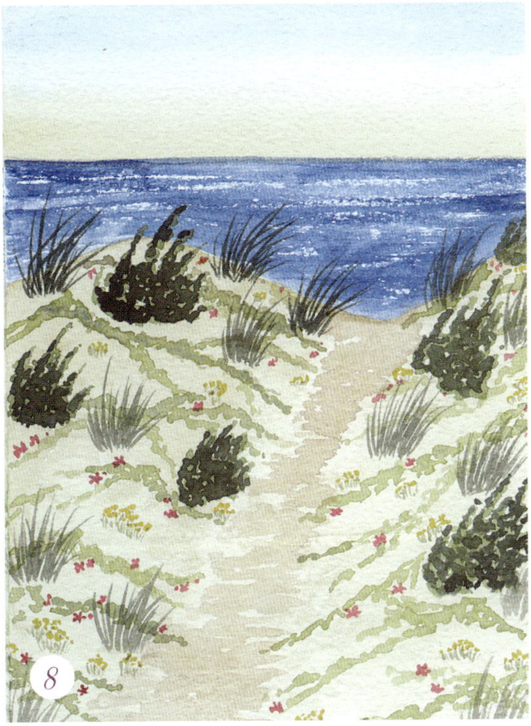

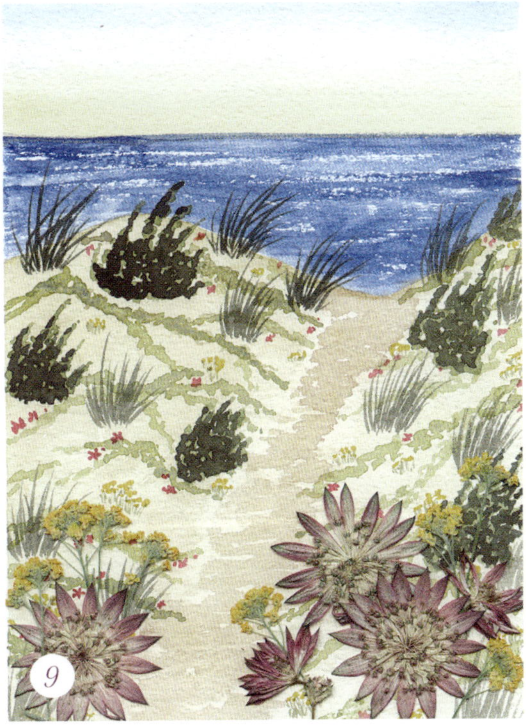

step 8

Mix some Perylene Green with Raw Sienna on your palette for just a little bit more of an earthy-green color (or use an existing mixture if you still have it). With your size 2 round brush, use the brush point to very lightly and quickly add short vertical marks beneath the clusters of yellow flowers. The lines do not need to line up exactly with the yellow marks; we are just giving the impression of little branchy stems that are short. Allow the painting to dry. The painting portion is complete!

step 9

Choose your pressed flowers, and begin laying them out on your paper. Due to the perspective of this painting, I chose to mount just a few flower heads without their stems, plus a few small filler flowers in the lower corners of the painting. Using your glue brush, carefully paint the back of each flower with a thin layer of glue and press them onto the paper.

Once they are all mounted, set a piece of waxed paper on top of your piece and weigh it down with a few heavy books. Allow it to dry for at least 15 to 20 minutes before carefully peeling away the waxed paper. If you do this too quickly, you can peel your flowers off your page or break them. (See Mounting Flowers on page 22 for more details.) Your piece is now complete!

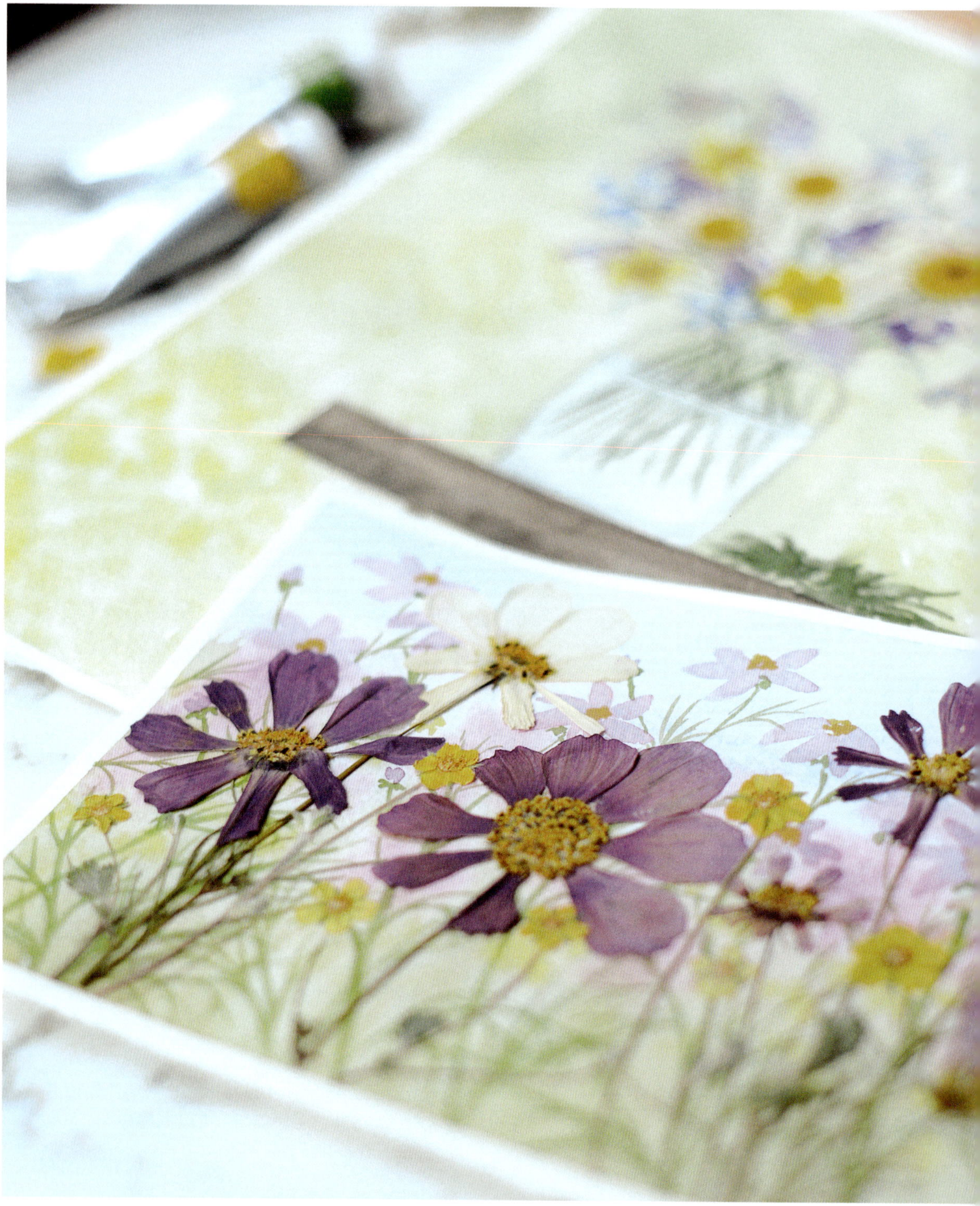

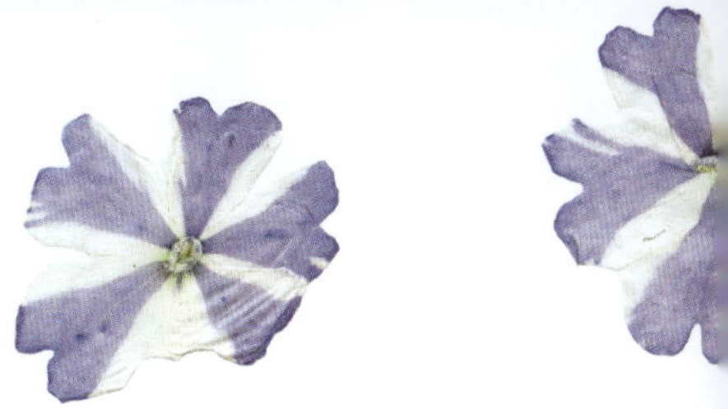

green thumb GARDEN

In this chapter, we will create cultivated floral landscapes rather than wild, naturally occurring ones. A container garden of spring bulbs in terra-cotta pots (page 177), a beautiful, loose floral arrangement in a glass jar (page 171) and an impressionistic view of the cut flower garden (page 185) are all subjects we will explore here.

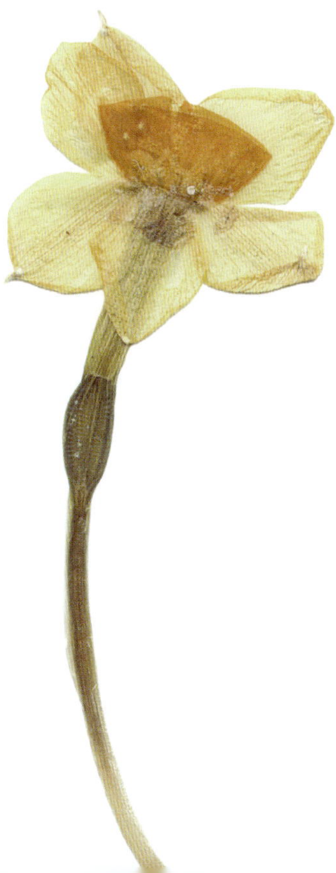

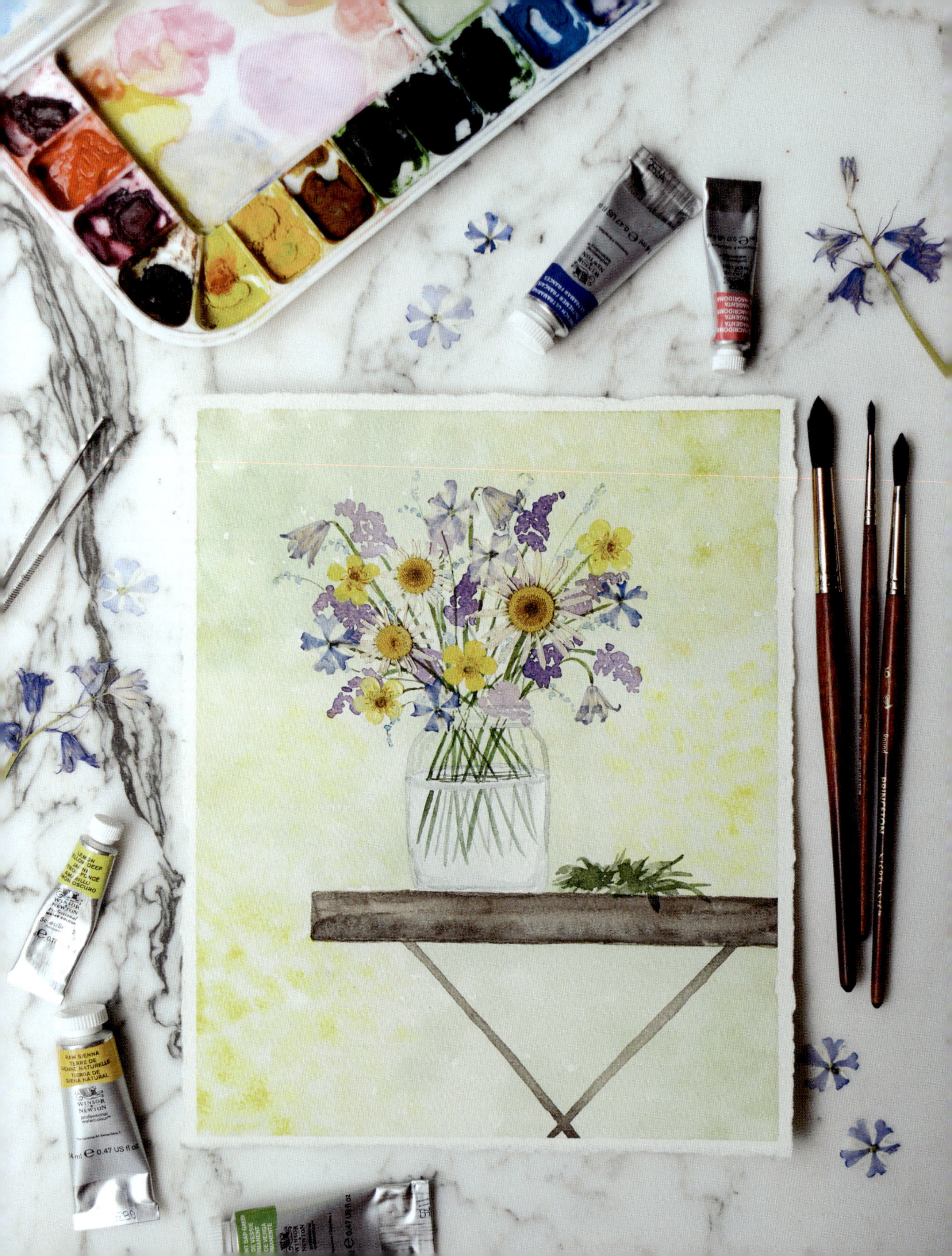
RAW SIENNA
TERRE DE SIENNE NATURELLE
TIERRA DE SIENA NATURAL
WINSOR & NEWTON
professional watercolour
14 ml ℮ 0.47 US fl oz

JAM JAR BOUQUET

Rather than a large, sweeping landscape, this project brings us closer to the subject: a casual floral arrangement made in a jam jar right in the garden. A painted jar of water and some loose, painted blooms form the backdrop for our pressed flowers, creating a unique mixed-media piece. For this flowerscape, I used daisies, verbena blossoms, buttercups and bluebells.

size

8 x 10" (20 x 25 cm)

brushes

Size 10 round brush
Size 6 round brush
Size 2 round brush
Glue brush

flower palette

Daisies
Buttercups
Bluebells
Verbena blossoms

materials

Tweezers (optional)
Scissors
Glue
Waxed paper
Heavy Books

color palette

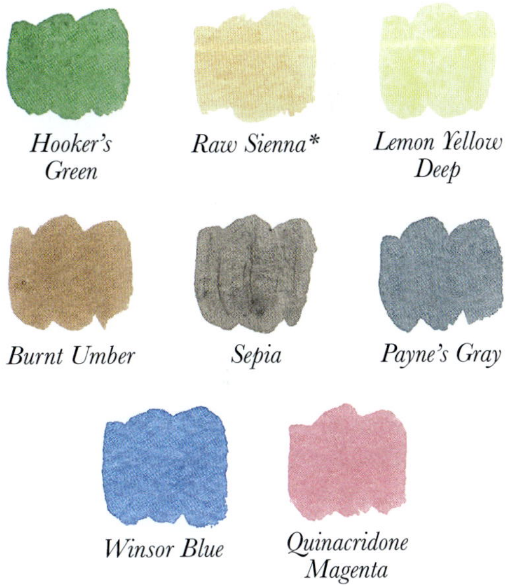

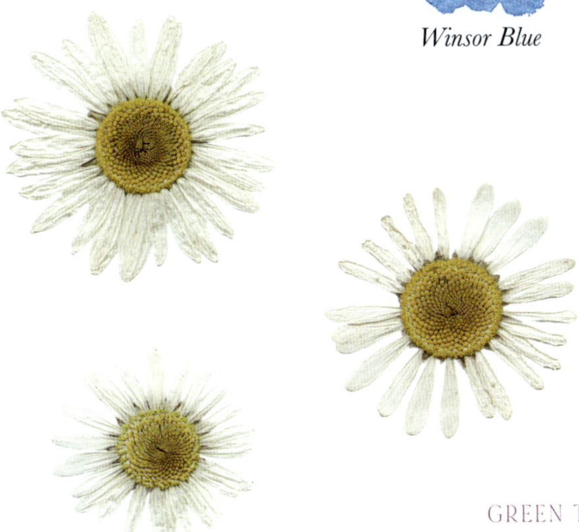

step 1

With a pencil, very lightly sketch a tabletop with a long, thin horizontal rectangle. Add legs extending downward off the bottom of the page. Then, atop the table, sketch a glass jar. To do this, you can sketch a cylindrical shape with rounded "shoulders" and a long rectangle on top for the mouth of the jar. Draw a flattened, thin oval inside the jar—above the halfway point of the jar—for the water line.

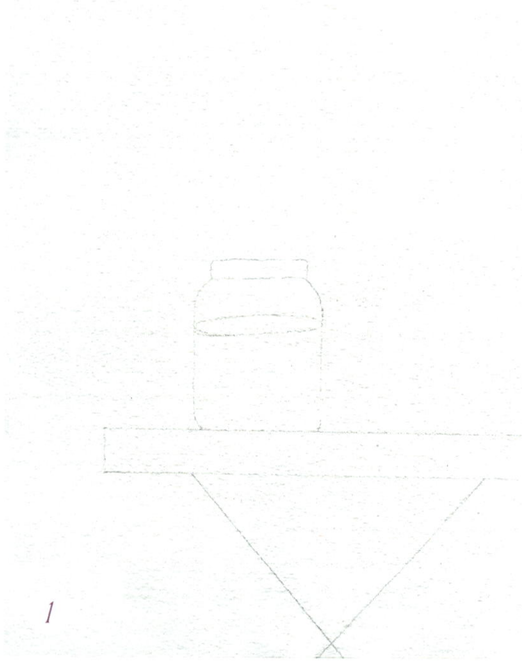

step 2

On your palette, create three watery mixes: Mix 1 is a watery mixture of Hooker's Green and Raw Sienna; Mix 2 is a watery mixture of Lemon Yellow Deep; Mix 3 is a watery mixture of Hooker's Green and Burnt Umber.

Using a size 10 round brush loaded with clear water, paint the entire paper except the table and the area inside the jar below the oval. (You can dampen the area above the oval.) Then, pick up some of the lighter green paint mixture (Mix 1), and begin tapping the brush to the paper, making marks throughout the dampened area. The paint should spread and bleed. Leave a few little areas open to add yellow marks to the left and right of the jar and under the table. Clean your brush, then pick up some of your yellow mixture (Mix 2) and make more marks within those areas. Pick up some of the darker green color (Mix 3), and add it in, sparingly, to the light-green areas for dimension. The paper should be covered in a dreamy wash of color. Allow the painting to dry.

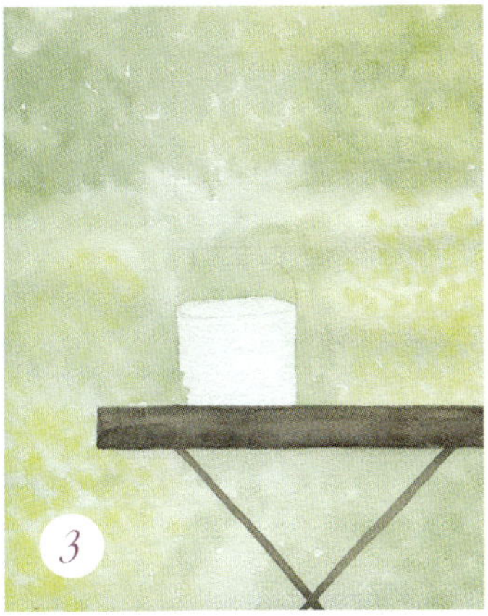

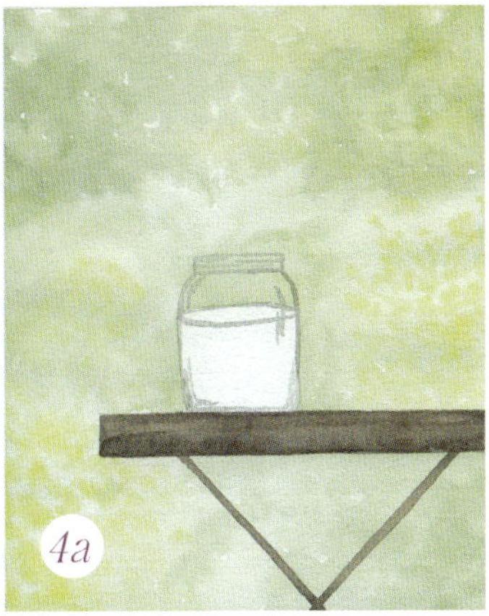

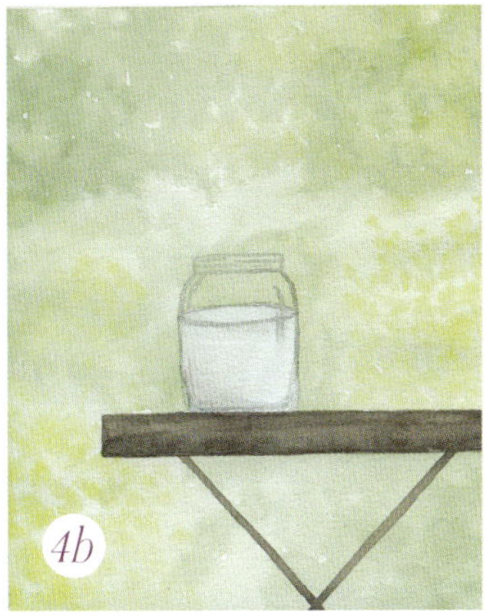

step 3

Create a pigmented mixture of Sepia on your palette, and load your size 10 round brush with this brownish paint. Carefully place the point of the brush in one corner of the pencil sketch of the table (which we left dry in the last step), and drag the brush sideways in a straight line to fill in the table with paint. Then, drag the brush along the table legs, keeping a steady hand so the lines are straight and even. While the paper is still damp, add a little bit of Payne's Gray to your Sepia mixture, and then use a little bit of that paint to add a shadow line on the bottom edge of the table. Allow the painting to dry.

step 4

Create a watery mixture of Winsor Blue with a little bit of Sepia on your palette. Pick up some of this paint with a size 6 round brush, and paint along the pencil lines of the jar—the outside shape, the rim and the oval (the water line). Add a few contour lines in the bottom-left and top-right corners of the jar.

Once those marks have dried, add even more water to the paint mixture, and use the same brush to fill in below the water line and inside the oval.

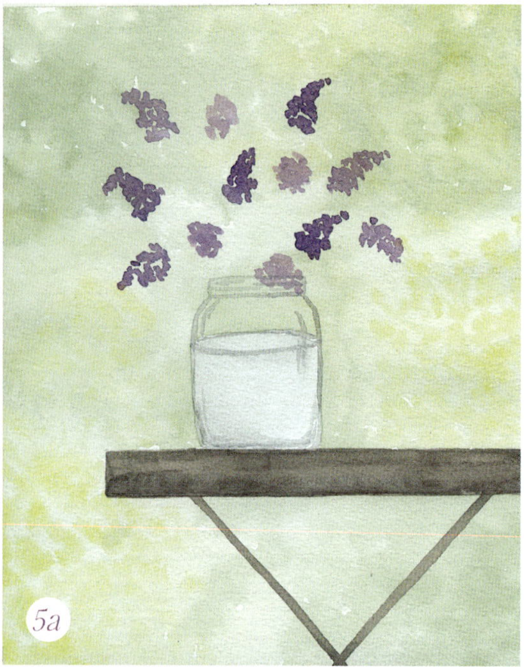

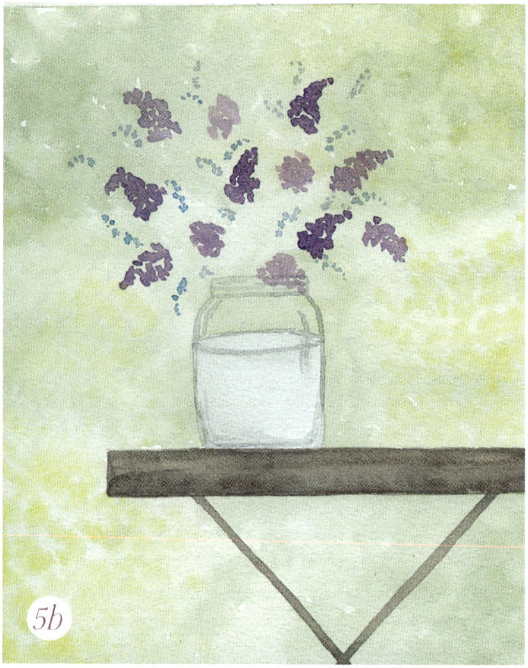

step 5

Create a moderately pigmented mixture of Winsor Blue and Quinacridone Magenta on your palette. Pick up some of this paint with your size 6 round brush, and begin painting dots and blobs in a small triangular shape somewhere above the top of the jar. These will be purplish lilac–type flowers, with their stems blooming from the jar, so keep that in mind when you are choosing the angle and position of each triangular cluster. Space your clusters out across the area above the jar; don't get too far into the corners or close to the edge of the paper.

Create a watery mixture of Winsor Blue on your palette. We'll add a few smaller flowers, like forget-me-nots, spaced between the lilacs. These can be small dot clusters painted with your size 6 or size 2 round brush, in little linear groupings. This doesn't need to be precise, because we are just adding some more color. You don't need to fill this space in completely, because we will be adding pressed flowers later.

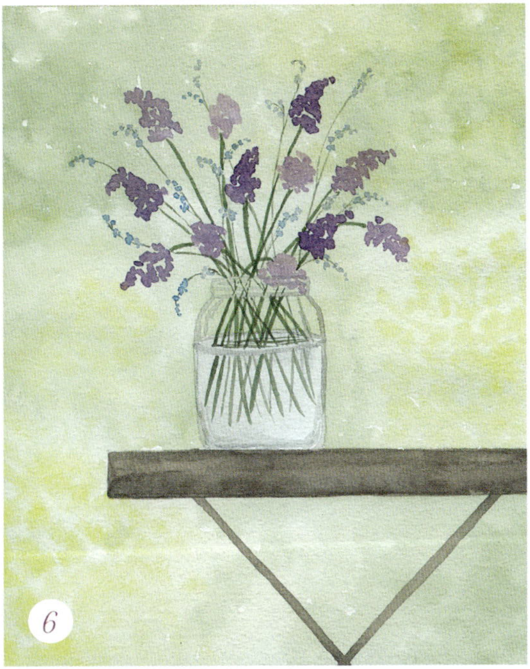

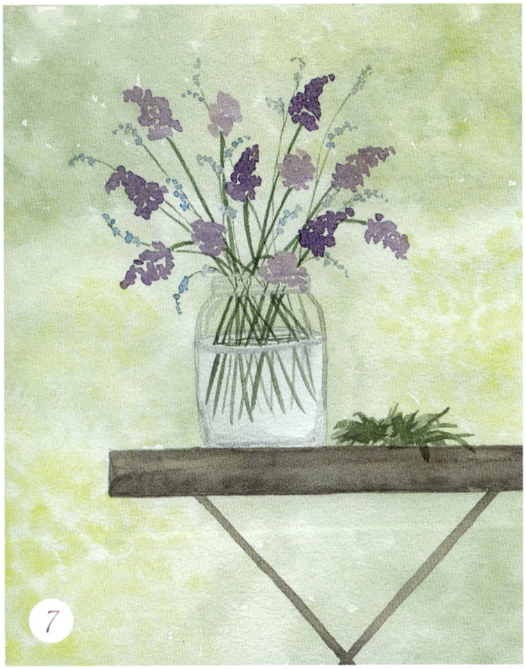

step 6

Create a moderately pigmented mixture of Hooker's Green and Sepia on your palette for an earthy-green color. Using your size 2 round brush, pick up some of this paint and lightly paint thin stem lines for the flowers. The stems will be visible all the way from the flower, into the jar and even into the water. I like to paint the stem from the water line (oval) up to the flower, and then add the below-water portion, separating it from the main stem slightly to account for refraction.

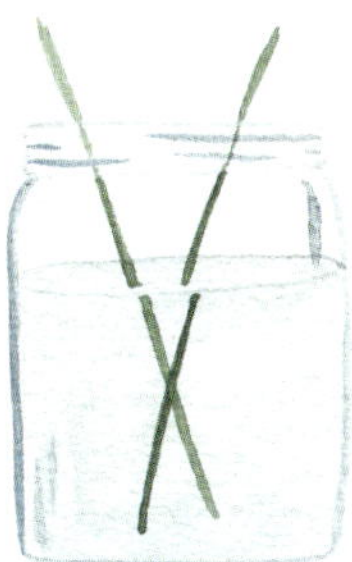

step 7

Using the same paint mixture and your size 6 round brush, paint some blobs and marks on the tabletop next to the jar—as if there is a small pile of leaves and stems that were cut from the flowers as the arrangement was made in the garden. To complete the look, make a combination of loose blobs and short lines by quickly swiping your brush point from the central cluster to create a sharp straight line. It doesn't have to be perfect!

You can add a little more paint of a darker or more concentrated color once the first layer has dried to add dimension. Allow the painting to dry.

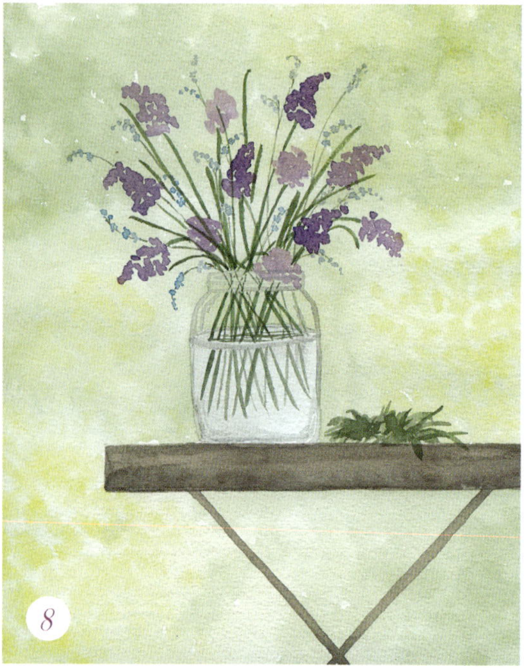

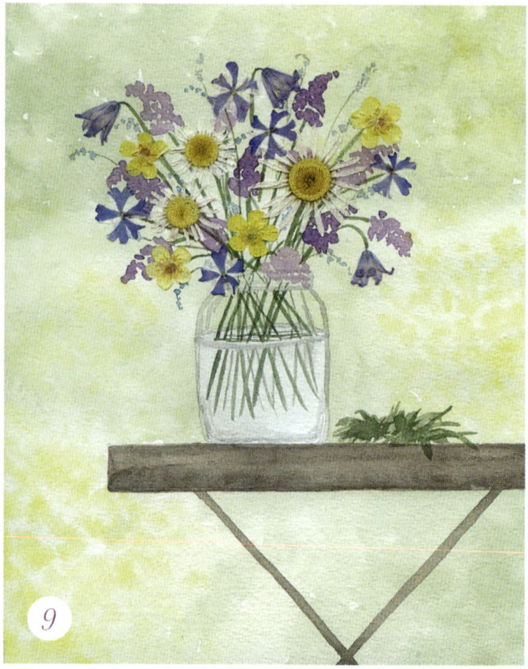

step 8

Gather your pressed flowers and lay them around the area above the jar, as if they are blooming from the vase. It's okay if they overlap the painted flowers. I like to use small individual blooms without their stems for this. Once you have laid them out, see where it looks like stems are needed before removing the flowers. (If you have a digital camera or smartphone, you can snap a photo of your flower layout for reference.) Paint some more stems to the areas where your pressed flowers will be mounted. To help you visualize where everything should go, you may want to do this by removing one or two flowers at a time, rather than all of them at once. The painting portion is complete!

step 9

Using your glue brush, carefully paint a thin layer of glue on the backs of each flower before pressing it onto the page. Use your photo as needed for reference.

Once the flowers are all mounted, set a piece of waxed paper on top of your piece and weigh it down with a few heavy books. Allow it to dry for at least 15 to 20 minutes before carefully peeling away the waxed paper. If you do this too quickly, you can peel your flowers off your page or break them. (See Mounting Flowers on page 22 for more details.) Your piece is now complete!

IN THE GREENHOUSE

A collection of terra-cotta pots, all bursting into bloom with bulbs and other flowers, is such a charming sight. In this project, we combine painted terra-cotta pots, along with painted leaves and a few loose blooms in the background, with real pressed flowers for a fun interpretation of the container garden. This arrangement of mixed containers could be set anywhere, but here we have our planters spread across a floor in an imagined greenhouse. Since this is a container garden of bulb flowers, I chose to use pressed miniature daffodils, muscari (grape hyacinth) and the blooms from my verbena plant.

size

5 x 7" (12.5 x 18 cm)

brushes

Size 10 round brush
Size 6 round brush
Size 2 round brush
Glue brush

flower palette

Miniature daffodils
Muscari
Verbena blossoms

materials

Tweezers (optional)
Scissors
Glue
Waxed paper
Heavy Books

color palette

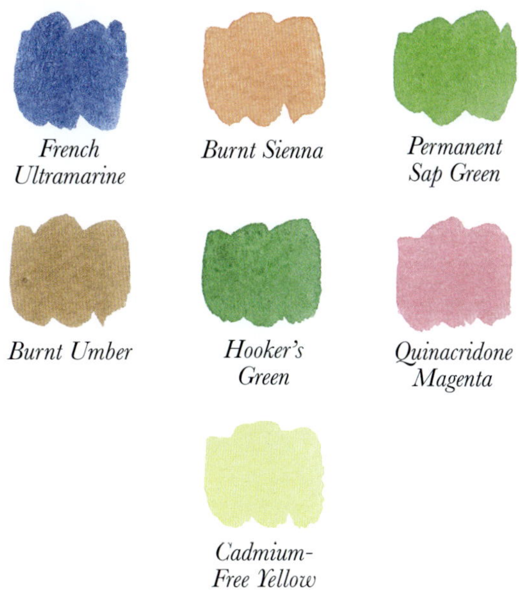

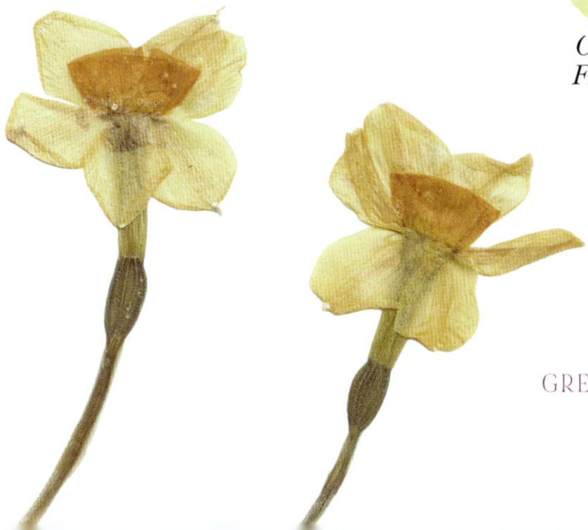

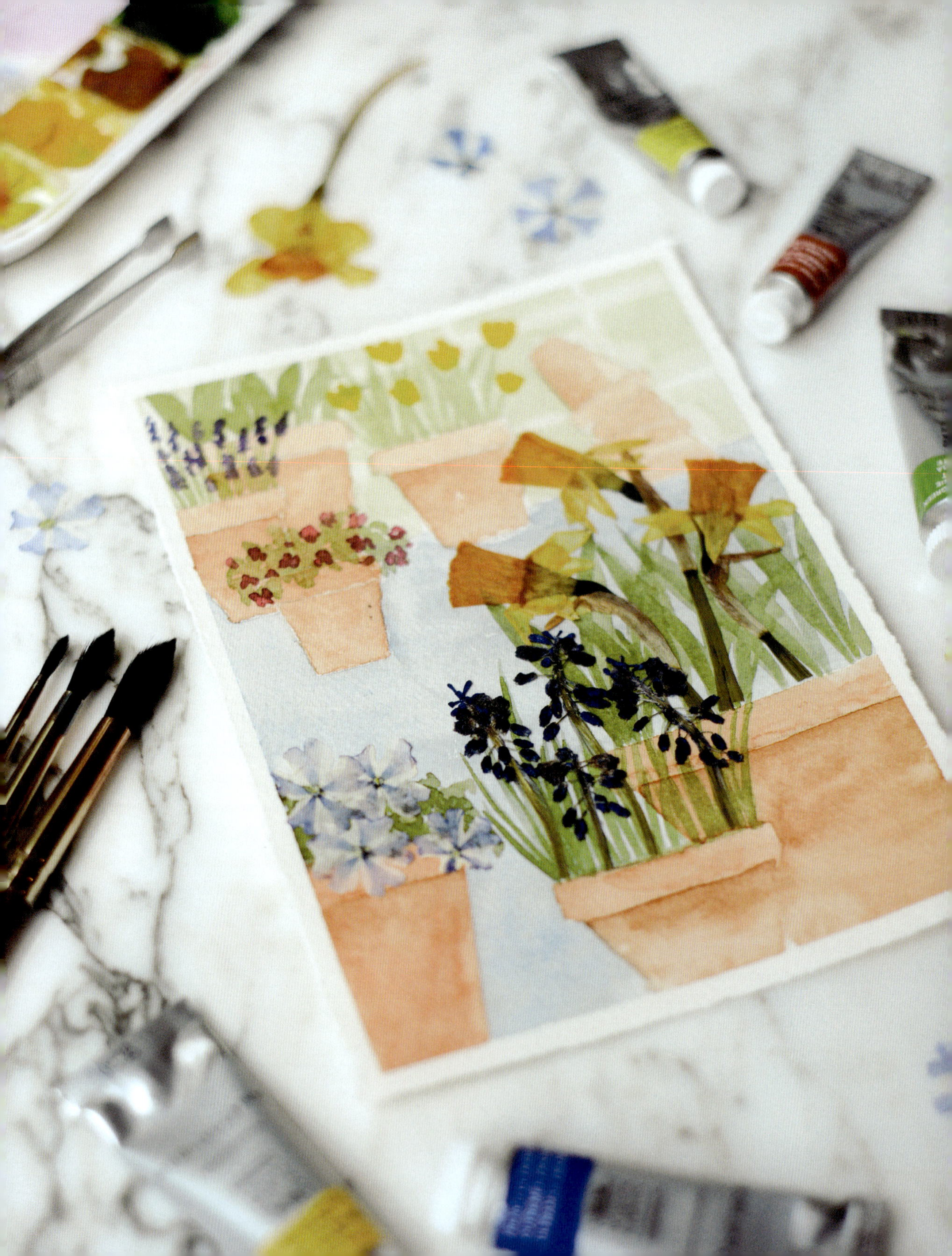

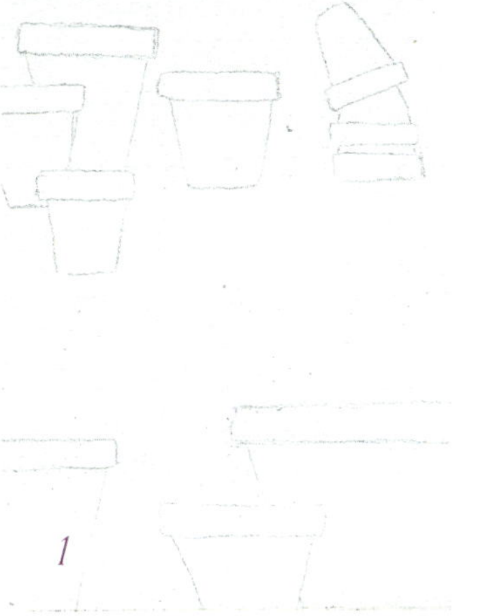

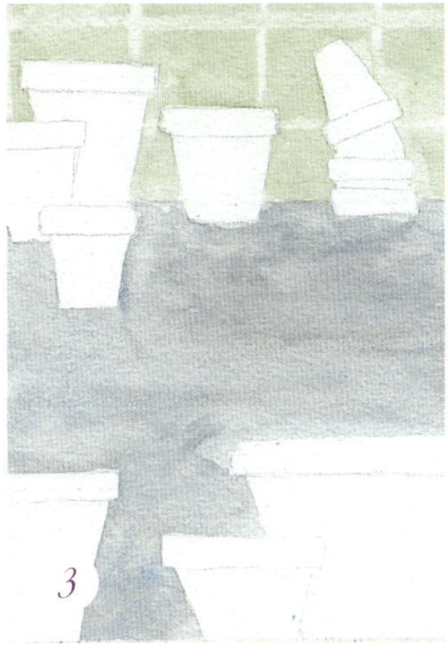

step 1

Using a pencil, lightly sketch a straight line across the paper about a third of the way from the top. Then, lightly sketch the shapes of some terra-cotta pots using short, stocky trapezoids for their base topped with rectangles for the rims of the pots. Start with three large ones across the bottom of the page, and create a collection of smaller ones up near the straight line near the top. I like to vary the sizes of these pots, placing some in front of others. You can even make a stack of upside-down, unused pots like I did in the back right. Carefully erase any unneeded marks, such as where any pots intersect.

step 2

Create a very watery mixture of French Ultramarine and Burnt Sienna on your palette. Load your size 10 round brush and paint in the area below the one-third line and the bottom of the page, surrounding the pots. This will be the greenhouse floor. Allow the painting to dry.

step 3

Create a very watery mixture of Permanent Sap Green and a little Burnt Sienna on your palette. Load your size 10 round brush and paint in the area above the one-third line to the top of the page, working around the pots. Then, dry your brush on a paper towel and use it to drag a line from the top of the page down to the floor, lifting some of the greenish paint. Dry your brush again and repeat, evenly spacing three or four lines from left to right. Then, after drying your brush again, repeat this process to make a few horizontal lines between the floor and the top of the paper. This is our greenhouse wall. Allow the painting to dry.

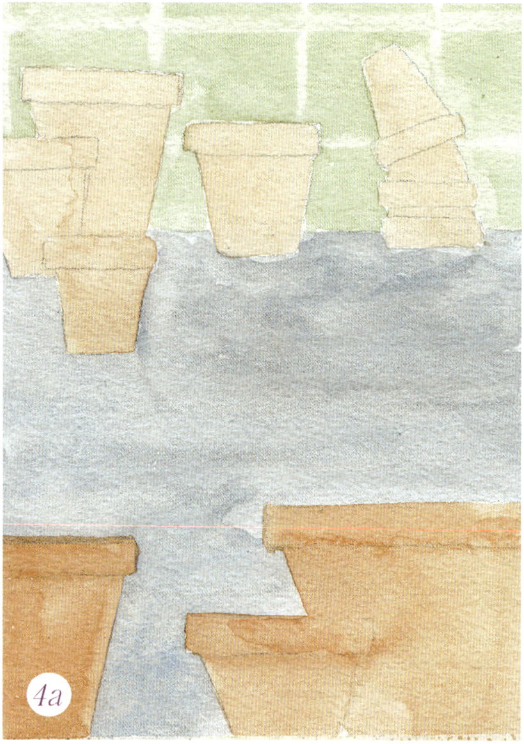

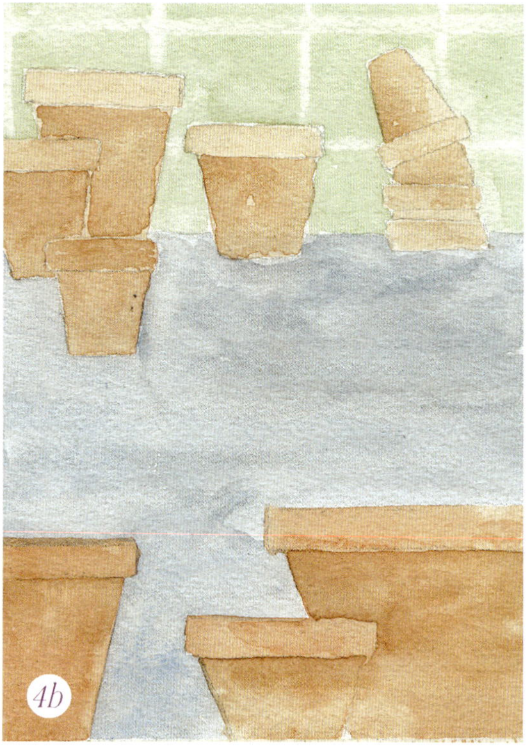

step 4

On your palette, make a moderately pigmented mixture of Burnt Sienna, and load your size 6 round brush with it. Using careful brushstrokes, begin to fill in the terra-cotta pots, starting with the pots at the bottom of the page. Add some more water to the mixture on the palette before filling in the pots farther up the page, so they appear a bit lighter in color. Allow the painting to dry.

Add some Burnt Umber to this mixture to darken it. Use the same brush and clean water to dampen the terra-cotta pots again (leave the rims dry). Then, pick up some of this darker paint mixture and tap it into the dampened area just below the rim in a line. The paint should spread and soften, creating a shadow and adding some dimension to the pots. Allow the painting to dry.

step 5

Create a few earthy-green mixtures on your palette: Mix 1 is Permanent Sap Green and Burnt Sienna; Mix 2 is Hooker's Green and Burnt Sienna; Mix 3 is Permanent Sap Green and Burnt Umber; Mix 4 is Hooker's Green and Burnt Umber.

Using your size 6 brush, pick up one of these green mixtures, and begin adding foliage to the pots in the background. Here are a few types of foliage to try:

* **Thin leaves**: Place the brush point carefully at the top of the pot's rim. Using light pressure, sweep upward, lifting the brush as you go to create a tapered end. Continue adding similar brushstrokes across the top of the pot. To give a natural look, you can bend some of the leaves by changing the angle of your brush at some point during each brushstroke (at the beginning, middle or end).
* **Thick leaves**: Place the brush point carefully at the top of the pot's rim. Using heavier pressure through the belly of the brush, sweep upward, again lifting the brush as you go to taper the end. Repeat, filling in the area along the pot rim. Again, you can bend some of the leaves as described above.
* **Small clustered leaves**: Using the brush point, tap the paper in the area above the pot rim, making lots of little dots and marks that connect. A few can tumble over the sides or front of the pot, but make sure they mostly all connect to each other so it looks like one cohesive plant.

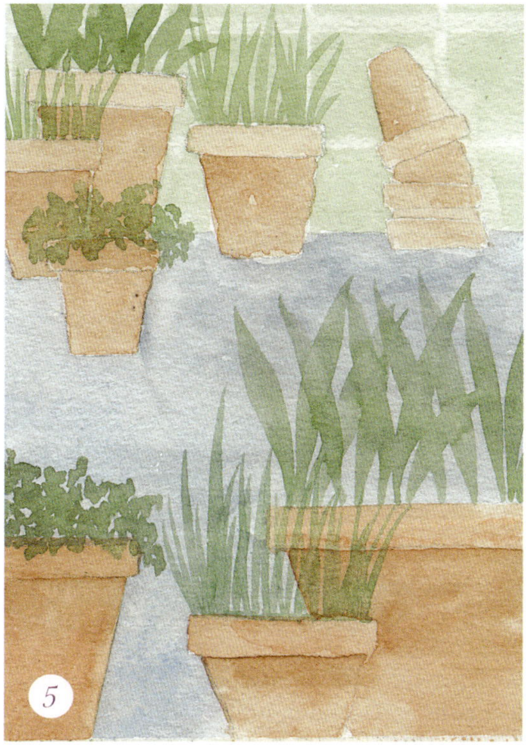

Use all three leaf styles (one per pot) and the different shades of green on your palette to add foliage to each pot in the back row. Then, with slightly more concentrated paint (or multiple layers), add leaves to the pots near the bottom of the page, in the foreground. These leaves should be larger (taller) than the ones in the back.

step 6

Once your leaves have dried, take a look at the painting to see if any need to be darkened. If they do, you can pick up some more of the paint and go over your leaves to strengthen the color, especially in the foreground.

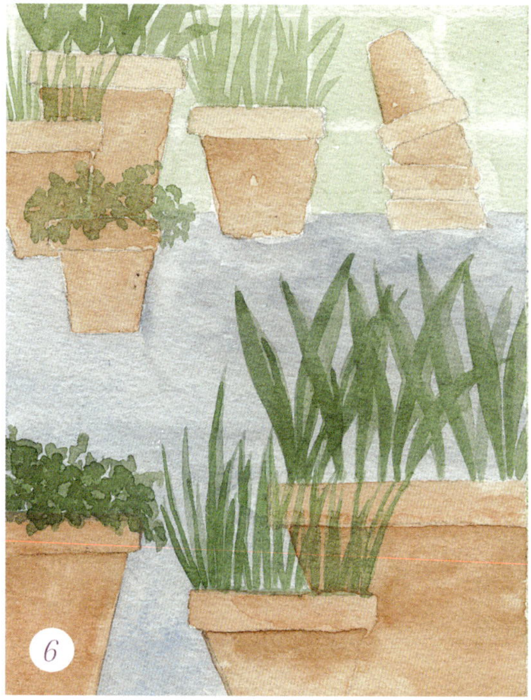

step 7

We will be adding pressed flowers to the pots in the foreground, but you may wish to paint some flowers in the background. Here are some ideas.

* **Pinkish cactus flowers**: Using a pigmented mixture of Quinacridone Magenta and your size 6 round brush, paint small blobs or miniature, roundish clusters of dots on any pot with *small clustered leaves*. Add these pinkish blooms among the leaves across the pot.
* **Purplish hyacinth flowers**: Using a pigmented mixture of Quinacridone Magenta and French Ultramarine and your size 6 round brush, paint small linear clusters of dots among the leaves of a pot with *thin leaves*. These little lines of dots should each rest atop a leaf (which could also be a stem).
* **Yellow tulip flowers**: Using a pigmented mixture of Cadmium-Free Yellow and your size 6 round brush, paint *V*-shaped or "cup" flowers among and above the leaves of a pot with *thin leaves* or *thick leaves*. Each flower should connect with a leaf or stem, which you can add with matching green paint if necessary.

The painting portion is now complete!

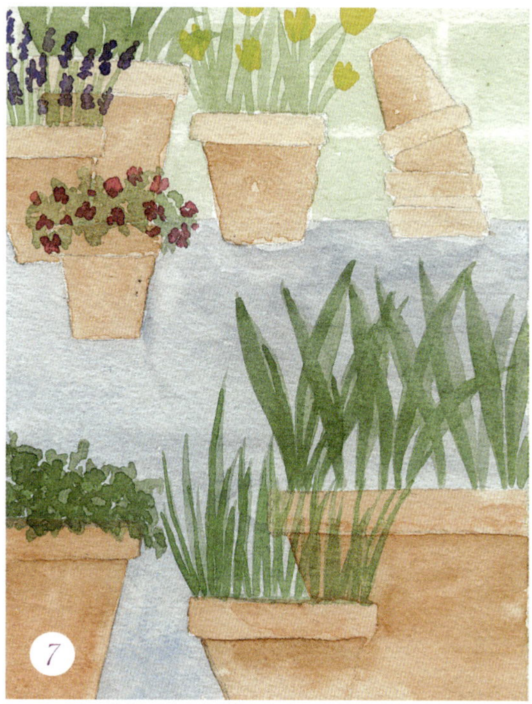

step 8

Choose your pressed flowers, and begin placing them so they appear to be growing out of some of the pots (the ones in the foreground), with the stems meeting the top edge of the terra-cotta. Once you are happy with your layout, trim the stems to length and begin picking up the flowers one by one. Using your glue brush, carefully paint the back of each flower with a thin layer of glue and press them onto the paper.

Once they are all mounted, set a piece of waxed paper on top of your piece and weigh it down with a few heavy books. Allow it to dry for at least 15 to 20 minutes before carefully peeling away the waxed paper. If you do this too quickly, you can peel your flowers off your page or break them. (See Mounting Flowers on page 22 for more details.) Your piece is now complete!

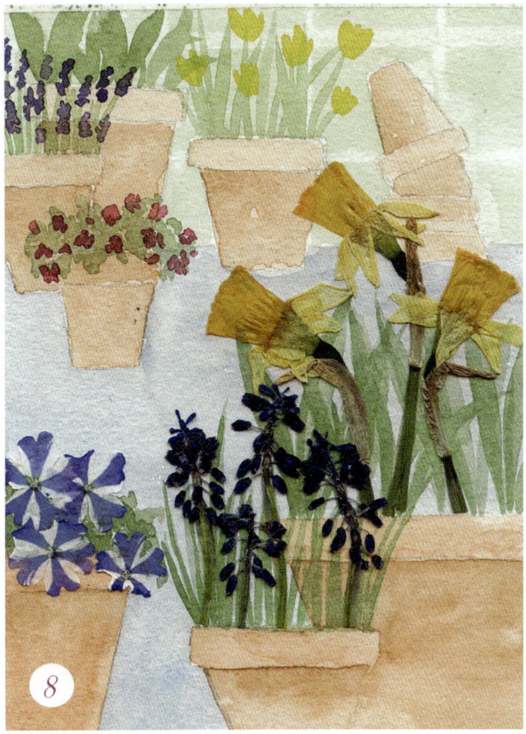

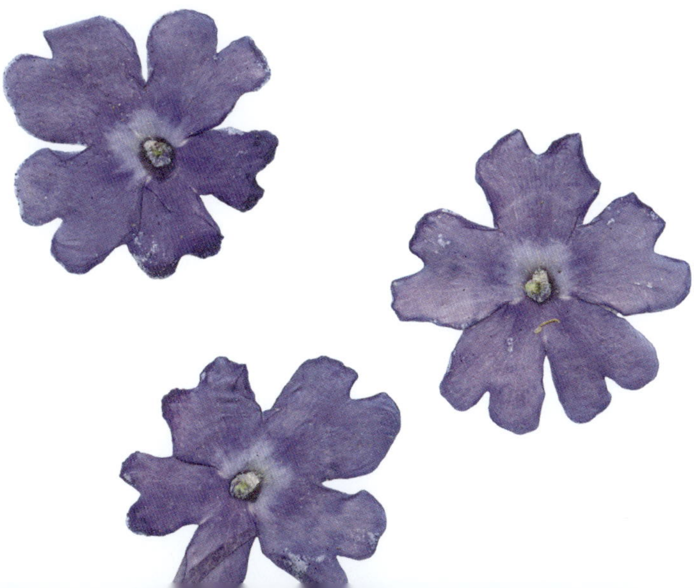

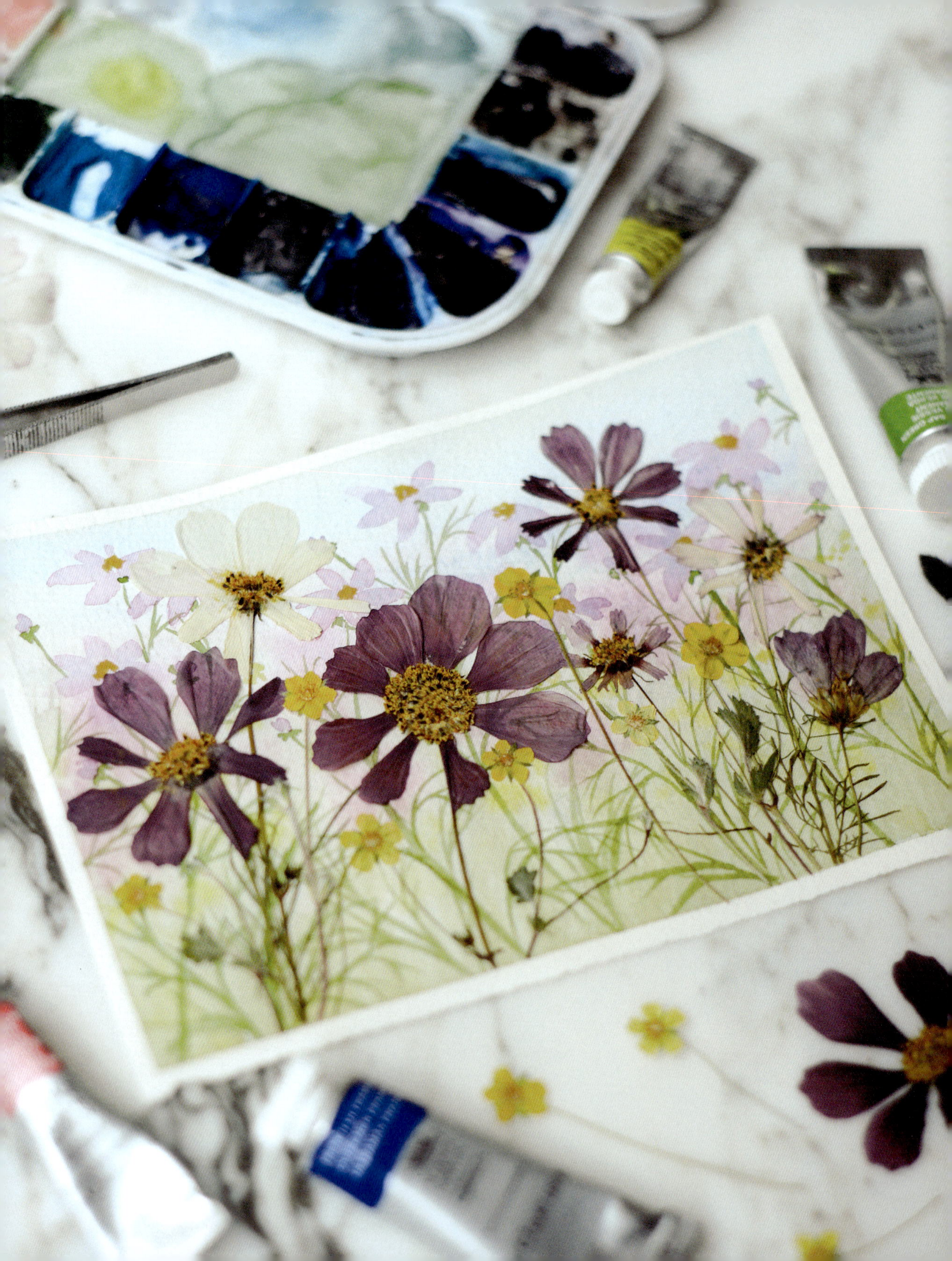

THE CUTTING GARDEN

Each fall, my wild garden bursts into bloom with hundreds of cosmos flowers. Their beautiful blooms come in shades of pink, purple, and white and float atop tall, bendy stems and loads of wispy, fern-like leaves. The flowers are fantastic for cutting and pressing and are fun to paint, too! In this project, we will paint an impressionistic view of the cutting garden and finish it off with pressed flowers. You can vary the colors of paint, the shapes of your flowers and your pressed flower palette to make countless variations on this theme. Since this piece was inspired by a garden full of cosmos flowers, that is what I am using here, along with some small cinquefoil blooms.

size

5 x 7" (12.5 x 18 cm)

brushes

Size 10 round brush
Size 6 round brush
Size 2 round brush
Glue brush

flower palette

Cosmos
Small cinquefoil or other yellow flowers

materials

Tweezers (optional)
Scissors
Glue
Waxed paper
Heavy Books

color palette

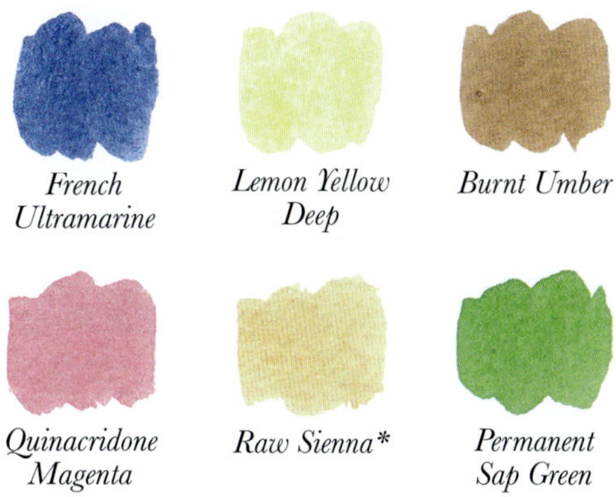

French Ultramarine
Lemon Yellow Deep
Burnt Umber
Quinacridone Magenta
*Raw Sienna**
Permanent Sap Green

step 1

Dampen the entire paper with clean water. Then, use a watery mixture of French Ultramarine on your size 10 round brush to paint sweeping curved and diagonal brushstrokes across the top half of your paper. You don't have to cover the space evenly; these brushstrokes and a few gaps will give the effect of a sky filled with wispy clouds.

While the paper is still wet, create a watery mixture of Lemon Yellow Deep, French Ultramarine and a little Burnt Umber. Using the same brush, pick up some of this paint and make broad, sweeping brushstrokes upward from the bottom of the page, merging up into the blue portion.

step 2

Create a moderately pigmented mixture of Quinacridone Magenta with a little bit of French Ultramarine. While the paper is still damp, load up your size 6 round brush with this mixture to paint star-shaped flowers in the central third (horizontally) of the page. (See Painting Tiny Flowers on page 37 for more details.) Since the paper is wet, these will bleed and soften—which is exactly what we want.

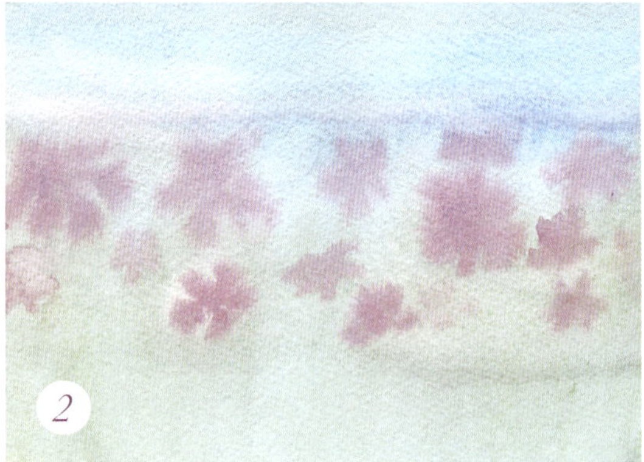

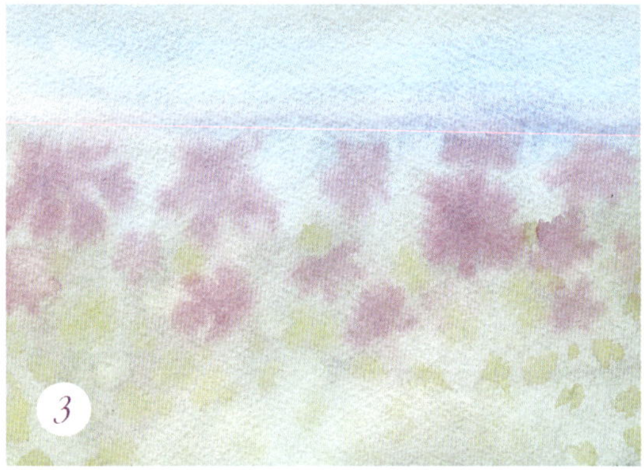

step 3

If your paper is still damp, proceed with this step, but if it has begun to dry and the marks aren't bleeding and spreading, dampen the lower portion of the paper with clean water and a large brush. Create a watery mixture of Lemon Yellow Deep with a little Raw Sienna. Then, using the size 6 round brush again, paint small clusters of yellow dots throughout the bottom third of the page, with a few interspersed between the pinkish-purple blobs from step 2.

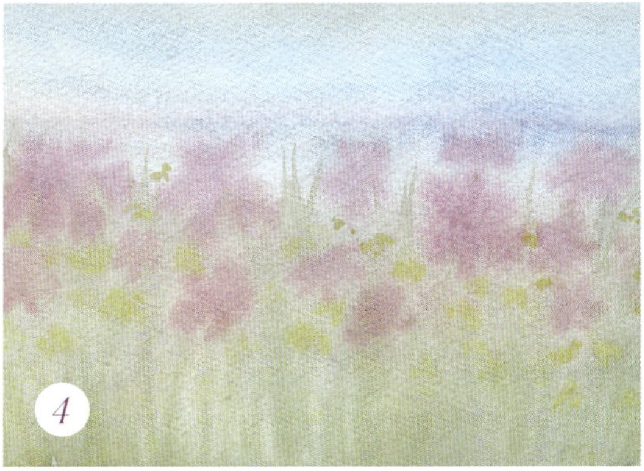

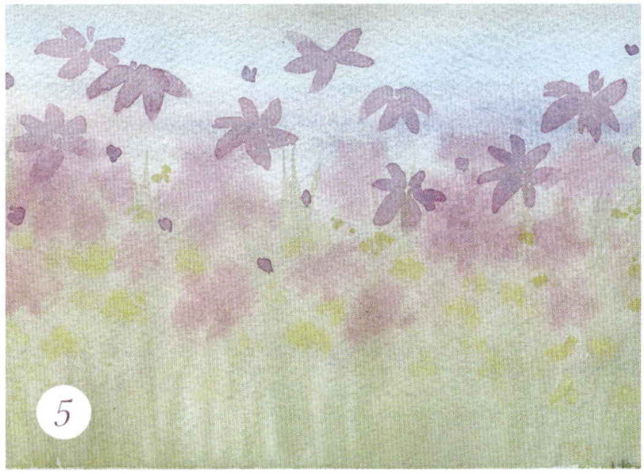

step 4

Dampen the paper again, if necessary, and create a mixture of Permanent Sap Green and Burnt Umber. Then, load your size 2 brush and paint another upward series of sweeping brushstrokes for grass throughout the bottom of the page, toward the pink and yellow marks. Allow the painting to dry.

step 5

With your size 6 brush, return to the purplish mixture of Quinacridone Magenta and French Ultramarine on your palette from step 2. Using this paint, create several star-shaped flowers across the top third of the paper, painting into the sky and overlapping the purplish blobs from earlier. Add a few small dots here and there as flower buds. Allow the painting to dry.

step 6

Create a moderately pigmented mixture of Permanent Sap Green and Burnt Umber, and load your size 2 round brush. Using a light hand and the point of the brush, drag thin, wispy branching lines from the base of each new flower (painted in step 5), down to the bottom of the painting. Feel free to cross stems, connect the buds to flower stems and allow organic movement.

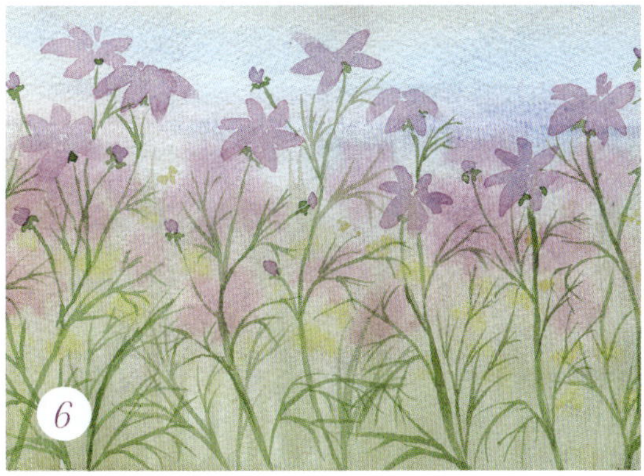

Add leaves at the bottom of the stems and along the length of them, with larger leaves at the bottom and smaller ones toward the top. These leaves are wispy and fernlike, and they are simple to paint with a series of *V* and *Y* shapes.

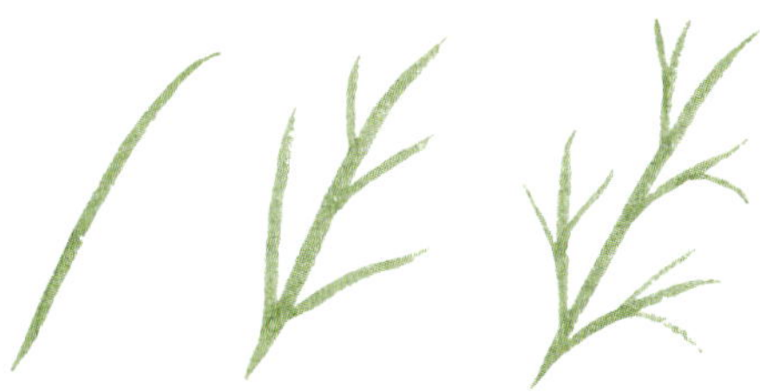

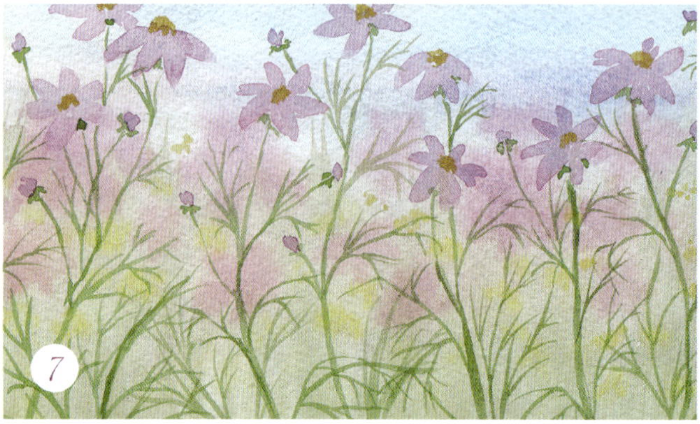

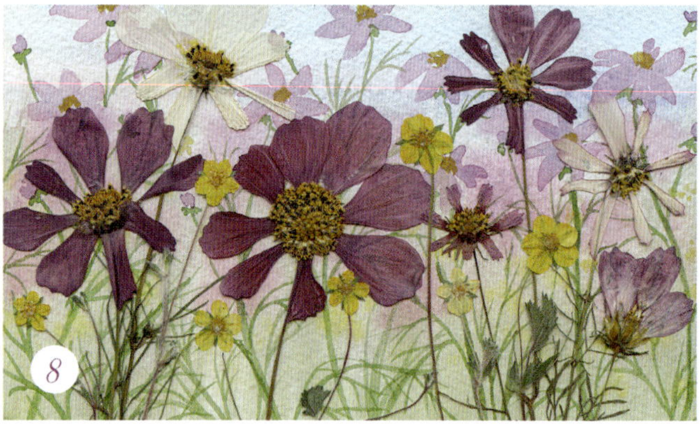

step 7

Create a pigmented mixture of Lemon Yellow Deep and a little Burnt Umber. Then, using your size 2 round brush, paint small centers on the new flowers by tapping the brush in a small cluster where the petals meet in the middle. Allow the painting to dry. The painting portion is now complete!

step 8

Lay your pressed flowers on top of your project, with their stems reaching to the bottom of the page. Once you are happy with your layout, trim the stems to length and begin picking up the flowers one by one. Using your glue brush, carefully paint the back of each flower with a thin layer of glue and press them onto the paper.

Once they are all mounted, set a piece of waxed paper on top of your piece and weigh it down with a few heavy books. Allow it to dry for at least 15 to 20 minutes before carefully peeling away the waxed paper. If you do this too quickly, you can peel your flowers off your page or break them. (See Mounting Flowers on page 22 for more details.) Your piece is now complete!

ACKNOWLEDGMENTS

This book would not be possible without the incredible network of support who helped bring it to life.

To my husband, Evin, thank you for your love, encouragement and listening ear as I worked through this big (and sometimes intimidating) project.

To Owen and Ellie, thank you for motivating me, making me smile and keeping me grounded.

To Lori and John, thank you for believing in me and fostering my creativity from the very start.

To Kathy and Kevin, thank you for your energy and support when I really needed to sit down and write.

To Lauren, Valerie, Emily, Kaitlin, Colin, Heidi and so many more friends, thank you for cheering me on throughout the process.

To my editors, Madeline and Alexandra, thank you for your faith in me and my work, for your support and encouragement along the way and for everything you did to help make this book the best it could be.

To Meg, Laura and the rest of the team at Page Street Publishing, thank you for your hard work transforming these words and paintings into a beautiful book.

To my community of creatives and supporters on Instagram and elsewhere, thank you for your kind words and support over the years. The amazing response to these Watercolor Flowerscapes, in particular, was key in the making of this book.

ABOUT THE AUTHOR

Karly Murphy is the botanical artist behind kmpressed. Her love for flowers and passion for creating and sharing beautiful things have combined to inspire her work with flower pressing and painting. As a lifelong Virginian, residing in rural central Virginia greatly influences her work, both through the local flowers she preserves and the painted artwork shaped by the surrounding landscapes. She enjoys exploring and sharing the natural world with her husband and their two young children, from the meadows and forests near their home to the lakes and beaches farther afield.

Her work can be found at kmpressed.com and on Instagram @kmpressed.

INDEX